Choosing to Live, Choosing to Die is an unusual and special book. It is at once a tribute to a beloved husband, an account of an extraordinary life and career built after a catastrophic childhood accident, an indictment of disability services and attitudes in the past, and a challenge for euthanasia legislation, both from the perspective of the subject and the family members so intimately affected.

Beautifully written and well-constructed, it alternates a narrative of the accident and its long and painful sequel (which builds a 'what happens next?' tension) with an account of the developing relationship between the author and the man who became her husband and stepfather to her two sons. It shines a searing spotlight on the hurdles, discrimination, and inadequacies of the disability policies and services then current, and the challenges that would have undone a less indomitable spirit. Neither partner is idealised, and the strains imposed on their special bond are not glossed over.

The medical deterioration that led Bill to the choice that his life was no longer worth living is graphically depicted, as is the challenge for his family in supporting his choice. At a time when Voluntary Assisted Dying legislation has been passed in several states – notably Victoria and recently S.A., and with Queensland about to vote on its own legislation, *Choosing to Live, Choosing to Die* will appeal to a wide community of readers.

Dr Gail Tulloch, author of *Euthanasia – Choice and Death* (Edinburgh University Press, 2005)

Carolyne Lee is an Australian writer, translator, and former university lecturer. www.carolynelee.com.au

CHOOSING TO LIVE,

a memoir of my husband

CHOOSING TO DIE

CAROLYNE LEE

ARCADIA

Published 2021 by Arcadia
the general books' imprint of
Australian Scholarly Publishing Ltd
7 Lt Lothian St Nth, North Melbourne, Vic 3051
Tel: 03 9329 6963 / Fax: 03 9329 5452
enquiry@scholarly.info / www.scholarly.info

ISBN 978-1-922669-02-5

Cover Design: Sarah Anderson

For my sons, and for Bill's family.

Mortality is the human condition … The learned consciousness that our time is not infinite adds a fundamental meaning and value to the time we have—an edge that would be missing were we immortal.

— Gail Tulloch, *Euthanasia – Choice and Death*[1]

Contents

Author's Note

Although this book depicts real events,
I have used pseudonyms for some people.

Acknowledgements

An earlier version of the final two chapters of this book was published in *The Saturday Paper*, 21 June 2014, at a time of urgent debate about Voluntary Assisted Dying. I am grateful to the following for permission to quote: Nick Couldry, from his book, *Listening Beyond the Echoes*; the family of the late Aidan Fennessy, from his play *The Architect*; Rhonda Galbally, from her autobiography *Just Passions*; and Gail Tulloch, from her book *Euthanasia - Choice and Death.* I wish to thank many people without whom this book would not have come into being. Bill's sister Merrilyn and her children, and his brothers Wayne and Grant strongly encouraged me to write the book, but also provided me with many stories about Bill's life before I met him. Bill's mother June was a great source of support. My two sons help to keep Bill's memory alive in innumerable ways. Andrew McRae is a tough but constructive reader of most drafts I produce, providing insight and editorial support for which I am always grateful. Gratitude is due to those who aided me in the following ways: providing primary source information, commenting on early drafts, encouraging me to seek publication, or giving the gift of their time and expertise: Mary Henley Collopy, Bryn Jones, Virginia Lloyd, Rosie Maddick, Jennifer Martin, Catherine Nowak, Penelope Nunn-Guinet, Annie Risk, Blair Sanderson, Robert Sessions, Margaret Simons, Kerry Sunderland, Gail Tulloch, the late Dr David Burke, the late Jennifer Cummins, and those who provided information anonymously. Thank you to Nick Walker and his team at Australian Scholarly Publishing.

Introduction

> [A]ll the characters are consumed by the process of trying to find their appropriate role in the stark spotlight of mortality. How are we meant to be? Anyone with an experience of death knows this. And in a broad sense, this is simply a concertinaed version of life itself. *Who are we and how are we meant to act?* And where is it that we might find the answers to this? I don't know the answer to this. But I remain curiously engaged …
>
> — Aidan Fennessy[2]

In many ways I was searching for answers when, several years after my 45-year-old husband's death by euthanasia, I finally began to write about his life. Given the enormity of the act of euthanasia, such a search was only to be expected.

For the final decade of his life Bill had been the major part of mine and my children's lives. I was 38 when we became a couple, and when Bill first took on the role of stepfather to my children, then aged 9 and 7. Ten years later, after too many years of serious illness, weak and in pain, Bill made the decision to end his life. He was weak only in the physical sense: in his mind he was stronger than most of us will ever be. So few at any age have the ability to face their own mortality, to take control of it, and to call time on a life that is no longer physically endurable due to pain and incurable illness.

During our time together, the chief elements constituting Bill's life and identity were his active roles as stepfather and husband, and as head of department in an Institute of Technical and Further Education. He valued these roles more than anything, for they imbued his world with meaning and purpose, providing a high quality of life, with all the aspects he'd long sought. He was uniquely qualified to judge what he deemed a 'high quality', given that he'd experienced the exact opposite for most of his teenage years.

When his health began to fail in his early forties, he continued his normal life for as long as possible, despite often feeling desperately ill and frequently needing medical interventions. But the day arrived when he could continue no longer. He may have been able to go on living for several more years; but a lot of that time would have been in hospital, in pain, completely helpless, and the active roles that gave his life the elements for which he'd fought so hard would have all but disappeared. He saw this as nothing less than a loss of self.

His were quite ordinary roles really, but what made them so important were the extraordinary efforts Bill had been forced to make in order to acquire and keep them. He was well aware of this, and rightly proud of it, and wanted to and should have written his story himself. I fully expected to see him make a start on it during our time together, but he never did. He was always so busy, and then when ill-health hit him in his final few years, he used all his remaining energy just to continue living his 'ordinary' life, especially working in his beloved profession.

We see people with a disability on the public stage if they are talented athletes or successful comedians, but rarely if they quietly lead seemingly ordinary lives, as the majority of people with a disability do. This absence or invisibility is a subtle form of discrimination, however unwitting, and undermines the identity of ordinary people with a disability, in effect delegitimising or denying their existence. To redress this denial is one of my motivations for wanting to tell Bill's story. At the same time, I worry that in doing so I'm usurping his voice. But as I began my first tentative steps in planning to write about him, urged by members of Bill's family, I started to see my remembering of him, and my reassembling of his story, as a new sort of relation with him, a type of conversation even, and one that continues because, in many cases, those whom we have lost can become part of us. If this is the case, then instead of usurping his voice, perhaps this ongoing conversation could enable his voice to be heard again in some way, mingled with other voices, but participating nevertheless in the telling of his story.

As well as redressing the denial I spoke of—the denial of the existence of four million Australians who live with a disability (10,000 of whom have a spinal cord injury such as Bill's)—by telling the story of an 'ordinary' man, I also want to make a record of Bill's achievements, for both the family and the general public, because there is a great deal about his life that is inspirational to others. I did not know the full extent of this when I started writing the book, as I had been with him for only the final ten years of his life. While I was witness to the success of his efforts, I lacked a deep and detailed knowledge of his life before I entered it.

To obtain information that I lacked, I certainly drew on what his family remembered, but such memories do not always tally; in this case, dates and details I was given seemed somewhat fluid at times, and over certain events different members sometimes contradicted each other. Those of us born in the 1950s (and right through to the 1990s) did not have many of our milestones captured by anything more than the odd black and white photograph. Clearly, to complement and correct the oral information, I would have to supplement it.

Through Freedom of Information requests, I managed to gain access to detailed hospital records of Bill's very lengthy and complicated medical history, records I never saw during his lifetime. These provide a rich primary source from which I have attempted to reconstruct an account of his life from the age of thirteen. Letters from teachers and doctors have also become an important source for me, as have in-depth interviews with significant people who knew him in his teens and twenties. From these widely diverse sources I have slowly assembled the jigsaw pieces, finally forming my own vivid picture of Bill's life.

The bare facts of the story are dramatic enough: almost killed and tragically maimed in a road accident at thirteen; incorrectly diagnosed by the medical system, struggling for nearly a year to communicate without a voice; regarded for at least the first six months post-accident as intellectually disabled; and not permitted until he was 19 to be integrated into mainstream education, mainly because he was confined to a wheelchair. After major and traumatising surgery requiring almost a year of lying in a hospital bed, he finished secondary school successfully, followed that with a university degree, and gradually began to build a professional career. Little by little he proved his capabilities, rising slowly but surely in his profession of secondary teacher and educational administrator, until he became the head of a department.

I met Bill in 1990 when he was in his penultimate position as head of the Evening School section of the Box Hill Technical and Further Education (TAFE) Institute. We married at the end of 1993. Eight years later—after being seriously ill for several years—he chose to die. It was then, and still can be, very difficult in Australia for those who are seriously or terminally ill to end their lives peacefully, and at the time and place of their choosing, except in very specific circumstances, and dependent on state legislation. But in December 2001, my husband managed to achieve such a death. But it is not his death I wanted to focus on in my memoir of him; rather, it was his life, the 'ordinary' but against-the-odds life of a man with the disability of paraplegia.

Although I do not want to focus on death, neither do I want to avoid it. Death is the only reason that life is so precious. More than anyone I have ever known, Bill saw life as extremely precious. And he wanted a death in keeping with his view of life, and with the way he had lived his adult years. He constantly challenged all expectations, especially conventional ones, not only to improve his own life, but also to help others—particularly all the young people who undertook the programs in his department—and to try to change aspects of society that were unjust or discriminatory. In a way, it was almost logical that he died the way he did, against mainstream medical advice and conventional wisdom.

It took me many years from the time of his death before I could physically write a word about Bill. Each time I tried to make a start, something strong but intangible prevented me. In the immediate aftermath of his death when others—not as close to him as I was—were writing his obituaries, I looked on uselessly, as if struck dumb, thinking: 'I should be writing that'. But I couldn't; I felt paralyzed. This paralysis continued until nearly a decade had passed.

In trying to make sense of my paralysis, I undertook research into the act of writing about a loved one who has died. As a result, I now understand that in addition to the reasons I've given above, I was also prevented by fear. While it may be a fairly common desire to want to 'bring back' a beloved by writing about them, it is also the violation of a taboo, of which for a long time I was afraid. This is hardly remarkable, given that our society is a death-denying one, an aspect that has been written about extensively; the bereaved are exhorted to 'get on' with their lives, to 'move on', and the quicker the better. Few people are comfortable about focusing on the reality of death and its centrality in life.

Even with people who are facing death, the topic is often not raised. I have been told by cancer sufferers that many doctors will not speak to them about dying. They simply do not want to talk about it. This is surely shortchanging the person who is dying, and does not serve anyone's interests.

It is hardly surprising that few of us really want to examine death in any reflective way. Even fewer would ask 'How do we learn to die?', a question intimately linked with the one posed by playwright Aidan Fennessy in the lines I have chosen for my epigraph to this introduction. And yet the last period of a person's life can in a sense be the culmination, transformative of everyone involved. As I began to write Bill's story, I realised this was very much the case, for him, and for us, his family.

If we see death in this way, as something more integrated into life, we are more likely to be able to accept our mortality and face it squarely, thus deepening our respect for the value of life itself. By accepting our mortality, I mean acknowledging a private awareness that one day we will die, an awareness that binds us to all others.

Bill indeed accepted and faced his mortality squarely, especially in his final two years, although he rightly kept this private until his final week, for it is an intensely personal undertaking, only to be shared at the appropriate moment. When it was shared, his acceptance and transformation was, for those of us who cared for him in his final week, a type of metamorphosis, an ongoing one. I cannot speak for others, but for me it was a long, often painful, and profound process, one that has continued to this day, enriching my life with a particular meaning I could otherwise never have grasped.

It is through the framework of this meaning that Bill's story needs to be told, but the framework has to be built, painstakingly, like the jigsaw I mentioned earlier; this one several metres long and wide, with tens of thousands of pieces, many requiring preternatural perception in order to be distinguished from each other. Of course, when I speak of jigsaw pieces, I'm really talking about words, and I've been searching for many years now for what I consider to be the appropriate words. The lack of appropriate words, of any words, following the death of a friend or a loved one is a common phenomenon. But it is important that they be found, for it can be too easy to forget the one who has died. It was this realisation, becoming stronger and stronger as the years slipped by, that Bill's life and achievements would be effaced or concealed—simply by time's passing and by my inertia born of inability—if I were not to tell the story of his life; and this is what impelled me, albeit belatedly, to finally find the words.

This choice of words is never an easy matter. It is not merely a question of bearing witness, of being faithful to the loved one, although certainly in such cases the writer would seem to be performing an act of fidelity. This very act is fraught with danger, though, as many writers have discussed. There is the ever-present risk, especially in describing one's relationship with the loved one, of appropriation, and as well of a type of narcissism, including the creation of pity for the survivor, so easy to construct inadvertently when relying on one's personal memory. One way to mitigate such pathos is to refuse to exclude all difficulties and conflict from the story of the loved one. This means resisting the urge to perform a whitewash over troublesome aspects of one's relationship with the person who has died. It is also important to guard against the ever-present egotism of the writer who is perhaps unconsciously seeking a 'last word'. I hope desperately to avoid this egotism, although of course it will not be me who will be the judge of that. But if anyone has a 'last word', I want it to be Bill.

To avoid these dangers, I felt I should let Bill speak as much as possible, so that my voice would only be heard following or responding to his. This, too, presented difficulties, as it is surely an over-faithfulness. I could end up with a story too stilted, without the friction and fluctuations of everyday life. This would be as bad as the inverse—where all the words come from the living and not the dead, annihilating the person a second time; yet it is only because of and through me, the writer, that Bill may speak. I wanted to find the words that would allow me to navigate this almost impossible choice, between Scylla and Charybdis, infidelities both; but then I never expected the voyage to be easy.

The voyage is also not easy in other ways: there is the pain of the re-evocation of the loss and grief that few are keen to endure a second time. The pain of this re-evocation is perhaps diminished the longer one waits before writing, as in my case, but it is still there: the price one has to be prepared to pay for 'keeping alive' the loved one. This concept of 'keeping alive' is an important one, mentioned by many bereaved people, as well as by writers on this topic. Once we write about our dead we affirm their existence within us, within our story, and thus we can no longer completely lose them. Many memoirs are written by those of us left behind, specifically to tell the story of a loved partner, or other family member. Through our writing we must be hoping to bestow a type of life, a bestowal that is not one-way. The dead can endow us with precious knowledge. This is something long known to humanity, as exemplified by various myths, such as the well-known story of Orpheus and Eurydice.

It is the knowledge of mortality that an intimacy with death brings us, a knowledge that can enhance our appreciation of life, that can encourage an opening up of and to the world. My own world, and that of my sons, was opened up by both the life and death of Bill. But to affirm this, to keep both the gift of knowledge and the gift-giver alive within us, the story must be given the shape of words. This means the story can then go out into the world of readers, and perhaps change that world a little.

And that is my hope for this memoir of Bill, that I ultimately came to feel was something he would have wanted to be written. As I mentioned before, I always expected him to write his own story. As well as his story of sheer survival, he also wanted to reveal the ignorance and ineptitude, the discrimination and exclusion, that still surrounded the treatment of disability, including paraplegia, in the nineteen-sixties and seventies. Equally, he would have told of the inspired contributions to his life that were made by many individuals; of the untiring support of his family; of the fight to receive a 'normal' education, to attend university, to obtain work as an administrator and teacher; of his interest in disability activism through his teenage years in the 1970s; and of his continuous efforts to be treated simply as an 'ordinary' man in many contexts that most of us take for granted.

Being with Bill every day, seeing him doing the ordinary things that most of us do—getting showered and dressed for work, wheeling out to his car, folding up the wheelchair with one hand before transferring it on to the roof of the car by means of a special hoist, then driving to work, and repeating that process in reverse—I used to think, admiringly, that he often expended more effort just preparing for his day than many of us exert in a whole day. Of course, had he written his own book he would very likely not have focused on these daily concerns, because for him they were perfectly ordinary. He would certainly have written of his professional life—of its joys and sorrows, and probably of marriage and raising children. He wrote a great many things in our time together—mostly to do with his work as a teacher and educational administrator—but never anything autobiographical. So the memoir I've written is inevitably different from the one Bill would have produced, and different from one that anyone else close to him might write. This is as it should be; each writer can only write what seems true to him or her at the time, what fits with his or her experiences, ethics and values.

A principal concern of mine in writing the life and death of another is an ethical one. Just because everything can now be captured on media and immediately put into the public sphere—from the tears of reality television contestants through to gruesome political assassinations—does not mean we should have no standards, no frameworks for judgment about what is ethically appropriate to be shared on a large scale. But how can an individual author hope to articulate such ethics, in the absence of any that are universally agreed-upon?

In addressing this question, media theorist Nick Couldry argues that ethics in this sense must focus on the issue of how we should live, with the most important question of ethics being how can we, as members of society, live together well? In framing the issue in this way, he is explicitly drawing on Socrates' recommendations of questions we should ask ourselves. The first is 'How should I live?' and the second, depending on our answer to the first question, is 'How should each of us conduct our life so that it is a life any of us could value?' Couldry believes that living well with others is about 'human flourishing', that is, to develop in a healthy or vigorous way.[3]

On this basis, I could say that there is only a purpose to publication if the material will help others flourish. At the same time, if we turn to the values that are supposed to underlie democratic society, they are the values of respecting and not harming others, values regularly neglected in the media. I'd like to argue strongly that, if or when any of us become involved in the media process in any form, we should make every attempt to adhere very carefully to the virtues of accuracy and sincerity, but balance these virtues with efforts to take very good care that our words don't hurt others. This is just as important for a memoir as for any kind of media text. I find this consideration—taking care not to cause hurt—to be a useful guiding principle, coupled with Couldry's notion of flourishing, of helping others to flourish, for this really was the leitmotif of Bill's whole life.

Bill was someone who inspired strong emotions in almost everyone he encountered. In most cases these emotions were positive, although not always. He was no saint, and no easier to live with than anyone else, and it's not my aim to write a hagiography. Following the principles I've outlined above, I simply want to tell his story. For I think it's one that can help us to live, to flourish, and to die, and along the way to seek if not to find answers to the question, 'Who are we and how are we meant to act?'[4]

Prologue

I was not there when it happened on that winter morning in late June 1969, in outer suburban Melbourne. How could I have been? We would not meet for another twenty years. But like him, I too was then a teenager, although living over three thousand kilometres away on the west coast of this vast island.

For each of us the day began like any other. That ordinary Monday when Bill's first life ended, as he sometimes described it. His life as a boy who could walk, run, kick a football; whose spinal cord, brain, and limbs all worked perfectly; who planned, 'when he grew up', to be a footballer with one of the major Victorian Football League teams. Unlike for most young boys with such plans, for Bill it had been a realistic goal.

Somehow I must tell of that day; I must recreate it. First in my own mind, for myself, but also for the readers of Bill's story. It is, after all, the initiating event of his story. It caused everything that followed: first, the bad, which endured for a long time. But also the good. This event set up the defining paradox of his life. To fight endlessly for a satisfying quality of life, but once that quality was gone, to face death with more than bravery; to embrace it.

Bill always marked 23 June. At the start of each year he marked it in his diary, although he hardly needed a reminder. As he said, it was the anniversary of a death. On those days he was quieter than usual, more reflective. I would take a little more care around him, be more circumspect; put extra effort into preparing something for our evening meal that I knew he especially liked. Over dinner he would perhaps refer to one or other of the details of his accident, but not always.

We did not often pass the place where it had happened, but occasionally we had to, for his parents lived in Croydon, an outer suburb of Melbourne, and sometimes his nephew played football in that area. The first time we drove through the intersection, Bill said quietly, 'That's where I had my accident'. So from early on it was always part of the geography of his story, of our story.

When I came to write Bill's story, something his family strongly encouraged me to do, seemed to need me to do, I became aware that I didn't know the full account of that day; the only person who did was Bill's brother Wayne. He generously agreed to revisit that day that had robbed him too of more than any child should have to lose, and to tell me what he remembered. I listened carefully and took notes.

Because I wanted to paint a picture of that time, over fifty years ago now, when most children were probably less cossetted than they are today, more independent, I asked the rest of Bill's family for their recollections of that period. As well as the tragic event, related a little differently by each family member, several humorous stories emerged as well, which I felt I must include in any account of Bill's adolescence.

Over several weeks, I drafted an account of Bill's life in the context of his family, which itself provided the context for his accident. This was the chapter in which I was most frightened of usurping Bill's voice, of appropriating his story. To counter this fear, I decided I would begin from the relatively safe position of a social historian, narrating the life of an ordinary family with four children in 1969, showing their roles, their daily activities and motivations, what they spent their money on, what media they consumed—an extremely sparse amount by today's standards. For the accident itself, I wanted to zoom in closer, to show the sequence of events through the eyes of the two boys, based on the information Wayne had given me.

The latter part of the chapter was the hardest thing I have ever had to write. I had to imagine myself into that day and that place, sometimes through Bill's eyes, but mostly through Wayne's. During this period of writing, my dreams were filled with these two harum-scarum boys, tearing around on their bikes in that new suburb in the foothills.

I wrote the first draft of the accident before visiting the actual location. Once I started writing, though, the location appeared in my imagination like a vivid dream. I felt the wheels of my imaginary bike crunching over the gravel as I pedalled along the road. In my peripheral vision I glimpsed the trees on either side, many of them Australian natives in full leaf despite it being midwinter. In my dream-vision, a large eucalyptus tree towered over the others, signifying a marker in the brothers' race along the road. I finished my first draft, and drove to the site of the accident in Croydon. It was a mid-week morning; mine was the only car moving in the side roads, and I crawled along in second gear, trying to take everything in, pulling over every so often to jot down notes.

Suddenly, the giant eucalypt from my imagination loomed ahead. Most trees of this type live for a couple of hundred years, so it would certainly have been there fifty years ago, even if a few metres shorter.

Reality's mirroring of what I had previously only imagined felt like a sign that I was on the right track. I don't believe in signs and portents, yet sometimes things happen that we can't rationally explain. I don't remember, but perhaps Bill had driven us down that road not long after we started seeing each other. Perhaps the tree had lodged in my subconscious, to resurface at the appropriate time. I'll never know.

My fear of appropriating Bill's story, of misappropriation even, fell away after I had driven along those roads. Or almost. There was still Wayne's response to hear. Had I represented his memories correctly? How would he feel when reading my reconstruction? I sent him the file, saying he should not hesitate to correct me. After a few days he sent back a short email. 'It's fine,' he said simply, in typical fashion; Johnson fashion.

1969: The Accident

There were few students or teachers at Croydon High School in the outer suburbs of Melbourne in the late sixties who hadn't at least heard of the two Johnson brothers. With an age difference only two days shy of twelve months, they were more like twins, and rarely apart. The two of them participated in every daredevil pursuit possible, both inside and outside school. Despite being the younger, thirteen-year-old Bill was slightly taller and more athletic than Wayne, and was the star of the school's under-16 football team, and the cricket eleven.

The brothers were especially fascinated by all things mechanical, and by household technology of the time. If the family radio or television broke down, and if their father was out, they would find his toolbox and try to 'fix' the problem themselves. Mr Johnson might return home to see the family radio—in those days a large apparatus often bigger than today's desktop computer—in pieces all over the boys' bedroom floor. The 'beltings' their father gave them for their efforts never seemed to deter them.

On one occasion, Bill and Wayne awoke very early one Saturday morning while their parents were still asleep, and decided to have some fun in their father's beloved Holden Kingswood sedan. With Wayne in the driver's seat, and Bill on the bench seat beside him, they managed to start the motor, back the car out of the garage, and were slowly edging it backwards down the steep driveway when pyjama-clad Mr Johnson burst out of the front door. He ran across the lawn towards the car, yelling for them to stop, his pyjama pants sliding slowly downwards. The boys managed to pull on the handbrake and stop the car, and hurled themselves out of the doors, intending to run away from him. But at the sight of their father hobbling along with his pyjamas around his ankles, they were laughing so hard that Mr Johnson had time to pull up his pants and catch both of them.

On Saturday afternoons the boys were obliged to help their father with his 'moonlighting' soft-drink round—in his main job he worked as a fireman—delivering bottles to houses in the other new suburbs around Croydon, Mooroolbark, Kilsyth and Bayswater, as did their younger sister Merrilyn once she was nine or ten. In the 1960s many women at home with small children did not have a car, nor any easy means of travelling to shops, which could be quite a distance in the outer suburbs. As well as milk, many items were home delivered, and bottled carbonated drinks were becoming popular. The three children loathed this chore imposed by their father, especially since he almost always remained in the car while they had to go back and forth to the houses with the orders; but they were each paid 70 cents for the afternoon's work, about seven dollars by today's standards.

As soon as Bill and Wayne had saved enough money, they bought themselves each a second-hand bicycle. Both bikes were old and well-used—that's why they were going cheap—and Bill's was really too big for him, but he knew this wouldn't be for long, as he was growing quickly. The bikes enabled the boys not only to ride to school, avoiding a long walk, but also to do their shared paper round much faster. For a couple of years they'd been doing an early morning paper round.

It's almost unimaginable nowadays to think of all those copies of *The Age* or *The Sun* being home-delivered in the mornings so that people could read them on the bus or train on their daily journey to work. And then the afternoon paper, *The Herald,* would provide fresh news for people to read in the evenings. This was the high point of newspaper readership, but it was not to last. Gradually, by the mid-1980s, the majority of people had their own cars and drove to work, causing the first dramatic dip in newspaper circulation, mainly because a person can't drive and read at the same time!

In early 1969 Bill and Wayne exchanged their morning paper round for an afternoon one, because they'd obtained work on Monday mornings at the Croydon market. For two hours of unloading goods from trucks and vans for the traders they were paid around a dollar, whereas a paper round only paid two dollars for the whole week. Once football season started Bill couldn't help with the paper round on two afternoons as he played for the under-16 team with compulsory twice-weekly training.

The boys' jobs were entirely their own initiative and the proceeds were all theirs. This was an era when pocket money for children was seen not as a right but a privilege, given only in certain families, and many parents like the Johnsons simply felt they had nothing to spare. The three jobs obviously left little time for homework although Bill, being academically very able, managed not to fall behind; but Wayne's performance at school was starting to suffer. Many thirteen- and fourteen-year-olds at that time, with only a fraction of the money and material possessions that most teenagers today take for granted, would have chosen part-time jobs over homework any day. And the two boys were earning a significant amount for children of that age: it was the equivalent of around fifty dollars between them, by today's standards.

They would use the money to buy the latest musical hits, then available on single or 'LP' vinyl records; or they would buy clothes or shoes that they would otherwise not have had; or, best of all, proper haircuts at the men's barbershop. This was to avoid the haircuts their father gave with his blunt clippers, which caused them to be, in their words, 'the laughing stock of the school'.

On the 23 June 1969, Bill and Wayne had risen at 5am as usual on a Monday, to start their work at Croydon Market. They often finished by 7.30, leaving plenty of time to return to their house in Taronga Crescent, have breakfast and go on to school. But today there had been more than the usual amount of stock, and it was almost 8.30 before they arrived home. Their mother, June, worked as a cashier three days a week at Woolworths Supermarket in Croydon, and was about to leave herself. As well as Wayne and Bill, and their ten-year-old sister Merrilyn, June also had Grant, her youngest, aged four, looked after by a neighbour on the days she went to work.

By the time the two brothers had changed into their uniforms, and grabbed a piece of bread and Vegemite, it was about seven minutes to nine, and they were running the risk of arriving late at school, a deed that was punished very severely. June reminded them there'd now be very heavy traffic if they took their usual route through the busy intersection of Hull and Dorset Roads where there were no pedestrian lights. She instructed them to turn right just before the busy road, take the small hilly road which bypassed the cross-roads, and turn left into Dorset Road. There they could push their bikes along the footpath before turning right at the crossing into the road leading to the school. They took this route if their mother expressly asked them, although they disliked it because part of the road was gravel, which made pedalling harder. But at least the final part, Beryl Street, leading into Dorset Road, sloped downhill, where they liked to race.

As they turned into the first part of the gravel road, Alwyn Street, passing the convent of Our Lady of the Sacred Heart on the left, they pedalled hard to pick up speed. There was no one else around, neither car nor pedestrian. Even today, almost fifty years later, this section of the road is still gravel, and resembles more a rural enclave, than it does the rest of suburban Croydon. The two boys hurtled around the right-angle bend, where the road becomes Beryl Street and the gentle slope begins, and continued pedalling fast to prevent their bikes from skidding on the gravel.

They liked to keep up the momentum until they could see the cars flowing along the main road, Dorset Road, ahead of them, by which time they were almost level with a large eucalyptus tree on the right, about thirty metres before the main road. This was where they usually started braking, by pushing backwards on the pedals, giving them enough braking distance before reaching the intersection, where they'd often execute spectacular skids, sometimes spinning their bikes around 360 degrees in the process.

Instead of the lever brakes attached to handlebars that are common today, many bicycles in the 1960s and 70s had what were known as 'coaster brakes', activated when the rider pushes the pedals in reverse. This type of brake, used since the early 1900s, required less maintenance than the more expensive lever brakes, and worked equally well in wet or dry weather. But in the rare event of the bicycle's chain breaking, coaster brakes would instantly fail.

On that morning in June, Wayne—the faster cyclist with his lighter, wiry build—was a few metres ahead of Bill, whose bike was larger and more cumbersome (although sometimes with a mammoth effort Bill could overtake him). Up ahead was the large eucalyptus tree where they'd usually begin braking, ready to stop at the main road. Suddenly Bill felt a huge jolt: he must have hit a pothole before bouncing out of it, although staying upright. But strangely his bike now seemed to pick up speed. Looking down, he realised what had happened. 'My chain's broken,' he shouted to Wayne.

'Yeah, sure,' Wayne yelled, without looking back. He'd heard this one a few times before, and on those occasions had stopped and turned around, only to see Bill whizz past him, laughing crazily as he took the lead.

He wasn't to know that this time it was for real. Unseen by Wayne, on the right-hand side of Bill's bike, the long end of the chain was lashing wildly around, defying gravity. Instinctively, Bill stuck out his right leg, trying to get his foot on to the road and stop the bike. Immediately, he felt as if giant jaws had snapped around his lower thigh. It was the broken chain leaping like a steel serpent until it had his leg in its embrace. The pain blocked out everything. Bill froze. He couldn't yell out. He couldn't let go.

It was another few seconds before Wayne applied his own brakes, oblivious to what was happening behind him and, with a neat curving skid, came to a stop just before the intersection. He now turned sideways and looked over his shoulder. Immediately Bill hurtled down the slope, straight past him. Clamped to the bike by the chain around his left leg, Bill careered straight into the flow of peak-hour traffic. There was the screech of car brakes, and then a terrible, terrifying thud.

Wayne saw his brother's trapped leg ripped off by the impact, while his body was flung to the grass verge on the other side of the road. It was not a wide road, and Wayne could see the blood gushing from what was left of Bill's thigh. He ran to the house on the corner, pounding on the front door, screaming, 'Get an ambulance, get an ambulance'. Then somehow he made his way across the busy road to his brother. Bill was lying very still, half on his side, facing away from the road, his eyes shut. Wayne tried to staunch the blood with his hand. Some passing cars stopped. A man ran over with a bag, saying he was a doctor. He took a strap from his bag and applied a tourniquet. He took out syringes and gave the boy two injections. Before long loud sirens and flashing red lights announced the ambulance had arrived.

Bill's leg, thought Wayne, *it's back on the other side of the road. They'll forget it.* He tried to say something, but the paramedics were conferring with the doctor, while leaning over Bill, doing something, he couldn't see what. He tried to talk to them, but no one was listening, no one heard him. Now they were putting Bill on to a stretcher, ready to put him in the ambulance. The traffic was thinner now, so he crossed the road, picked up the torn-off part of his brother's leg, and took it back to the ambulance. One of the paramedics now noticed him, took the leg gently from him. 'Are you his brother?' Wayne nodded dumbly. 'Hop in,' said the man, and then he climbed in behind the boy, and sat next to him on the bench beside Bill, lying very still and pale on his stretcher.

'We're taking him to hospital,' said the man. 'He's lost so much blood, and we don't yet know about his internal injuries. We've done everything we can, but we don't think he's going to make it.'

1990–91: The Man in the Wheelchair

Late one August afternoon I approached the Evening School administration area, an expanse of open-plan office just inside the entrance to a large red-brick building, a few minutes' drive from the Box Hill campus where I was based. My stomach was jumping around, my mouth was dry and I felt a little light-headed. There were two reasons for this. It would be the first time I'd ever taught a module of a final-year subject (known as the Victorian Certificate of Education, or VCE). And I had to report to Bill Johnson, who was in charge of this section. I'd met him briefly the previous December, in my first year at the Institute, and since then had seen him only once or twice in staff meetings of our combined sections. But his name came up frequently in discussions in my department. He seemed to be known as a bit of a larrikin, but also as someone who lived for his work and was extremely efficient at managing the Evening School, as well as teaching his academic specialty, VCE Politics. Ever since meeting him, I'd wanted to see him again, and now I had a perfect excuse. I didn't want to blow it.

As soon as I entered the administration area I saw Bill seated behind his desk. He was bent over some papers, a pen in one hand. I had plenty of time before my class started and had been hoping we'd be able to have a chat. Holding my heavy pile of books in front of me, I approached him, worrying that he wouldn't remember me, given that our introduction had been eight months ago, and very brief.

I took a deep breath. 'Hi, I'm Carolyne. I teach in Paul's Writing course. Paul introduced us last December, if you recall?'

He looked up slowly and smiled, somewhat ironically I thought, before saying, 'How could I forget?'

Gesturing for me to sit down on the chair in front of his desk, and with merely a hint of gentle impudence in his slight smile, he asked, 'So what are you planning to do in *my* Evening School?' I knew he was well aware of why I was there, but I played along. I told him that my Head of Department had asked me to teach the four-week Writing Workshop segment of the VCE English class, during which the students would prepare a folio of different types of texts.

'Ah yes, I heard they'd managed to hire a few of you "real writers" to teach in the new writing course,' he said, openly playful now. But then he became serious, asking, 'So what do you write?'

'I've been freelancing for newspapers for a few years,' I told him, 'mainly for *The Age*, writing feature articles on various aspects of culture, as well as book reviews—that sort of thing. Plus my co-edited book has just been published.'

This had only happened recently; it was my first book. To compile it, my co-editor and I had collected essays from thirty-six women about how they had chosen whether or not to have children, discussing their reasons, or detailing how they had not consciously chosen. In writing the Introduction and also my own chapter, I'd written about ten percent of the book myself as well as doing the co-editing. It had been published by Angus and Robertson.

Because I'd been planning to show a copy of it to the new group of students, it was at the top of the pile of books I was carrying, so I handed it to Bill. He pored over it at once and seemed very interested. 'Where can I get a copy?' he asked. I told him I'd bring one to work the next day, and send it to him in the internal mail. I wanted to get it to him quickly. For some reason it seemed terribly important to me that he should read it straightway so I could hear his opinion when I arrived at the Evening School the following week. As it turned out, I didn't even have to wait that long. A few days later, I found a letter from Bill in my staff pigeonhole. I felt very moved that he'd gone to the effort to read the book, or most of it, in such a short time, so that he could discuss it with me.

In his letter, he told me he'd expected from its title *Who'd be a Mother?* that the book's contents would be rather strident. He was instead surprised to find enormous variety in the thirty-six points of view, many that he'd never considered before; the book had left an overall impression on him, he said, of motherhood being excessively hard work because of the way our society was structured, yet overall worth the effort.

He pointed out that as a man he felt it was problematic for him to make pronouncements about motherhood. His own views on the topic, he said, were very much shaped by his mother's and his sister's ways of mothering, both women seeming fiercely maternal; at the same time both had worked outside the home and were very strong and assertive. His mother June's strength, in particular, had been crucial in supporting Bill during his long period of rehabilitation.

For each of the next three weeks I arrived early to teach my class, and Bill and I would chat in his office. I looked forward to these evenings very much and took great care about what to wear. Bill always wore colourful shirts and matching ties, with a brown or navy suit jacket. I still have a framed photograph in my study, taken at that time, in which he's wearing a deep blue shirt with a brightly patterned tie, mostly red, but patterned with swirls of the same blue as his shirt.

Bill and I moved on from discussing my book, and various teaching matters, to sharing details of our lives. He gave me a brief outline of how, following his accident and several years of hospitalisation, he'd spent four years in the Yooralla Special School for children with disabilities, a place he didn't remember fondly. In those days, there had been widespread discrimination at most levels of society, and he and his mother had been ridiculed by the authorities and committees to which they'd had to apply, for wanting to move Bill out of Yooralla and into a regular school to complete his secondary education with a view to going on to university.

Despite having taught some children and young people with various disabilities, I'd never had close contact with a person confined to a wheelchair. How many do we come into daily contact with? Even today, although elite sportspeople like Dylan Alcott and Kurt Fearnley deservedly receive much publicity, we still see very little media coverage of people in wheelchairs leading ordinary lives in all parts of society. Perhaps this is because many of our public places and buildings are still not wheelchair friendly, nearly forty years after the first International Year of Disabled Persons was proclaimed in 1981 by the United Nations. As recently as the end of 2018, there was a demonstration in Sydney Road in the Melbourne suburb of Brunswick by people in wheelchairs and those pushing prams, protesting at Public Transport Victoria's broken promise that by the end of 2017 ninety percent of tram stops would be accessible.

Bill told me that although it was now 1990 he certainly couldn't use public transport independently, something that had motivated him to learn to drive with hand controls. I told him I'd had a small glimpse of accessibility issues during my time of pushing a pram and then a stroller when my children were small; I'd even mentioned these difficulties in the chapter in my book. After meeting Bill I tried to imagine having such accessibility problems for a whole lifetime.

Was it the enormous effort required of people like Bill to lead an ordinary life that so impressed me the first time I met him? It had been the previous December, when our Institute's CEO had invited all staff for end-of-semester afternoon drinks; two teachers from my staffroom, Paul and Marie, were planning to attend, so I trailed along behind them. The large hall was packed with people, and we stood amid the noisy roar of several hundred voices. Paul disappeared briefly, returning with drinks, and led us into a small space at the side. A short distance away, what looked to be a tall slender man, perhaps in his early thirties, was sitting in a wheelchair beside a large man who was bending over him, probably to converse over the noise.

I couldn't take my eyes off the man in the wheelchair. For a man so tall and broad-shouldered, he sat neatly, replying to the other man from time to time, and occasionally sipping from a glass of beer. I wanted to take in every detail. He was wearing a light brown jacket and a cream-coloured shirt with a button-down collar, but no tie. I also noticed immediately that he had only one leg, his left. His face had the symmetry of an intricate sculpture, and his hair was dark brown, receding slightly and curling on to his shoulders at the back. His neat, slightly pointed beard was a lighter, golden brown. But his large intense eyes were the most arresting of all. I thought he was the most beautiful person I'd ever seen.

He seemed to be assiduously avoiding looking in my direction, even though I must have been staring at him; instead, he was focused on the man to whom he was talking. Worried that he might notice my staring and assume it was the rude stare that the able-bodied sometimes inflict on people with a disability, I turned back to Paul, but kept him in my peripheral vision. From time to time I felt the slight frisson that indicates one is being looked at. I hoped it was him but didn't dare check.

Noticing the two men had finished their conversation, Paul started to move towards them, indicating with a tilt of his head that I should follow him. 'Hi Bill,' he said to the man in the wheelchair, 'how're you going? Haven't seen you for a while.' They exchanged a few words, but I couldn't hear much over the background babble of the crowded hall. Paul grabbed my arm, pulled me closer, leaned towards Bill, and said, 'This is Carolyne, Bill, a new member of our department; Carolyne, this is Bill. He's in charge of our Evening School.' Bill and I nodded at each other politely, but he didn't smile or show the least interest. I found this intriguing. I was thirty-five but looked much younger, and was used to rather more enthusiastic greetings when introduced to men! I later discovered that he was several years into a rather tempestuous relationship which would continue for another eighteen months.

Paul and Bill chatted for a while longer, although the noise meant I couldn't hear or participate. The CEO started his speech and everyone fell silent. Afterwards, a few people began leaving. Bill said goodbye to us with a nod of his head, spun around in his wheelchair, and sped away, the crowd in front of him parting left and right, leaping and laughing to get out of his way, as if they were used to this. I promised myself to try and get to know him better, if the occasion presented itself.

That night I dreamed about Bill. I was looking out of the window of the front room in my house and saw him walking up the path. He knocked at the door. When I opened it, he towered over me; he was wearing a tan-coloured suit. I was expecting him, and wore one of my favourite dresses, heels, and makeup. In the dream it seemed surprising that he was calling on me like this. There the dream ended, but the memory of it is with me always.

On the evening of the final week of my classes at the Evening School, I said to Bill, 'I'll really miss our chats'.

'So will I,' he said, looking at me more seriously than usual.

I took a deep breath: 'Why don't we have lunch together one weekend?' I asked.

'Great idea,' he said, brightening, 'this coming Saturday?' And he scribbled his address on a piece of paper and handed it to me. 'Twelve sharp!' he said, swiftly turning his wheelchair around with a squeal of the tires and speeding off into a colleague's office, before yelling back over his shoulder, 'And bring the boys—I've got a big backyard, they'll love it!'

I was happy that he'd invited my sons, who were aged seven and five, and next day I told them that on Saturday we'd be driving up into the hills to visit a new friend of mine from work. They loved meeting new people and doing anything different, and 'into the hills' sounded like a phrase from a storybook to them. I didn't expect Bill to prepare lunch for us all, so I rang him and said I'd bring something. Did he like pumpkin soup? He did, so it was settled. He said he'd supply a salad, drinks and dessert.

I decided to tell the boys in advance that Bill was in a wheelchair, so while we were having dinner on Friday night, I said, 'My friend that we are going to see tomorrow …'

'Yes, the man who lives in the hills!' shouted the five-year-old, excitedly.

'That's right,' I said. 'Well, when he was only thirteen he had a very bad car accident and lost a leg and damaged his spine, and so he couldn't walk after that.'

'Oh, so is he in a wheelchair, like the lady who came to talk to us at assembly once?' asked my elder boy. I'd forgotten about the recent talk given by the head of a state government department which dealt with disability services. 'She told us she had a very important job, and lives in a flat all by herself, and everything,' my elder son continued. 'She said the only thing she can't do is go up and down steps!'

'Ah yes, well, Bill's a bit like that lady. He has a good job, drives a car, and lives by himself too.'

Bill's house was easy to find, just off Burwood Highway in the outer Melbourne suburb of Ferntree Gully, not far from the start of the forested green belt leading into the Dandenong Ranges National Park. His driveway led past the side of the house to a wide concreted expanse at the rear with a large garage and a small wooden ramp to the back door. Beyond the concrete was a long lawn dotted with fruit trees, divided from the green belt by a narrow creek. My little boys, accustomed to the smaller backyards and closer-spaced houses of North Balwyn, were visibly impressed. It was a fine day, and they'd remembered to bring their football, and were already dying to run around on the grass. I introduced them to Bill and they politely said 'Hello', before the younger one blurted out, 'Can we go and play in your backyard?'

'Of course you can,' Bill replied, 'but I expect your mother will want you to have something to eat first'. In the kitchen I re-heated the soup and sliced up the crusty loaf that I'd brought.

'I know I promised to make a salad,' said Bill, 'but I had an unfortunate incident in the supermarket, and the lettuce got away!'

'Got away?' said both children at once, sensing an amusing story.

'Yeah, I should have put a basket on my lap, but I thought as I only needed one or two things, it wasn't necessary. I went over to the veggie section and grabbed a lettuce. I put that on my knee, but as I was wheeling away, the lettuce started rolling off. I tried to grab it, but leaves just came away in my hands, and the lettuce rolled off and down the aisle. I didn't think the staff would approve of their lettuces being rolled around like lawn bowls, and I was obviously the culprit as I had my lap full of lettuce leaves! So I quickly brushed them off before anyone could see and sped out of there as fast as I could!'

This story made the boys roar with laughter. But, more than that, it made us realise that a simple activity like supermarket shopping was a challenge if you're in a wheelchair. 'So there won't be any salad,' said Bill, playing to the audience, and pausing for effect, 'but I do have ... Coke!' This was something I only allowed as a rare treat, so the boys thought they were in heaven. They finished their meal so quickly that Bill and I had hardly begun to eat ours.

'You can take your dessert to eat outside, if you like,' Bill said to them.

'Dessert?' I almost never gave them dessert after lunch. Bill told them to go to the freezer where they'd find a box of 'Drumstick' ice-cream cones, and to help themselves to one each. With a chorus of 'Thank you', they did as advised, and ran outside with them.

With the boys out in the garden, serious conversation became possible, and we talked for a long time, mostly about teaching, the great passion for both of us. I'd recently begun my Master of Arts, and Bill said he hoped in the near future to do a postgraduate degree in Educational Administration.

I asked him how long he'd lived in his house. Seven years, he said, adding that for six years before that he'd lived in a bungalow behind his parents' house. After a few years of working he'd decided to buy his own place. It had been difficult to find a house that was wheelchair-accessible, but eventually he'd found this one; it had been adapted and made accessible by the couple who'd owned it, for their elderly parents, one of whom used a wheelchair. All the rooms were on one level, the kitchen counters and stove were a little lower than usual, and one of the bathrooms was wheelchair accessible with a wheel-in shower.

I was surprised to learn that ideologically Bill was against the whole capitalist concept of private ownership, with big mortgages, and large profits for the banks. He thought a society's resources should be shared, and people shouldn't own houses while others went homeless. I argued that if he didn't own a house, he'd very likely have to rent one, and that would then contribute to someone else's private property, a point he admitted was true. We agreed we'd like a fairer society, with more public housing, more funding for state schools, and greater access to higher education for groups that historically lacked it.

'Do you know that only ten percent of Australians have an undergraduate degree?' he asked me. 'That figure hasn't improved for decades, and is one of the lowest among the OECD countries.' I hadn't known it and was surprised. I think he'd be happy to know that thirty years later the figure has nearly doubled. It's not that we believed the only route to success was via a university degree, but we regretted that many more Australians lacked the opportunity and the choice.

That was the first of many conversations about discrimination. Bill was very committed to fighting all forms of it, and had been involved in some of the demonstrations organised by disability groups during 1981, the International Year of the Disabled. His fierce dedication to equal opportunity for all disadvantaged groups was why he was so passionate about his work. His department catered for people aged from sixteen years upwards who had either not had the opportunity or had not succeeded in formal education elsewhere. Sometimes a mother or father in desperation would bring in a teenager so depressed they were almost catatonic, while other parents and children arrived in his office hurling abuse at each other. I already knew from department folklore that Bill almost always managed to calm them down, begin a dialogue, and encourage the young person to attempt a return to study in some form or another, with the ultimate goal of attaining the Victorian Certificate of Education.

It was becoming harder and harder for young people to obtain a job if they'd discontinued their studies before finishing year 12 and obtaining the VCE. But if they did, they could either go on to university if they had the required marks, or to one of the TAFE trade or technical courses such as veterinary nursing, library technician, beautician, hairdressing, even the professional writing course in which I taught.

We talked about our own goals. I'd already told him during our Thursday evening chats that I was separated, relatively amicably, from the father of my two children. I'd only resumed my teaching career eighteen months earlier, after staying at home for several years while the children were very young, and I was keen to complete my Master's, and even do more study and see where it led me. I also wanted to edit and perhaps write more books. Bill's ambition was to rise further in the Institute, he said. He hoped to apply for the position of Head of Department soon, once the amalgamation of his Evening School section with the larger department in which I worked had taken place.

I could have talked to him all day, but I'd heard nothing from the children for some time, so I went out to call them. They soon came running, both very muddy, and I had to help them remove their shoes and wipe dirty patches off their trousers with an old towel before they could sit on the chairs. Bill was laughing, 'Oh don't worry about it, these chairs have seen much worse with my three nephews!' It was late afternoon by now, and I thought we should head home.

As we drove west, leaving the hills and forest behind, the sky was darkening with the lovely orange glow for which sunny winter days in Melbourne are famous. In the back seat the children were calm and contented, tired out, chattering occasionally. I felt overwhelmed with admiration and respect for the new friend I'd made. I'd never known anyone so passionate about his work, his beliefs, and about his desire to make a difference to the lives of the educationally disadvantaged. He seemed to me completely without self-pity, narcissism, and all the other unpleasant traits from which most of us suffer.

I felt privileged to know Bill but couldn't see how we could get to know each other better; he'd told me that for several years he'd been with a woman in an on-and-off relationship which they were about to try and mend. Separated for only a year, I'd recently started seeing someone, but thought it best that I not become serious with anyone any time soon.

1969: Coming Back to Life

Mid-morning, Monday 23 June: a police car speeding along Mount Dandenong Road braked with a sickening squeal before turning into the Woolworths carpark in Croydon. In the front of the car were two police officers; in the back seat slumped Wayne, who'd told them to come here, knowing his mother would be at work.

One of the men and the boy left the car and hurried into the store. Wayne led the policeman to his mother, on the second cash register from the door. The man told June her son had been hit by a car and was in Box Hill Hospital. No! she thought, there must be some mistake. Wayne was here and the two boys were inseparable, so Bill must be …

But he wasn't. She looked expectantly at Wayne, waiting for him to say something. Hunched over, he looked grey and ill, dishevelled, his school jumper covered in dark stains, but at least she could see he was in one piece. So it must be Bill who was hurt. 'Madam, we must hurry,' said the policemen.

Numbly, June called out to her supervisor, mumbled something about a road accident, grabbed her jacket and, still in her cashier's tunic, followed her elder son and the policeman back to the car. As they drove out of the carpark, she realised she hadn't thought to phone her husband, Adrian, still asleep at home after his night shift with the fire brigade.

Once the car was back on the main road, June noticed they were speeding through the red lights, siren wailing, the other traffic slowing or stopping to let them through. Still confused, she turned to Wayne. 'What happened? Is he badly hurt?' Wayne nodded mutely, and stammered, 'His bike, it …' He couldn't say any more. He couldn't find the words for what he'd seen happen to his brother. The policeman in the passenger seat turned and said, 'We're trying to get you there before he …' When he saw her face, he simply could not finish his sentence.

Bill's medical records do not make easy reading, even now, all these years later. In our first year together, Bill told me the story of his accident and its aftermath. He recounted summaries of his long years of hospitalisation. His narrative seemed so remote and distant to me and was delivered so unemotionally, often in short instalments, that I always had trouble visualising him in a coma, unable to talk or breathe properly for years on end, his spinal and neurological condition undiagnosed during the first six months. I just couldn't associate all of this with a man who'd achieved so much, who during our first few years together seemed in such good health, and who'd overcome most of the physical obstacles more than a decade before we met. Revisiting Bill's medical history now, for the first time in detail, I'm struck by the almost superhuman physical and psychological efforts he must have made.

Once the most urgent of his medical problems were under control, which took over three years, Bill had to reconstruct an active, meaningful life for himself, in a situation where many would have given up. He had to re-learn almost everything—to cough and breathe normally, to talk, use a wheelchair, to manage a body with greatly reduced physical capacities. He had to do almost everything for himself with his left hand, including writing, since fine motor control never returned to his right hand, nor much strength to his right arm.

The enormous psychological efforts Bill had to make seem almost inconceivable. First, coming to terms with the devastating injuries, followed by years of hospital treatment; then the need to construct a new 'self', the complex interaction of psychic processes that we all try to make more or less 'normal' and coherent, and which we need in all our interactions with others and the world in general. We know that everything that happens in childhood and adolescence helps shape one's psyche, for good or ill. It's almost too painful to reflect on the psychic damage to a thirteen-year-old boy caused by such devastating injuries, by the inability to communicate for a long period, by his schooling being interrupted for years; worst of all, perhaps, the awareness of being seen as a huge medical 'problem' for at least the first six months in hospital. Such thoughts serve to set in relief what it must have taken for Bill to reconstruct a 'normal' selfhood from the ruins of a young life, following the effective loss of most of his teenage years.

Immediately after the accident Bill was taken by ambulance to the nearest large hospital, Box Hill and General Hospital, as it was then called, in the eastern suburbs of Melbourne. He was in a coma and frighteningly pale when admitted to Intensive Care. The staff gave him a blood transfusion and took him to the operating theatre to have the remaining part of his right leg closed. Bill told me that originally his leg had been severed just above the knee, but it became repeatedly infected, necessitating further amputations; by the end of that year barely a quarter of his thigh remained.

I once asked Bill why the doctors didn't try to re-attach his leg, for he'd told me how Wayne had ensured it was taken in the ambulance. He explained that for several weeks he'd not been expected to live, nor, if he did survive, to be anything beyond a 'vegetable', as his parents were told; in any case he didn't believe such operations were even considered feasible in 1969. He was right. The first case in Australia of a successful lower limb reattachment, of a foot, was in 1972, although upper limb reattachments had been taking place in various countries from 1962. But it was still experimental surgery, and the successful reattachment of the bottom third of a child's leg, by Japanese doctors, did not occur until 1974.

Bill was in a coma and had obviously lost a great deal of blood, but there was no visible evidence of any damage to his body other than the severed right leg, and some abrasions on his torso. The medical staff had no idea that his spinal cord had been damaged because it had occurred, apparently, without his spine having been fractured, or certainly not noticeably enough to show up on an X-ray. Children and adolescents, because of the flexibility of their bones, can sustain significant damage or even rupture of the spinal cord through extreme bending or stretching of the spine, without an X-ray revealing any detectable evidence, and this was the case with Bill.

It wasn't until he was seen by the spinal specialist Dr David Cheshire, six months later, that he was correctly diagnosed as having 'from the moment of impact … a complete paraplegia below the level of the 5th dorsal'. The paralysis also affected the muscles between his ribs, the intercostal muscles, which prevented his lungs from working properly, and so the coma was probably caused mainly by a lack of oxygen to the brain.

Bill must also have sustained a significant internal brain haemorrhage in the crash, causing some paralysis and damage—cerebral hemiplegia—to the right side of his body; this also contributed to his coma. But this wasn't properly diagnosed either until he was transferred to the Spinal Injuries Centre (since renamed the Spinal Unit) of the Austin Hospital over five months later, on the first of December 1969, when retrospective diagnosis was made by the spinal specialists.

Two days after admission to Box Hill Hospital, while still in a deep coma, one of Bill's lungs collapsed due to the muscle paralysis. Lung collapse leads to cardiac arrest and death, usually within minutes, but someone must have been attentive, for respiratory arrest can be hard to detect in patients who are unconscious. Bill was resuscitated and immediately given emergency surgery—a tracheotomy—to insert an artificial windpipe. To do this, the surgeon creates an opening in the hollow that one can feel at the base of the neck between the two bones in the centre at the front. A tube is inserted through the opening into the trachea or natural windpipe to provide an airway for oxygen to enter the lungs, enabling the lungs to be cleared when necessary. Bill's first artificial windpipe stayed in place for around three weeks.

Bill would experience several more cardiac arrests during his time in hospital. It's not an uncommon event, and many who have been successfully resuscitated often describe it as 'dying and returning to life'. This is certainly how it entered Johnson family folklore, and it was a story that was passed down to Bill's nephews and nieces, and to my children too once Bill became part of our lives, but no two family members could ever agree on the number of times it occurred to Bill. His mother June used to say it was 'a dozen times'; his younger brother once told me it was 'nine times'; Bill himself used to say 'at least four times'. The oft-embellished story was repeated so much by family members including our two boys, even after his death, that I wonder if it served as a parable for the almost superhuman efforts Bill had made, and for his seemingly miraculous achievements on the journey from an almost-dead adolescent to a successful professional man.

Bill used to describe the experience in a very matter-of-fact way, saying simply that his heart had stopped and he'd been resuscitated, but he never contradicted his family's description of the experience as 'dying and coming back to life'. When he read accounts of other people who'd had 'near-death' experiences, who'd seen bright lights or other strange manifestations, and who often regarded it as proof that there is more to human life than our physical bodies, Bill would disagree. He wasn't strident about it and never mentioned it around people who were believers in an afterlife, and probably never said it in front of the children; but he did say to me once, at a time when the topic was for some reason prominent in the media, 'I know there's nothing more beyond this life, because I've been clinically dead, and I've seen that there's nothing'.

His view was that of an atheist and I respected his view. Or at least his conscious view. Much later, when I learned about Buddhist views of such experiences, I wondered whether Bill could have been subconsciously altered by these brushes with death. Others who've had similar experiences have been described by researchers as having a reduced fear of death, a deeper acceptance of mortality, and a focus on the importance of love; they were also found to be very motivated to help others, and to show little interest in material pursuits, which necessarily enhances a person's spiritual side. Everyone who knew Bill would have felt these were fitting descriptions of him.

While Bill was in Intensive Care at Box Hill Hospital, June visited him every day, and Bill's father Adrian too if he wasn't scheduled to work during the brief visiting hours. June would spend the entire time talking to her 'Billy', as she called him all through his childhood; she felt sure he could hear her, and besides, she'd read somewhere that people should continue speaking to patients who are in a coma. Always a talker, she'd tell him what Wayne, Merrilyn and Grant had been doing, about her work, what she'd watched on television. Every so often, she'd say, 'If you can hear me, Bill, open your eyes'. She said this every time.

After a week or so, she noticed slight movement in his eyelids, and he did indeed open his eyes when she asked him, but closed them again after a few seconds; it was clearly an effort for him. By the second week he was opening his eyes more as she spoke to him. June tried to tell him what had happened to him, as much as she knew, for his condition was mystifying even to the medical staff. Her recollection of that period was that no one expected Bill to survive, and that if he did, he'd be a 'vegetable'; that terrible word again. She felt quite alone in believing this to be untrue, and maintained a strong belief that he could hear her talking to him, and that his intelligence was not impaired.

At the end of the second week Bill was observed moving his arms slightly; at times he looked distraught. Both reactions are common in coma patients. When he seemed distressed, June would stroke his head and try to reassure him that he would get better. She explained to him that he couldn't make any vocal sounds because the tracheotomy tube in his throat caused the air supply to bypass the vocal cords. She had no evidence that he was hearing her, but she kept talking anyway.

Over the next ten days, Bill began gradually to surface from the coma. The tracheotomy tube was removed after three weeks, on 16 July, and he began breathing through his nose and mouth; but the damage to his throat from the tracheotomy and some muscle paralysis from the brain haemorrhage and resultant hemiplegia meant he could still not talk. Years later he would say that he still wasn't sufficiently awake on 20 July to be among the 500 million television viewers who watched Neil Armstrong and Buzz Aldrin walk on the moon; even if he'd been awake, hospitals in 1969 certainly didn't have television sets at the end of each bed. In any case, everyone was still talking about the moon landing when he did finally become conscious nearly a month after the accident.

Bill's return to consciousness may have seemed to his family like an immense milestone, but it was only the start of a very long journey. The paralysis of Bill's intercostal muscles meant that for some years he wouldn't be able to breathe normally, and in particular would have great difficulty coughing. We take coughing for granted, and barely notice ourselves doing it unless suffering a respiratory infection. Even when we're well we cough frequently in a minor way throughout the day in order to constantly remove saliva, excess mucus or dust from our lungs; without this, infection quickly sets in.

The inability to cough and clear his lungs was Bill's most serious health problem in the first few years, as is common with spinal injury patients, and he frequently encountered respiratory problems. The tracheotomy tube was re-inserted and removed many times, especially in the first six months. As he gradually returned to full consciousness, Bill didn't know any of this; for him the worst thing was the knowledge of his missing leg. He would glare at June and gesticulate angrily at his amputated thigh. June would stroke what was left of his leg and kiss him, saying, 'Yes I know, I know, it's very upsetting, but your brain is okay, and you can have an artificial leg later'. Recalling this period decades later, June said to me, 'It was the anger I saw in his eyes that told me his brain was relatively undamaged'. At the time no one else shared her view.

It's now well recognized that many people coming out of a coma require therapy to re-learn many everyday skills such as speaking, walking or eating, but it seems that this information was not communicated to the family. In any case, so many of his injuries and so much of his condition were a mystery to those treating Bill, that no one would have been able to say precisely what brain function he had or would be likely to regain.

Fourteen-year-old Wayne saw his brother come out of the coma radically altered, unable to do almost anything unaided, with no speech and greatly reduced muscular control even in his upper body. Where was the brother, only twelve months younger and with whom he'd done everything, who was like a twin to him? Where was the talented footballer who had played for the under-16 team at the age of 13? Wayne believed he'd lost him forever. Few fourteen-year-olds could witness such a terrifying event and not suffer intense emotional and physical reactions, heightened reactivity to stimuli, anxiety and depression; in other words, post-traumatic stress. But this condition was not named until the 1970s, mainly in response to Vietnam Veterans, and was only officially recognized in 1980.

Unable to face returning to Croydon High without Bill, and determined to leave home, Wayne managed to secure a hairdressing apprenticeship with René Henri in South Yarra, a renowned Melbourne salon at the time. In 1969 fourteen-year-olds were legally permitted to leave school to enter an apprenticeship. Wayne wasn't interested in hairdressing as a career but just wanted to get an apprenticeship, any apprenticeship, as quickly as possible so he could earn some money and leave home. Even though it took most of his wage, he rented a small room in a boarding house in Carlton. One day his aunt, June's younger sister, visited him, and was so appalled at the state of the place that she insisted he go to live with her and her family, which he did. A few years later he left both hairdressing and Melbourne, and went to work for a cousin's company in Mount Gambier in South Australia. Before long he bought a car and would make the six-hour drive to Melbourne to see Bill as often as possible.

In the immediate aftermath of the accident it's not surprising that virtually no one except June thought Bill's brain was functioning normally, or ever would again. All that anyone knew at the time was that he'd been so traumatically and severely injured, and had lost so much blood, that it was highly likely he'd suffered significant brain damage. That was why, after about eight weeks at Box Hill Hospital, Bill was transferred to the Neurology ward at Saint Vincent's Hospital, at the time considered to be one of the two or three best hospitals in the state, with a well-developed neurological team. The Box Hill Hospital doctors didn't know what else to do with him; as noted in Bill's records, he represented a 'nursing problem [that] was beyond the capacity of the Children's Ward at Box Hill Hospital'.

1991: History in the Making

'Hey, got anything exciting organised for your birthday?' I asked Bill, trying to look as if I didn't care, but unable to suppress a grin at my uncharacteristic sassiness. It was early December 1991, and we were having one of our Friday after-work chats in his office. Earlier in the year we'd told each other our birthdays—they were within ten days of each other towards the end of the year—and I'd carefully noted Bill's in my diary.

All day I'd been wondering whether or not to ask him this question because I wasn't sure how he'd respond. I fully expected to hear him say he planned to spend his birthday with his girlfriend, so I was bracing myself for disappointment. On the other hand, it wasn't inconceivable that he might suggest we do something together, the answer I was secretly hoping for. I tried to achieve a tone of light-hearted banter, as if I couldn't really care less. But as the words came out of my mouth, I realized I cared very much.

I wasn't usually this audacious, not with anyone, but something had given me the courage. Perhaps it was because recently his manner towards me appeared to have changed slightly; for a month or so Bill had seemed somehow a little different. Since our lunch at his house over a year ago, we'd become good friends, getting together semi-regularly for long conversations over lunch or the occasional dinner. At the start of the year, Bill had achieved his goal of promotion to Head of Department, a new larger one encompassing all Adult VCE and several other programs. His office was now at the Institute's Whitehorse Road campus, where I'd been working. If, in the recent restructure of departments, my course had not been transferred to another area, Bill would have been my boss.

From the beginning, Bill had always been warm and friendly to me, but lately he was warmer than usual, and on several occasions I felt he'd been almost on the point of saying something to me but had stopped himself. It must have been this slight change in demeanour that made me bold enough to ask him out for his birthday.

'I'm very glad you asked,' he said slowly, with a sort of studied calmness, before breaking into a wide, mock-wry grin, 'because … I'm officially single! So, for my birthday … well, I'm open to suggestions.' We locked eyes and laughed like children with an unexpected gift.

'Right then,' I said. 'It's a date. What would you like to do?'

'What about dinner at my place?' he said. 'Tell me what your favourite food is, and I'll get it in.'

'Lobster!' I almost yelled. 'But let me bring some things for entrée, and of course the cake. It's your birthday, after all. What type of cake do you like?'

He looked sheepish. 'Promise you won't laugh?' I assured him I'd try not to. 'Okay, then … it's ice-cream cake.'

I might not have laughed, but I couldn't help a grin. 'Right. Lobster followed by ice-cream cake. It's a deal.'

Even while obsessively researching ice-cream cakes sold by various shops in the eastern suburbs, I told myself to be careful; Bill's girlfriend had broken off with him several times even in the relatively short time I'd known him, and each time they'd seemed to repair things and get back together. The current rupture might not last. I felt as if I were taking a leap into the unknown. In any case, did I really want to start a relationship with Bill? I'd already attempted some hard self-reflection on this subject.

As Bill and I had become closer, I'd thought about whether our friendship might lead to an eventual relationship, assuming that both of us wanted it to, and if we both found ourselves single at the same moment. I'd even begun to consider seriously what an intimate relationship with a paraplegic man would involve.

My entire knowledge of what a man with paraplegia might be like came from the character of the disabled Vietnam Veteran Luke Martin, played by Jon Voight, in the film *Coming Home*, made in 1978 but still well-known throughout the 1980s. It had been produced by Jane Fonda, who also starred in the film, the first to be made by her anti-war-themed production company, Indochina Peace Campaign. The story, told through the eyes of a military wife, shows the damage the Vietnam War did to many of the servicemen.

I'd loved the film when I first saw it. What I especially liked about Voight's character was his lack of self-pity, except briefly at the start when he first became disabled. Once he became rehabilitated, he lived independently. Contrary to the stereotype held by some people, of the disabled being somehow asexual, Luke's sexuality was as evident as any other man's, something the film dealt with quite explicitly. Played by Jane Fonda, the woman he falls in love with—Sally, the wife of a Marine Captain away in Vietnam—was depicted as having her first orgasm with Luke. What also interested me about the Luke Martin character was that he had firm and idealistic opinions, and the courage to stand behind them; on one occasion he chained himself to the hospital gates in an anti-war protest. His strength of character transformed the rather vapid Sally.

The representation of the Luke Martin character, and his and Sally's romance, was not a bad introduction for me in seeking to understand a little of what it might be like to be in a relationship with a disabled man. I also read one or two autobiographies by people with paraplegia or quadriplegia, telling of their daily lives and their relationships with partners. They at least helped me to imagine the amount of medical equipment and intervention that would be required as a normal part of daily life for a person with this type of disability. But my ignorance was still immense, and I didn't even think of trying to find organisations that had been set up to help people with spinal injuries, and which would have been very helpful to me, had I approached them and asked for information. In Melbourne, there was the Paraplegic and Quadriplegic Association of Victoria (since renamed

Independence Australia), which I discovered only later once Bill and I were together; this organization would have been able to add enormously to my knowledge.

Today I would be able to acquire this information in seconds in my own home; but in 1991 the internet was in its infancy and it would be a long time before 'google' became a verb. Today, when I 'google' the phrase 'living with paraplegia', one of the most poignant of the many links on the first page of results is christopherreeve.org. The former Superman star did not become quadriplegic until 1995, after which Bill and I keenly followed Reeve's subsequent activism to improve the lives of people living with paraplegia and quadriplegia, and his lobbying for more research into spinal cord injuries. Sadly, Reeve also died from complications linked to his condition at the age of fifty-two, three years after Bill's death.

Bill's birthday, Thursday 19 December, was a fine, warm day. I didn't have to go into work as we teachers had started our summer break, but Bill intended to put in several more days' work at the office. I'd bought the ice-cream cake earlier in the week and hidden it in the back of the freezer behind several bags of frozen peas and packets of pastry. I didn't want the children demanding it for dessert. After lunch I took both boys to their friends' houses where they were to stay overnight. I then shopped for smoked salmon, artichokes and a soft French brie, all intended for our entrée before the lobster.

When I returned home the phone was ringing. It was Bill. I barely had time to wish him a happy birthday before he was asking me what I thought of the news, his passion for politics energizing his voice. I recalled hearing something on the radio that morning, but had been too excited preparing for our evening to pay much attention. I wasn't about to admit this, though, and asked him what he thought would happen, playing for time, and hoping he'd give enough information that I wouldn't need to reveal my ignorance.

'I can't believe it,' he said, 'Bob Hawke's our longest serving Labor PM, they've won four Federal elections under him. But leaders become unpopular in recessions. And Keating's already challenged him once before, if you remember.'

I did, vaguely, and tried to make it sound like I'd been following events too, but really I was just stalling for time. 'Well, if he wasn't successful then, do you think he will be this time?'

'I think so,' replied Bill, really warming up now. 'The ALP's been bitterly divided lately and needs some new ideas. Hawke was asked by his ministers to resign last week but refused. I think this'll see him off, though. Keating's such a wizard with economics, he could introduce all sorts of reforms. Anyway, he's nominated himself to be leader now, and there'll be a Caucus Ballot at 6.30 tonight.'

Great, I thought, just as I'll be arriving at your place.

'Hey, there's a news bulletin starting,' he yelled, 'I've gotta go. See you tonight.' And he rang off.

I visualized Bill glued to the television in his office. I knew he also had a small radio in his desk drawer, these two devices being the only ones for keeping up with breaking news in those days before the internet. As a politics teacher and ALP supporter, Bill was riveted to the media whenever there was any political drama playing out. Now that I had the background to the story, I switched on my radio and for the rest of the afternoon I followed the news bulletins with at least half an ear.

Later, entering Bill's house by the back door, I could hear the sound of the television news drifting from the lounge-room at the front of the house. Calling 'hello', I put the cake in the freezer, and the other items in the fridge, before going through to the lounge. Bill swivelled his chair around quickly, saying, 'I hope you don't mind if I finish watching this, but it's history in the making. If Keating wins, it'll be the first time an Australian Prime Minister has been unseated in a caucus or party room ballot.'

'No, I don't mind,' I said, smiling at his excitement. 'Go ahead.' And I really didn't mind, as this distraction conveniently hid my nervousness.

'There've been attempts to do this in the past,' Bill said, 'but the challenger either didn't win, or if he did, it was when the party was in opposition, so it didn't change the Prime Minister. It's a pity classes have finished for the year, as it would be great to discuss this with my students.' I often wonder what Bill would think of the situation now, with the deposing of an elected Prime Minister four times in eight years, a tendency which caused a BBC journalist to dub Australia the 'coup capital of the democratic world'![5]

Bill and I watched the rest of the report, which contained footage from earlier in the day: politicians arriving at Parliament House in their cars; Bob Hawke striding down corridors, giving terse answers to reporters' questions, his white hair gleaming as usual, his face stern. I was starting to feel swept up in Bill's passion for politics. Now a commentator was saying it was 'the showdown Labor had to have'. The Caucus Returning Officer, Senator Jim McKiernan, soon appeared, carrying what looked like a wooden box. He announced in his lilting Irish accent that the ALP had just elected Paul Keating as their new leader, with a vote of 56 to 51. Australia had a new Prime Minister, to be sworn in by the Governor General the following day. Bill had been correct about 'history in the making'.

Bill switched off the television. He turned to me, his blue eyes glittering. 'Who'd have thought this would happen to the most successful Labor Prime Minister we've ever had? Mind you, after nine years it's time for a change, and I think Keating will be good for Australia.'

How I envied him his passion. Why had I not seen how exciting politics was? How could I have been so unmoved by it until now? Perhaps a secure job with decent pay had made me complacent during the economic recession that Australia, along with much of the world, was experiencing. Bill's optimism about Keating was to be proven correct: the Labor government would go on to win their fifth victory in a row in the election 15 months later, setting a record for the ALP of 13 years in power. Under Keating the Australian government would introduce native title for Indigenous Australians, increase the basic wage and family benefits, and advance the idea of Australia becoming a republic. But this was all still in the future. So were the negative outcomes of the years of Labor government, outcomes that most of us didn't fully grasp until much later. I can only imagine Bill's disillusion, if he were alive today, at the way the earlier period sowed the seeds for later political action of great shame to many of us in the second decade of the twenty-first century.

Already, in 1989, Hawke had legislated to allow immigration officials to detain boat arrivals of asylum seekers suspected of being 'illegal', mostly Cambodians fleeing their country's guerrilla war. In 1992 Keating, with Liberal party support, would introduce mandatory detention for all arrivals without valid visas, and would build at Port Hedland the first of Australia's onshore detention centres, a concept hitherto unknown in most advanced democratic countries. The cruel fallout would not be widely evident for another eight years.

Politics seemingly forgotten for the moment, Bill wheeled across to the table in the dining area. On my way in I'd spotted two champagne flutes on a silver tray. Now I noticed that the table had been covered with a white damask tablecloth. 'If you could get one of the bottles of champagne from the fridge,' Bill said, 'we can have our long overdue drink'.

I fetched the bottle, and the entrée, which I arranged on the silver tray and took into the lounge. We clinked glasses and drank a toast to his 36th. As the tiny cold bubbles bounced up my nose we smiled at each other. 'I won't forget my 36th birthday in a hurry,' he said, laughing, 'for several reasons!'

'You look happy,' I said.

'Too right!' he replied. 'Do you realise it's almost two years to the day since we first met?'

I'd forgotten, but now I was back in that crowded function room, seeing this lovely man for the first time. Tonight he wore a blue open-necked shirt that matched his eyes. And his hair was even longer, curling on to his collar; I wanted to touch it. He was such a positive person, so engaged in every detail of both our society and the department of which he had charge. I'd developed enormous respect for him, and lately I'd also begun to feel very attracted to him. I wasn't sure if he felt the same way about me.

Bill poured us each a second glass of champagne. He wasn't quite ready to finish talking about politics, so we reminisced about how Hawke had entered parliament ten years earlier. Bill recalled the landslide 1983 election, and how Hawke had done so much to improve education, establishing national curriculum standards in schools, and national training and qualification standards for post-secondary education. Most importantly for us, he'd seriously upgraded the TAFE sector in which we worked. Politics hadn't been my field at all, but listening to Bill's impassioned accounts I could see its appeal. He had the knack of narrating events like the plots of novels, with intrigue, cause and effect, flawed and complex characters. My interest in politics was born that evening.

The smoked salmon and its accompaniments having been devoured while we talked, we decided to proceed to the main course. There wasn't much to prepare as everything was ready. I'd already seen the two halves of a lobster in the fridge and a glass bowl full of salad. On the kitchen counter I found crusty rolls, a bowl of dipping sauce and lemons. For carrying things from one room to another Bill used a lap tray with a raised rim, fixed to a small beanbag cushion to keep the tray stable on his lap. This was perfect for transporting most objects that he'd otherwise have found too difficult to carry, like plates or bowls of food, or full glasses of wine, since he had to use his left hand to propel his wheelchair. Together we transferred everything to the dining table.

When Bill had told his mother that 'a new friend' was coming to dinner she'd offered to help with the preparations. She and Bill's father had brought everything over, including the beautiful tablecloth, when they'd come to wish him a happy birthday earlier in the evening. As we'd demolished the entrée, it was time for the main course. I served salad on to each of our plates, and the chunks of lobster meat. Bill showed me how to gently bite the lobster legs to crack their shells before sucking out the meat.

I took the ice-cream cake out of the freezer and placed two candles, a '3' and a '6', and lit them, before carrying the plate into the dining room. 'I'm sorry but I'm not going to sing "Happy birthday",' I said. 'I have the most terrible voice!'

'That's okay,' said Bill, laughing. 'I'm glad to hear it. Otherwise I'd have thought you were perfect.' Suddenly serious, he reached out and touched my arm, 'Thanks so much for this, you've thought of everything'. We returned to the lounge. I was delighted to be the object of his enthusiasm at last.

'There's something I've been meaning to ask you,' said Bill, as he wheeled over to his bookshelf. He came back with the copy of my book that I'd given him the previous year. 'You forgot to inscribe it,' he said. I felt honoured, and fetched a pen from my bag. After a few moments' thought I wrote some lines on the title page: 'For Bill, one of the few people whose intelligent feedback can always be relied on'. I dated it, signed my name, and put the book on the coffee table.

Bill went to the CD player and held up the album *Hot August Night II*, asking, 'Is this okay?' Anything was fine by me except heavy metal, although Neil Diamond wasn't my favourite singer, by any means. After a few songs, Bill said, 'I want you to pay particular attention to the words of this next one'. And so began the famous hit, 'Sweet Caroline', very familiar to me and most of my demographic. The lyrics may not be poetry, but they simply express how it feels when you meet and feel strongly drawn to someone you never imagined you'd meet. This was clearly a message Bill wanted me to hear. We locked eyes and laughed and sang along with the chorus and some of the lines that we knew. By the end of it we both knew that the attraction was mutual.

'Come and sit on my lap,' Bill said.

I felt a tiny frisson of fear. Did I have the courage to cope with what I was getting us into? I quickly pushed the feeling away and climbed on to Bill's knee.

I didn't go home until the next morning. As I drove down the long highway back to my place that summer day, I believed I'd never been so happy.

1969: The Lowest Ebb

Eight weeks after his accident Bill was transferred from Box Hill Hospital to Saint Vincent's in Fitzroy, a large hospital half an hour's ride by ambulance towards the centre of Melbourne. Able to do very little but lie in bed, he couldn't even sit up unaided. There were tremors and some paralysis in his face, especially in his right eye and his mouth, and his right arm appeared useless although there seemed to be some feeling in it. His lungs couldn't function properly without assistance. The doctors at Box Hill Hospital had needed to re-insert Bill's tracheotomy tube at the start of August because he'd been having serious lung problems again. Each time he caught a cold there was great anxiety among the hospital staff and his family because the inability to cough and clear his lungs meant every minor respiratory infection would likely turn into broncho-pneumonia. During the early months those treating him struggled just to keep him alive, and no one treating him doubted that if he were to survive to adulthood it would be a miracle.

Would this period have been less traumatic if he'd been correctly diagnosed with a severely damaged spinal cord, a diagnosis which would likely have seen him sent straight to the new Spinal Unit at the Austin Hospital? The director of the Unit, Dr David Cheshire, who took over Bill's care in December, certainly thought so, and wrote in his scathing report the following year that he could not 'begin to comprehend the reasons which motivated those at Box Hill Hospital' to transfer Bill to Saint Vincent's Hospital rather than to the Spinal Unit.

As Dr Cheshire noted, the three and a half months at Saint Vincent's were spent 'almost entirely in the management of the respiratory problem' with the result that 'less than adequate attention was paid to the prevention of deformity' of his right arm, the 'prevention of a contracture at the right hip, and in physically and psychologically preparing Bill for life as a triplegic', as he termed it. His summary was that the whole episode was unsatisfactory.

For Bill's family his time in St Vincent's was perhaps the lowest ebb in the long years of his recovery and rehabilitation. He'd been sent to St Vincent's to be cared for by the neurological team because the doctors at Box Hill believed him to be suffering from significant brain damage that had seemingly robbed him of most of the necessary abilities to lead any sort of meaningful life. Apart from that view, there was no correct diagnosis, and no one knew whether this was a permanent or temporary condition.

In St Vincent's Bill was put into the children's ward, but under the management of the Neurology team. It may seem unbelievable today that a damaged spinal cord and a linked brain injury resulting in paraplegia/hemiplegia (or triplegia) could go undiagnosed for nearly six months. But a look at the relatively short history of spinal medicine, at the connections between spinal cord and neurological injuries, and the lack of knowledge about these two conditions that prevailed at the time, does help us to understand the ways of thinking that were still predominant in the 1960s.

Dr David Burke, who joined the Austin's Spinal Unit in 1965, and was first its Deputy Director and later Director, was one of the few specialists practising during those years who was still able to give me his views before his death in late 2019. Dr Cheshire, the Director during most of Bill's time there and the main doctor treating Bill, died in 2005, some years before I began researching this period of Bill's life. According to Dr Burke, in the 1960s very little was known about either spinal cord injuries or brain injuries. He told me, 'Most of the doctors were good people, but there was widespread ignorance about these conditions. The attitude towards spinal and brain injuries then was that they were incurable conditions and you didn't treat them much.'

It was a reaction against the prevailing view, in the belief that spinal cord injuries were not only treatable but should be treated immediately after occurrence, that had led to the specialisation of doctors in spinal medicine, and to the setting up of Spinal Units like the one at the Austin in the late 1950s. The idea was that a lot more could be done for people with paraplegia and quadriplegia than just keeping them alive, that they could undergo rehabilitation and resume independent lives including attending ordinary schools and participating in open rather than sheltered employment.

But this thinking was extremely new and other parts of the medical profession were mostly in ignorance of the dramatic shift in attitude. The unit at the Austin, recalled Dr Burke, was still being built up; it was only gradually that patients were being referred to it from other hospitals, and the spinal doctors often had to lobby for the transfer of patients from elsewhere, assuming that the injuries had been correctly diagnosed as spinal in the first place.

There had been very little research on patients (usually children) with a spinal cord injury caused by stretching—which in both doctors' views was what had happened to Bill—rather than by a severing usually caused by fracture of the spine surrounding the cord, so doctors couldn't educate themselves from research published in medical journals. Dr Burke noticed the gap in the research and produced his own paper on the subject using a sample of the children being treated at the Spinal Unit.

Previously, children with this particular injury were always assumed to have sustained neurological damage, especially in cases where X-rays couldn't reveal evidence to the contrary. As Dr Burke explained, 'a severe brain injury "mimics" quadriplegia or paraplegia. But at the same time the brain and spinal cord are so connected that when the spinal cord is stretched and badly injured or broken this can also damage the brain.'

Time would show that Bill's brain injury caused no intellectual impairment, and once fully out of his coma he seemed to have intuited that this was the case, even during the long period when he couldn't express himself verbally. Once his speech returned he was able to demonstrate his intelligence beyond any doubt. Lack of verbal expression was regarded at the time (as it had been for centuries) as a marker of intellectual disability, possibly as a result of the standard 'testing' for 'mental disorders' being heavily based on expressive language skills.

It was a classic Catch 22 situation; if you couldn't talk properly you'd be tested for 'mental impairment', but with a test that asked you to perform language-based tasks! It wasn't until the 1970s that research into non-speech communication began, using communication boards bearing letters or symbols or both. Once personal computers became more common many different communication programs were invented, making life for people with communication disabilities much less frustrating.

There's no doubt that the four months he spent in St Vincent's Hospital had an indelible effect on Bill, mostly negative. What must it have been like for a 13-year-old adolescent boy who'd excelled at all sports and been 'above average' at schoolwork, according to his reports, to suddenly find himself being treated as a severely brain-damaged child? In later years, Bill would explain that the uncertainty was one of the worst aspects of this period. Because the paralysis of his leg, lower body and right arm was also thought to be caused by brain damage, some staff occasionally voiced the view that it might not be permanent. Members of Bill's family tell of how someone in the hospital even suggested that if he could only 'try harder' he'd be able to 'walk by Christmas'. Perhaps the long-forgotten person was simply trying, in a bizarre way, to cheer him up, but it has entered family folklore as a symbol of the unsuitability of Bill's placement in St Vincent's. Bill used to tell me that he already somehow 'knew' deep-down that his spinal cord had been irreversibly damaged and that the paralysed parts of his body were never going to work again.

There was one area in which Bill did make significant progress in St Vincent's. As anyone who has had any major abdominal surgery knows, in the period until everything is healed all normal activities are painful: sitting up, walking, even laughing. This is doubly difficult when all the muscles below the chest are paralysed. The remaining muscles can be trained to replace some of those that are paralysed, but this takes specific and lengthy guidance and exercise. This is where physiotherapy comes into the picture. In 1969 manipulative procedures had only been practised with patients for a decade, although earlier forms of physical therapy had been developing since the early twentieth century.

The first move towards regaining some quality of life for the broken and battered thirteen-year-old was to help him retrain the muscles of his upper torso and his one good arm to enable him to sit up and maintain his balance sufficiently to use a wheelchair. A 22-year-old physiotherapist named Jenny was on her first professional placement after gaining her qualification and, under supervision from the senior physiotherapist, she began working with Bill soon after his admission to St Vincent's. She started with only ten minutes a day, gradually working up to two hours. She was teaching him how to use the muscles in his upper body to steady himself sufficiently so that he'd be able to sit upright. She also worked on strengthening his undamaged arm, and helped him to build up strength in his head movements in order to remediate to some extent the neck and shoulder muscles that had been damaged.

After about two months of helping him achieve sufficient balance to sit up, Jenny was able to put Bill into a wheelchair for the first time. This too had to be done gradually, starting with half an hour's sitting in it each day, building up to longer periods, but only on the days when he was well enough. During all of this time, Jenny recalled, they were still struggling 'just to keep him alive'. He was constantly fighting chest infections and had the tracheotomy inserted into his neck more often than not. She remembers that if the tracheotomy opening was covered, he could briefly whisper, although his speech was very soft and slurred, and could be hard to understand.

Bill seemed to develop a special bond with Jenny. He was always happy to see her, eager to try hard to work the muscles she asked him to exercise, and she found him a pleasure to work with. She must have presented the tasks in a light-hearted way, with some joking around; she remembers Bill as laughing and cheeky, very surprising considering how unwell he was most the time. Jenny had no difficulty in communicating with him, and he always followed her instructions as far as he was physically able; most importantly, he understood her jokes and they'd laugh together. I remember Bill's quiet, almost-wheezy laugh, so I can picture him at thirteen with a wide grin, eyes lit up, shoulders and upper body shaking with mirth.

The first photograph of Bill in a wheelchair was taken at Jenny's wedding in early November 1969. Bill rarely got dressed in those days; he was ill so often that he stayed in pyjamas. Jenny and two of her colleagues hatched a plot to take the two most gravely ill children, Bill and another boy with very serious head injuries, to attend her wedding. One of the women had a car and could drive the children and her colleague, and somehow found room for Bill's wheelchair. When recounting these memories to me, Jenny did not recall exactly how they managed to obtain permission for the outing, but it must have been well planned as Bill's mother would have had to bring in a clean, pressed outfit of clothes. Perhaps those in charge thought that these children were so likely to die they might as well have a little enjoyment by doing something out of the ordinary. The happiness of that day, captured by the photographer, is evident in Bill's face as he shakes the box of confetti over Jenny, getting more of it on himself than on her!

Following her wedding Jenny took six weeks' leave, and when she returned to St Vincent's in mid-December 1969 Bill was no longer there. She asked someone where he was. The person mustn't have known he'd been transferred to the Austin Hospital, and because everyone had expected Bill to die, Jenny was told that this was probably what had happened.

Not thinking to check the records, Jenny took this as true, for a cardiac arrest could have taken him at any time during that period. She always regretted that she'd never had a chance to say goodbye to Bill. Forty-four years later she received some consolation when in 2013 I managed to find her and tell her by telephone about Bill's rehabilitation, university degrees, professional success, and our marriage.

During his time at St Vincent's, although Bill could follow instructions quite well and answer questions by pointing or holding up combinations of his fingers, he was increasingly frustrated by his inability to communicate on any level beyond that. On one occasion, for example, when Bill's parents were visiting him for their allotted hour (visiting times were very short in those days and had to be strictly adhered to), neither June nor Adrian was wearing a watch and they were wondering aloud what the time was. Bill might have been lying facing the door, over which there was a clock, but as both parents were turned towards Bill they couldn't see it. When his father said, 'What's the time?', Bill held up his left hand with the five fingers open, then rearranged his fingers so that he held up only two, and lastly three; he was trying to tell them that it was five to three in the afternoon. When he gestured the five, then the two, June said, 'Five plus two equals seven?' He gestured impatiently that she was wrong and held up the fingers again. Finally she got it.

This gave June a glimmer of an idea. She remembered something she'd seen on television recently: a board that people without speech could use to communicate. No one had a clue how long it would be before Bill would be able to talk clearly again, for even during the periods when the tracheotomy wasn't in place, speech was still difficult for him.

Before June had her children she'd worked at the renowned Melbourne confectionery shop, Darryl Lea, in the city centre, and ever since she'd remained in touch with her former workmates. Many shop signs were still hand-painted, and at Darryl Lea this was done by a woman who worked in a room above the shop. June's current and former workmates knew about Bill's accident and regularly asked June what they could do to assist. June asked the sign painter if she could paint an alphabet board for Bill.

It was soon finished, and his parents brought it into the hospital. Made of lightweight plywood, it was around the size of a manila folder, and set out like a grid, with each letter of the alphabet in its own large square. The squares were around 2.5 by 3 centimetres, and the letters inside each square were painted different colours—red, blue, green, and yellow, on a white background. The most frequently used letters, including the vowels, were in red. The sign painter had also made a stick for Bill, wide at one end for him to grasp, and tapered at the other for pointing to the letters.

June never forgot how Bill's face lit up when he saw it. She put the stick into his one good hand, his left, and he understood immediately what to do. June watched as he pointed shakily first to the T, and then to the H. The first word he spelled out for his mother was 'Thanks'. At the time, June probably had no idea how revolutionary this gadget was. In the 1960s very few communication devices were in use for those with speech difficulties, and those that existed were mainly produced informally, by family members or friends.

Now that he had the board, Bill could have more complex conversations, even if it was a laborious process to spell out the words; this removed all doubt for June and Adrian about his intellectual ability, even if others still had some reservations. A short while later, another important event enabled Bill to use the alphabet board again to express his gratitude.

It's hard to render the event with the significance it had for Bill, a thirteen-year-old in 1969. Nearly fifty years later everyone over the age of about two seems to spend a good deal of their waking life glued to one type of screen or another, from smart phones to almost cinema-sized flat screens embedded in lounge room walls. If Bill were alive today he'd be in his sixties, and people of our age still remember the coming of television in 1956. Most homes, even in the early 1970s, had only one black-and-white TV set which took pride of place in the lounge room, the watching of it strictly controlled by parents, usually the father.

Later generations of children came to demand their own TV sets, in their bedrooms. My own children would have liked this, but Bill and I firmly rejected it and controlled very strictly their TV watching. My elder son, Alex, having been told that he could do as he wished once he'd completed his VCE, went out immediately he'd passed that milestone and bought himself a small portable set for his room. But in 1960s Australia a personal television set would have been absolutely unthinkable for most children. There were no sets installed for each hospital bed either, although they could be hired for a weekly fee. So when Bill's classmates and the rest of the students from Croydon High School told June they'd raised $400 (equivalent to about $4,000 today), she knew exactly what he'd want it spent on. This was more than enough money, and there was even some left over. To understand how Bill might have regarded this gift, we should perhaps imagine a thirteen-year-old today receiving a state-of-the-art laptop together with a full supply of all the latest games and TV series, as well as a premium Netflix plan.

Four months later Bill was able to take his TV with him when he left Saint Vincent's Hospital. The catalyst for his transfer to the Spinal Centre at the Austin Hospital is as unknown as it is intriguing but, given the widespread ignorance of spinal injuries, and Dr Burke's view of the difficulty of persuading doctors at other hospitals to refer patients to his centre, there must be a story behind it. Certainly the spinal doctors could lobby for patient transfer, as Dr Burke told me, but that could only happen if they knew of a patient with suspected spinal injuries at another hospital. I can find nothing in Bill's medical records that provides any clue.

June Johnson, an inveterate storyteller, used to recount her version of how the transfer came about. By late that year, along with Bill, both she and Adrian had come to suspect that Bill's spinal cord was his chief problem. At the time June was helping a friend raise money for her very ill daughter, and had phoned the radio station where legendary Melbourne radio presenter Norman Banks worked. Banks commanded a huge following and was renowned for his fundraising work, especially his yearly Christmas Day appeal for the Austin Hospital. He'd been instrumental in raising the money for a new children's wing, and it was he who started the famous Melbourne institution 'Carols by Candlelight' in 1938.

Banks was a very famous, even revered, public figure in Melbourne, considered 'almost a deity at the Macquarie Network', and June had been listening to him broadcast since she was a child. He was certainly the logical person to contact, if one was fundraising for good causes. According to June, Banks responded to the message she'd left for him at the radio station by telephoning her at work and asking how he could assist with her friend's fundraiser. After giving him the details, and well aware of his large financial contributions to the Austin hospital, she told him about her paralysed son languishing undiagnosed in Saint Vincent's, and asked if Banks could have any influence in getting Bill transferred to the Spinal Unit at the Austin.

'He'll be there by this afternoon,' Banks is supposed to have said. Given Banks' sense of his own influence, he could well have said this; if he didn't, the dialogue could perhaps be attributed to June's inventiveness and astute sense of narrative plotting. Equally likely, Banks may well have phoned the doctors at the Austin and, given his history of strong support for the hospital, the director of the Spinal Unit, Dr Cheshire, might have contacted Saint Vincent's and asked for Bill's details. Whatever the truth, Bill was duly transferred, although it's most unlikely it was that very afternoon.

1991–92: Love and Forgetting

Two days had passed since Bill's birthday dinner. A whole weekend. I knew he was busy with his nephews and niece, and I was driving my children here and there, and trying to finish my Christmas shopping. I wasn't anxious that I hadn't heard from him. I needed time for reflection, and I suspected Bill did too. Neither of us wanted to fling ourselves into a relationship simply because we'd spent a night together. We were colleagues, after all, so we needed to think carefully through the next steps. Bill wasn't my boss, thanks to the recent restructure, but our two departments were close. Many of the staff were cliquey and quick to judge, usually negatively. There was a lot at stake. And then there was Bill's disability. Could I handle it? If we became a couple I'd face a number of adjustments and compromises. Was I up to it?

No contact for two days after a night together wasn't abnormal for the early 1990s; back then, my phone—like everyone else's—was neither mobile nor 'smart', and the future inventor of Facebook, Mark Zuckerberg, was only about six years old. Any call I received at home had to be taken in the lounge on a fixed line phone; there was little prospect of privacy.

Late in the evening of the third day after our dinner, as soon as the children were asleep, I rang Bill. I could tell from his voice how happy he was to hear from me. 'I was planning to ring you this evening,' he said. 'But you've beaten me to it. I didn't want to phone straightaway, as I thought that would make you feel pressured.' I was touched by his sensitivity. There's nothing worse than someone assuming too much too early and bombarding you with phone calls.

We discussed what we'd like to happen. We'd been good friends for over a year, and we'd suddenly, unexpectedly, become lovers. Nothing could be taken for granted. We were both fiercely attached to our independence and neither felt ready to pin down exactly what our relationship should be. We decided we'd spend an evening together once a week or so and see how things progressed from there. We'd keep things to ourselves for a while. Fortunately, it was now the Institute's summer break so we didn't have to be in contact with colleagues.

Christmas was in three days' time and we each had longstanding plans for Christmas Day; Bill was going to spend it with his family, and I with friends. But the Saturday after Christmas, 28 December, would be my birthday. 'How about another birthday dinner on Saturday night?' Bill asked. 'At my place, since the last one went so well.' His grin was pure complicity, and I smiled widely in return. I'd been so hoping he'd suggest it. So together we planned an evening of 'dinner, dope and poetry', as Bill put it, as we'd decided we would share and discuss our favourite poems.

After the usual Christmas over-indulgence, on my birthday neither Bill nor I felt like eating much for dinner, so he ordered in roast chicken and salad, and for dessert we had thin slices of the remains of his birthday ice-cream cake. He'd also bought me a gift. A few days earlier he'd asked me which edition of Shakespeare I had on my bookshelf, and had been taken aback when I said I didn't possess one. I explained that when I included a Shakespeare play in the literature subject I taught, I'd buy a small paperback version of the play, one that included an academic introduction and annotations, as it was more accessible and affordable for the students and enabled us all to work from the same edition.

Bill presented me with a three-volume edition of the *Complete Oxford Shakespeare*, in blue linen and navy leather binding, embossed with gold lettering. I had never owned such beautiful volumes, and I was—for once—speechless. Even today, when every word Shakespeare ever wrote is freely and easily available on the internet, my volumes with their gold curlicues marching across embossed blue spines are amongst my most treasured books.

As Bill began rolling a joint, I took up volume II, turned to *Twelfth Night,* and began to read aloud Orsino's opening lines:

> If music be the food of love, play on,
> Give me excess of it that, surfeiting,
> The appetite may sicken and so die ...

'Stop!' Bill yelled. 'That's the last thing we want to be hearing right now, about appetites sickening!' But he was laughing. Of course, I'd done it deliberately. Even back in the early 1600s, apparently, love never remained for long the way it was at the beginning. This bothered me a great deal. Must love peter out after a while into an apathetic, dull routine? I knew we'd have to tackle this prospect before long. But not tonight.

Smoke was curling from Bill's nostrils as he wheeled towards me with another book in his hand. He passed me the joint, flicked through the book, and in his gravelly drawl began reading Robert Frost's enigmatic and emotionally rich love poem, 'Two look at two'.

> Love and forgetting might have carried them
> A little further up the mountain side
> With night so near, but not much further up.
> They must have halted soon in any case
> With thoughts of the path back, how rough it was ...[6]

Frost had been *de rigueur* for every undergraduate literature syllabus of our generation, and we'd all cut our poetic teeth on his work. The poem has a quiet, calm certainty, with its first and last words being 'love', and in between a meditation on love as almost an emanation from the natural, animal world.

This called for a counterpoint. I'd brought along the book The Fact of a Doorframe, by Adrienne Rich, a poet Bill and I had been discussing in our Friday afternoon conversations for some time, as I'd been studying Rich's work in one of the subjects of my master's degree. I wanted to read aloud from her poem, 'From a Survivor', a current favourite of mine.

It's hauntingly lyrical, the narrator addressing her ex-husband who had committed suicide. But it was the first part I was concentrating on, a part that in my view is about the inherently unequal nature of conventional relationships between men and women, inequalities that most of us aren't aware of beforehand, that ultimately fail us all. I wasn't consciously linking the poem to our lives, I simply loved Rich's way of expressing these themes. I read aloud the first four stanzas, down to the lines where the narrator implies that she and her husband were in blissful ignorance of what lay ahead and, in any case, saw themselves 'as special'.[7]

Looking back nearly 30 years to that night, the prescience of our choosing those two poems astounds me, summing up the best and the worst of times that Bill and I spent together. And yes, we thought we were special, so very special, that's for sure.

Later, in bed, after making love, we talked for hours: about our lives, our commitment to teaching, about feminism, and 'ableism'—discrimination against people with disabilities—and finally about how we were going to physically organise ourselves to go out together in Bill's car. It was not as simple as just hopping in the car as most people do. After climbing into the car via the passenger door, Bill would pull his folded-up wheelchair on to the front bench seat. So when he took another person out in the car they had to sit in the back seat, unless it was someone strong like his brothers who could put the wheelchair in the back seat or the boot. I didn't like the idea of sitting in the backseat while Bill drove me like some sort of chauffeur. Why couldn't I just lift the chair into the back seat or the boot? 'Too heavy,' he said. 'You can't. I've not had a girlfriend yet who could lift it.'

The word 'can't' has always been for me like the proverbial red rag to a bull. 'Huh! You know how I spell "can't"? Like this: T.R.Y.' I jumped out of bed. The wheelchair was on Bill's side. I folded it up vertically as I'd seen Bill do a few times, then I turned it so it was side on to me and, bending my legs to keep my lower back braced, I reached down and grabbed the armrest nearest to me and the wheel rim furthest away. I straightened my legs and levered the wheelchair against my body. In this way I somehow managed to raise it to hip height, still levered against me, and I thought this should be high enough for me to manoeuvre it into the back seat or the boot. While I was practising various holds to see which was most efficient, Bill was rolling around on the bed, gasping with laughter. Not because he'd doubted I could manage it but because he said that seeing someone trying to carry a wheelchair around a bedroom at 2.45 in the morning was like something out of Monty Python.

I got back into bed. 'Right. That's that, then. We're going out in the car tomorrow. And I'm sitting in the front seat, next to you.'

Suddenly he was serious. 'You're so caring,' he said. 'I've never known anyone like you.'

For our first outing in Bill's 1979 HZ Holden Kingswood, we went to a chemist in the large shopping centre a few kilometres away from his house and had our ears pierced. I had two piercings already, but wanted a third in my right ear. Bill wanted to wear a stud in his left ear. He asked me which one he should buy. 'The one with the deep blue stone,' I told him. 'To match your eyes.' Looking back, I now laugh at such silly antics. But I remind myself we were still quite young, only 36 and 38, after all.

In the weeks and months following that evening our lives felt irrevocably changed. We now knew we loved each other and wanted to be together as much as possible, but there seemed endless insurmountable hurdles. One was my own house; while it was a comfortable home for me and my boys, it wasn't accessible for Bill. There were steps up to the veranda and front door, and the toilet and the glass-walled shower simply weren't large enough for access by the wheeled commode chair Bill used for showering, so it would be impossible for him to stay over. I could spend nights at his house, which is what I did when the children were visiting their father, usually on a weekend. But they didn't do this every second weekend as is typically arranged, as their father frequently worked on weekends, and in any case he had a new partner and a baby on the way. I couldn't see why the boys and I couldn't just stay at Bill's place on the weekends, but Bill wanted us to take things gradually as far as the children were concerned.

As Head of Department, Bill returned to work in mid-January, and as the boys were still on school holidays and Bill's staff hadn't yet returned, the three of us took the opportunity to visit Bill in his office so we could all go to a nearby café for lunch. The boys already knew Bill from our lunch at his place a year before, and from their occasional visits to my office when I'd taken them to say hello to Bill. Sometimes, if one or other of them had a cold and couldn't go to school, they might spend a couple of hours in my office, drawing or reading, while I was teaching a class.

I wasn't sure how much the boys understood about Bill's disability. I didn't think they'd ask him embarrassing questions (they never did), but I wanted to be as frank with them as possible. I'd told them about Bill's accident before they'd met him, and now I explained how he needed to be in a wheelchair full-time, how his right arm had limited ability, and how he'd lost his right leg in the accident. They seemed to take in all the information I gave them, accepting it without judgement, and quickly became very fond of Bill. This was because he showed a lot of interest in them, asking them each time he saw them what they'd been 'up to', and listening and taking them seriously when they replied, just as he did with all the young people who arrived in his department wanting to resume their studies.

The 1992 school year started. I usually arrived home from work at about the same time as the children returned from school, and I'd then take them to one or other of the many extra-curricular activities they had until about six o'clock. On some evenings we'd drive back to the Institute where Bill would be just finishing work. There were many 'cheap and cheerful' restaurants in Box Hill and the four of us would go on foot, with my elder son always wanting to push Bill's wheelchair. He wasn't yet ten years old, but tall and strong for his age, so I let him, making sure I walked close by. Bill said that every family member who'd pushed his chair had tipped him out at least once. This wasn't deliberate, of course, but if the front wheels chanced to lock on a stray stone the momentum would tip the wheelchair forward and Bill would end up on the ground. I wanted to make sure this never happened to us.

A Vietnamese café near work, called Tien Dat, quickly became our favourite. The boys also liked the large chain restaurants promising 'all you can eat'; they were an occasional special treat. I also wanted Bill to join us for dinner at my house, but he couldn't even get from the driveway on to the front veranda.

Looking for inspiration to solve this problem, I went searching in my garage, which was full of old bits and pieces, much of it dating from when the house had been built in the 1950s. Finding an old door propped against the wall, I thought I might have found a solution. The door was plain and flat, and more or less undamaged. I carried it around to the front steps and it fitted over them perfectly, with one end of the door resting on the concrete path. The remaining step up to the front door wouldn't be a problem as I could easily help Bill with that.

Bill was also making changes at his house. He bought a new bed, queen size with brass railings at the top and bottom, and what he claimed was the best orthopaedic mattress on the market, and a king-size doona. He'd bought new bedding for the two single beds in his spare room too, as my boys had already started asking for 'sleepovers'. When Bill's parents saw all this activity they realised things were serious and said they'd like to meet the boys and me. We were invited to dinner the following weekend. June and Adrian usually went to Bill's house every Sunday afternoon and June would cook her specialty, roast meat and vegetables, while Adrian assisted with any tasks around the house or garden that Bill couldn't manage by himself.

I found Adrian quiet and shy, as Bill had described, but June's volubility was legendary in the family and we chatted non-stop. She asked me all about my own family, where I'd grown up, about my studies and my job. She was very interested in my Master's thesis and asked if she could read it once it was finished. No one had ever asked me this before! The boys behaved beautifully; a roast was one of their favourite meals, and they told June that they'd never had a more delicious meal.

Three weeks later we were invited to a Johnson family gathering at the home of Bill's sister Merrilyn and her husband. There we met the rest of the family, including Bill's beloved maternal grandmother, 'Little Nan', so-called to avoid confusion with Bill's mother June who was 'Nan' to all her own grandchildren. Little Nan was indeed little, and quite deaf, but seemed to enjoy being among us.

Merrilyn and Dave had four children: twin boys a little older than my first born, Alex, an older son, and a daughter slightly younger than my second boy, Patrick. My two children quickly made friends with the other four and they played together for hours, football or cricket in the backyard, or skateboarding on any concreted area they could find. Bill's younger brother, Grant, a Melbourne DJ, was there too. My boys couldn't believe they'd met a real DJ, plying him with questions about his job.

Wayne and his wife came across from South Australia for the weekend with their daughters Kate and Kelly. I found Wayne very serious and thoughtful, the quietest person in the family. By now Bill had given me an outline of his accident, and I couldn't look at Wayne without remembering that he had been with Bill on that day, had witnessed it all, aged only 14, and had carried his brother's severed leg to the ambulance. I thought I could see the tragedy etched in his gaze, no matter how jovial a manner he was able to construct. Bill's accident had meant the end of childhood for both of them.

The Johnsons were lively and talkative, and seemed to treat Bill no differently despite his disability. They deferred to him in educational matters, though, seeing him as the family intellectual, the only one to go to university, which he wouldn't have done, he told me, had it not been for the accident. 'Until then, I was going to be a footballer! Once I realised that wasn't going to happen, I had to develop different goals,' he said, laughing.

Life with Bill in it made me feel fulfilled and excited, intellectually, physically and emotionally. No matter what subject I raised, Bill was always able to comment wisely or help me solve any problem. I felt I could share everything with him—my writing, my thesis, and especially bringing up the boys. I felt very proud of all he'd achieved, of which the pinnacle was his promotion to Department Head the previous year. With over a thousand students and forty staff it was a demanding role. Yet after little more than one year in the job, the pass rate in the major program in his department, Adult VCE, had increased so dramatically that *The Age* newspaper had sent its higher education editor, Carolyn Rance, to interview him and write a profile.

The article began: 'When Bill Johnson tells students: "If I can do it anyone can," they take notice'.[8] He told the journalist he believed the sort of program he ran was well suited to its target cohort—people who hadn't completed school, often because of problems with the school system or at home—because of its emphasis on self-directed learning and adult relationships between teachers and students. The article's headline was 'Bill is an inspiring motivator', not failing to recount the history of Bill's accident at 13, and the steps he'd taken to rebuild his life afterwards.

It was the courageous character he'd forged along the way that now enabled him to handle the most difficult situations with calmness and sensitivity, whether it was hostility or discrimination, the daily problems that beset most workplaces, or the odd contretemps or conflict between the two of us. But as foreshadowed by the Adrienne Rich poem I had read on our second night together, we did think of ourselves as special, never articulating any hard times ahead. Who does at these moments? It's natural enough for one to forget or dismiss one's own failings and the impact these could have on the other. This alone would make the path ahead rough going indeed, a path that would also be strewn with several obstacles not of our own making.

1969–71: The Sparks of Resilience

A few weeks before his fourteenth birthday, still seriously ill, Bill was transferred from St Vincent's to the Spinal Unit at the Austin Hospital in Heidelberg, in suburban Melbourne. It was the first day of December, nearly six months after the crash.

Bill saw this transfer, at least in retrospect, as a 'breath of fresh air'. Many years later he told me that after all these months of uncertainty, the director of the Spinal Unit, Dr David Cheshire, had been able to diagnose his condition correctly and had told him the truth. How was Dr Cheshire able to do this when a number of doctors had failed?

Dr Cheshire, a British specialist in rehabilitation, had treated acute paraplegics in the famous Stoke Mandeville Hospital in southern England. Home to one of the largest dedicated spinal units in the world, it was established after World War II by the pioneer in the new specialty of spinal cord rehabilitation, Sir Ludwig Guttman. Guttman's work not only led to the creation of the Paralympic Games but generated the development of similar dedicated spinal units around the world. The unit at the Austin Hospital was set up in 1957; two years later, recommended by Guttmann, Dr Cheshire was appointed its full-time director.

The central mission of the unit was to integrate acute care with the rehabilitation of newly injured paraplegic and quadriplegic patients from day one after their accident. A whole team of experts was employed—occupational and speech therapists, physiotherapists, a remedial gymnast, and a social worker—with the spinal doctor playing a central coordinating role between the team and all the other doctors treating the patients with spinal injuries. The overall goal was rehabilitation, the resumption of as independent a life as possible. For this reason these specialists are also known as rehabilitation doctors.

For some time other doctors viewed this interdisciplinary method of treatment as controversial and were reluctant to cede authority to the new spinal/rehabilitation specialists, a view that might account for Bill's not being referred much earlier to the Spinal Unit. It's therefore very likely that as soon as Dr Cheshire learned—perhaps thanks to the radio star Norman Banks—about a spinal-injured boy who should have been in his unit, he would have lobbied for him to be transferred to the Austin.

Dr Cheshire recorded in his notes how difficult it was, so long after the crash, to tell Bill, still only thirteen, that his paraplegia was permanent. In Dr Cheshire's expert opinion, Bill had sustained 'a traumatic paraplegia at the time of the original accident … caused by longitudinal traction of the spinal cord in an over-flexed spine' and 'a right hemiplegia of cerebral origin …' The latter injury referred to Bill's right arm and shoulder, which manifested partial paralysis and spasticity; the term cerebral origin denoting the damage to the brain from interruption of its blood supply (a cerebrovascular accident, or 'stroke'). This was thought to be due to the traumatic injury caused by the stretching of the spinal cord, given the close connection between the spinal cord and the brain. This injury and its results were also of particular interest in the research of Dr Burke, Dr Cheshire's deputy in the Spinal Unit, who contributed to the correct diagnosis of Bill's injuries.

I can't even imagine how hard it would be for a thirteen-year-old to hear definitively that he would never walk again. Bill had suspected for months, though, that this might be the case. Dr Cheshire explained to him that his paralysis commenced at the sixth thoracic vertebra (or T6), just below the level of the shoulder blades. Now at least, and at last, Bill knew exactly what was wrong with him, could receive targeted treatment and, once well enough, would begin the long road to rehabilitation. Already he could sit in his wheelchair, thanks to Jenny his former physiotherapist at Saint Vincent's, although he wasn't yet adept at propelling it himself.

The next major challenge was to get Bill's breathing working optimally, as this problem had caused him to almost die twice in the preceding two months and could kill him at any time. He'd arrived from Saint Vincent's with a tracheotomy tube in place and a lung infection. But even with the tracheotomy tube Bill was frequently struggling to breathe. The Austin's thoracic surgeon found a constriction in Bill's trachea equal to four-fifths of the normal diameter, meaning he could inhale with great difficulty only one fifth of his normal intake. The surgeon dilated the constriction and inserted a new tracheotomy tube.

But here was another Catch 22: a tracheotomy tube is often vital for people who are paralysed, and yet long-term use of it can cause constrictions lower down in the trachea. Because it bypasses the vocal cords, a tracheotomy tube also greatly impedes speech, allowing barely a whisper. Much later, in 1985, the world-famous English physicist Stephen Hawking, paralysed and made paraplegic by motor-neurone disease, became gravely ill with pneumonia. Remaining alive only by means of a respirator, he had a tracheotomy tube inserted to try and save his life; but this caused complete loss of his speech, already quite weak. Technical advances meant that he could be fitted with an electronic device that emitted speech at his command. This wasn't yet available in the 1970s.

Bill's spinal doctors didn't waste any time. As they saw it, six months had already been wasted, seriously setting back Bill's rehabilitation. They requested from the Department of Labour a test of Bill's 'mental ability' (as it was then termed), to be conducted by a qualified vocational psychologist as soon as Bill had recovered from his trachea operation. The test indicated that Bill was 'about average' for his age but 'above average' in Arithmetic. His physical limitations and fatigue were noted by the psychologist but, curiously, no mention was made of the likely impact on his test results of his horrific accident, his six months' hospitalisation and numerous operations, extreme difficulty in talking, nor that he'd done no reading or schoolwork all this time. From the testing, though, Dr Cheshire confidently concluded that Bill had suffered no intellectual impairment from the accident, and in any case knew from an earlier letter he'd received from the principal of Croydon High School that the school regarded Bill's academic abilities as 'rather above average'.

Not long after the 'mental assessment', the Spinal Unit arranged for Bill to resume schooling via correspondence lessons, with a teacher's aide assisting him in the Austin's schoolroom. Occupational therapy also soon began, and immediate training in the use of his left hand for writing. He began to learn to type on a typewriter, initially very slowly but accurately, and soon he was able to type some of his school exercises. His weak and partially paralysed right hand was fitted with a wrist-stabilising splint.

As a result of the cerebral hemiplegia, Bill's shoulder, right arm and hand were stiff and contracted, with much spasticity, and were gradually becoming worse. This was a huge loss since he'd formerly been right-handed. The splint was an attempt to support the hand so that Bill could learn to use it again, albeit minimally, as fine motor coordination in that hand was greatly impaired. In addition, Bill was given regular physiotherapy for this weak right arm, and also for his left, the latter in the form of weight training since this arm would be needed to do most ordinary activities once Bill became independent.

The loss of the right leg below the upper thigh was causing posture problems due to asymmetry, and it was this that Dr Cheshire was worried about, as it was very likely to develop into a permanent spinal curvature. The resulting poor posture would lead to grave consequences necessitating the most torturous medical intervention of Bill's life.

But that was more than two years in the future and, for the moment, only two months after Bill's admission to the Spinal Unit, the Occupational Therapist reported that Bill was displaying 'great enthusiasm' for all these activities, noting he'd expressed frustration only once at his disability. She also reported that Bill could now slowly propel his own wheelchair around the wards, using his hands on the wheel rims, with a wheeling mitt and the splint on his right hand to increase traction. Her aim was to teach Bill the skills to perform all the usual activities of daily life—eating, dressing, self-care, and communication.

Bill wasn't keen on speech therapy—who would blame any teenager for lacking the enthusiasm?—but it began anyway; in his case, the tracheotomy tube made talking very difficult. When the opening in his neck was temporarily covered he could speak only in a hoarse whisper, lacking clarity. The muscles in Bill's larynx were very weak, unable to fully control his vocal chords; he was suffering from what speech therapists term dysarthria. Its effect on the movement of the tongue, for example, leads to slurred speech, impeding clear enunciation and the normal resonance of a voice; it also weakens the five muscles of the soft palate which play an important role in breathing and swallowing.

The speech therapist continued working with Bill in hourly sessions twice a week throughout 1970. The quality of his speech fluctuated according to his physical and mental states, improving markedly whenever the tracheotomy tube was removed, which occurred with finality only at the end of that year. Even then, the speech therapist felt he did not seem to make sufficient effort to be intelligible. Bill could certainly be stubborn; but it's hard to believe that he would not have done his best to regain normal speech. Many years later, during our time together, I sensed that he had to make more effort than the rest of us in enunciating and projecting his voice, and that was after the muscles in question had had 25 years of rehabilitation. By that time he was able to lecture to a large, crowded classroom and to use his voice for most of his working days in a high-level managerial role.

But in 1970 he simply couldn't try any harder; the speech therapist's view was likely informed by the strong expectation in the Spinal Unit that all the paraplegic and quadriplegic patients should receive a wide range of therapy and rehabilitation and make the utmost effort to prepare for an independent life. This meant returning to ordinary schools, where possible, or to the workplace if adult—which many were capable of doing—rather than going into sheltered workshops which had long been the default for people with a disability.

The Spinal Unit was an adult ward; Bill had been placed there instead of the children's ward to enable him to receive the specialised spinal care he required. There was really no other choice in Dr Cheshire's view. There were a few other teenage patients in the Spinal Unit with whom Bill enjoyed some camaraderie, but he told me later that he had effectively 'lost' his teenage years, and this was true.

Spinal Unit patients were mainly young men, survivors of car accidents or from diving into shallow water. Bill said that when hot weather was forecast for the weekend, the mood in the ward became sombre as it meant more patients than usual would be brought in. Bill recalled how, as new patients were admitted, their spinal injury classifications would be discussed. One might hear, for example 'The guy that came in today, he's a C2 from diving off a pier', or 'She's a T10, car accident', referring to whether the spinal cord was injured or severed in the Cervical section of the spine, or the Thoracic or Lumbar, with an 'L3', say, representing the Lumbar section. Patients naturally compared and contrasted their injuries and noted each other's progress, or failure to progress.

A patient around Bill's age, admitted at roughly the same time, with paralysis at a thoracic level just below Bill's, was making faster progress than him, and by April was talking of returning home soon. Bill knew that he would remain in the Spinal Unit for much longer, and this caused understandable jealousy and anger, a sort of sibling rivalry, according to the occupational therapist. The same therapist had noted a few months earlier Bill's enthusiasm in rehabilitation activities; she now recorded that his performance was influenced by mood swings which could fluctuate daily, often making her feel she was the 'target' of Bill's anger and frustration at what he saw as his slow progress.

In one area at least Bill could not rail at his slow progress; this was in chess. It's likely Bill was already proficient before the accident, and resumed playing in hospital. As observed in testing, he was above average at maths, an ability often linked to skill at chess. In mid-1970 the Victorian Chess Association organized a special exhibition match at the Croydon shopping centre, where Bill played the then Monash University chess champion, Robin Hill, who also lived in Croydon. The local paper reported it in a small article, referring to Bill as Croydon's 'miracle boy' due to his very survival, and now his ongoing rehabilitation. Frustratingly, the report did not mention the result of the match, and if Bill did tell me, I have forgotten.

In fact, Bill's progress was not slow at all, considering the gravely ill state in which he'd arrived at the Austin and the slow regaining of his health. Early on in his time in the Spinal Unit, as well as his respiratory problems Bill was often ill with the chronic urinary tract infections that would plague him all his life, another condition with which spine-injured patients become unhappily familiar.

During the first months alone Bill suffered frequent periods of nausea, probably related to urinary infections, frequently coughed blood, and—in the words noted on his medical records—could be 'depressed and uncooperative' with nursing staff. He was also taking Valium, prescribed from his time at Saint Vincent's, whether for depression or to reduce the spasms which are a side effect of paraplegia, especially in the first few years. Most newly injured spinal patients have suicidal thoughts, according to research.[9] Although very few persist with these thoughts, it might nonetheless explain why anti-depressants would be prescribed in the first year of spinal injury.

Two weeks after his arrival in the Spinal Unit, Bill was well enough and in sufficiently good spirits to ask if he could go out to a Christmas party at a relative's house. Dr Cheshire gave his approval, and also permitted Bill to have 'day leave' to go home for Christmas Day.

March 1970 saw the beginning of a period during which, when he was well enough, Bill managed to go on some evening outings with his aunt and uncle or a family friend, and went home for some weekends. He'd return from most outings happy and upbeat, according to his medical records, although a health issue the next morning could plunge him into depression again.

The cycle of illness alternating with recovery, and their corresponding psychological states, was to continue for the whole time Bill spent in the Austin, and indeed for the rest of his life. But the years of rehabilitation were the hardest for him, not even knowing how much independence he would ultimately achieve, nor whether he would ever again have a life that could be called 'normal'.

A few weeks after Christmas, Bill encountered the scourge of every person with paralysis—pressure sores on the buttocks from the long hours of sitting in a wheelchair, which can occur anywhere on frail skin that lacks muscle tone. He had to return to bed for days until the sores healed, lying prone and being turned every two hours. If a pressure sore becomes infected it can lead to fatal sepsis, as sadly happened in 2004 with former *Superman* actor, Christopher Reeve.

In addition to the pressure sores, several times a day Bill's lungs required suction through the tracheotomy in order to be cleared, while a nebuliser would deliver a drug to combat infection. Bill began to channel his energies into joking and 'cheekiness', as the nurses labelled it, something his sister Merrilyn clearly remembers. Two years Bill's junior, when visiting him in hospital she often ran ahead of her parents and arrived at Bill's bedside on her own. On one occasion, Bill whisked the sheet away to show her his severed leg, which had still not completely healed, in order to make her scream and turn away, while he shook with laughter.

Bill could be assertive when he didn't agree with some aspect of his treatment. Soon after arriving at the Austin, he began to refuse the dose of Mandelamine prescribed for urinary infections, very likely a result of previously experiencing the drug's side effects, such as vomiting, and difficulty breathing. This assertiveness, as well as the joking and sassiness, surely signalled that he was slowly moving towards 'bouncing back' from enormous adversity, an ability known as resilience (from the Latin *resilire,* meaning to 'spring back' or 'rebound').

This ability has been a growing area of research in psychology and medicine since the 1970s. Although there is no one definition of resilience, people who display it share a number of similarities including self-reliance, having a purpose in life, caring for others, and spirituality. These traits have been collectively described as 'wholeheartedness' by Brené Brown, a researcher and writer who has recently converted her findings about resilience into inspirational bestselling books.[10]

After ten months' physiotherapy in the Spinal Unit, Bill was finally able to breathe independently and the tracheotomy tube could be removed. Such progress made plausible a return to living at home and a resumption of his schooling.

To this end, it was decided that at the start of the next school year Bill would attend the Yooralla Hospital School for Crippled Children, as it was then called. Its very name shows how much has changed in the past 50 years in the way disability is viewed by society. The school was chosen for a number of reasons. Dr Cheshire believed Bill still needed the hospital context. Although he'd finally been able to do without the tracheotomy tube from the end of October, Bill was still frequently susceptible to respiratory problems, urinary tract infections, and pressure sores which appeared periodically, needing prompt treatment to prevent them becoming abscessed. In addition, as the doctors noted, Bill required the 'continuation of physical therapy and speech therapy'.

As well as primary teachers with 'special education' qualifications, and some teachers' aides, Yooralla was staffed by therapists and nurses who could provide a continuation of the treatment and therapies not available in ordinary schools. So it was logical for Dr Cheshire to decide that Bill should be admitted to Yooralla. It was also logical that Bill should board there from Monday to Friday, as Croydon was three-quarters of an hour from Yooralla by car, and in any case Bill's father worked full-time and his mother was then unable to drive (no 'disabled taxis' in those days). His parents agreed to Dr Cheshire's plan.

On his 15th birthday, after 18 months in hospital, Bill left the Spinal Unit for his parents' house in Croydon, where he'd spend the summer holiday before starting at Yooralla in late January. He was very much against the plan but was powerless to prevent it.

1992:
The Independent Candidate

'A great many people have a disability but, unlike mine, it can't be seen in most cases.' Over dinner in our early months together we'd been discussing what we called 'ableism'—an attitude we sometimes encountered that ranged from outright discrimination to mild patronising. Those with 'invisible' disabilities could at least avoid that problem. Among Bill's many students who'd returned to study in order to complete their VCE, he knew of a range of disabilities, some visible, some not. He regarded psychological problems in particular as disabilities that could be every bit as disabling as physical ones. I never once heard him judge others for not having been able to overcome their particular disability or illness.

We were to recall the conversation later in the year, a year in which Bill would display—as if he hadn't already—his ability to shrug off what an 'ableist', as he put it, would regard as the restrictions imposed by his paraplegia. At the same time he would introduce into our relationship a brutally realistic presaging of how he had already circumscribed what was possible and acceptable in a life with such challenges. In those early days together I too would introduce something problematic; it was a time when we both made discoveries about the other.

I'd suffered from both anxiety and depression on and off since the birth of my first son nine years before, although it wasn't diagnosed until many years later. A slow recovery after the caesarean birth, a lack of support—domestic help and babysitting—with all my family members thousands of kilometres away, and my previous husband in a high-stress, irregular-hours job, must all have contributed to my depression. I did little about it, bar a prescription for anti-depressant tablets, which I found did little for me and which I didn't renew.

It's difficult, towards the end of the second decade of the twenty-first century, to imagine a time when people simply could not admit to, nor talk about feeling anxious or depressed, a situation exacerbated by there being few resources to help sufferers find information. The internet didn't exist for domestic users in the early 1980s, and there were no obvious forums where people could share experiences; generalist medical practitioners did not ask pointedly at the end of a consultation if the patient had 'anything else' to discuss, as almost routinely happens today; there were no support organisations such as 'beyondblue' in those days, either. Unless you had the strength to admit that you might have this type of illness (and how? to whom?), you were on your own.

Unlike Bill, I lacked the quality of resilience, and couldn't admit to nor overcome my 'disability' for a long time. But quickly Bill realised I was suffering from something more than a 'bad temper' and encouraged me to seek professional help. If I wasn't going to do that, he wanted me to work at controlling the worst symptoms, my negativity and horrible temper. I felt this was perhaps at last achievable now I had such loving support in everything I was doing, from raising the children through to my busy teaching schedule; but it would be a few more years before I took Bill's advice and obtained targeted treatment.

For his part, Bill admitted he'd had a penchant for partying and drinking to excess, especially when out with his brothers or male friends. I'd always consumed very little alcohol, and this made me less tolerant of others' drinking. I explained this to Bill and he understood my feelings. He argued that as he went out with his brothers only about twice a year, if I were not there to see it surely it didn't matter how much he drank. I understood the logic of this and hoped I never would see it, although once we began living together I couldn't see how I'd be able to avoid it. I was as dismayed about this as Bill must have been about my depression; I idolised him and wanted nothing to shatter my view of him as the perfect partner.

We spent a lot of time discussing and analysing everything, including acknowledging our weaknesses. It was clear to both of us that our failings, with their origins in the past, had the potential to drive us apart at this fragile stage. But we had the sense that we were constructing something special and knew we must consciously confront and curb damaging behaviours. Our efforts were more or less successful.

By mid-year Bill and I knew that we wanted to be together for a long time. We bought each other matching gold rings, plain gold bands, each with a diagonal line of small diamonds, which we each wore on the third finger of the left hand. We decided we wanted to live together as soon as it could be arranged. The easiest way of doing this seemed to be to renovate my house to make it accessible for Bill, sharing the cost of the renovations. A builder who'd been recommended came and talked to us, listened while we explained our needs, then drew up some plans and gave us an estimate of the cost.

We hadn't really known what to expect, but the extent of the changes we'd asked for should have warned us that it would be expensive. And it was; way beyond our means. We both had sizeable mortgages on our houses so couldn't borrow any more. We were both dispirited, and I was despairing.

Bill's house was big enough for the four of us, but it was too far away from the boys' school, their friends and all their activities, and we didn't want to uproot them from the house they'd lived in all their lives. I couldn't see any way out of this impasse, and Bill blamed himself for not having enough money readily available. He'd invested most of his savings a few years earlier in the milk bar/fish-and-chip shop that his sister and her husband had bought in Mooroolbark. Now Bill decided it was time to sell his half of the business; he'd use the money for setting up home with me, and it would free him of other obligations before forming his own new family with me and my children.

As soon as Bill broached the subject with them, Merrilyn and Dave said they'd been thinking for a little while that they were ready to sell the business, as it took too great a toll on their family life, needing to be open seven days a week in order to be financially viable. The challenge now was to attract a buyer willing to pay a decent price, no easy matter in a depressed market for this type of business. They soon put the shop into the hands of a very capable commercial agent, but it still had to be kept open and running so that the agent could sell it as a viable business with an established customer base. Each week, Bill—who did the accounting for the business—would anxiously add up the numbers, for any downturn in sales figures would affect the attractiveness of the business for potential buyers. The fish-and-chips and takeaway food side of it was doing quite well, thanks to Dave's superb cooking, but the grocery side was increasingly losing out to supermarkets.

The sale would take time, the agent said; there was nothing to do but make the best of the situation. We decided it was wiser not to rush into living together anyway, and gave ourselves the long-term goal of setting up home—a fully accessible one, either my house suitably renovated or a new place—by the end of the following year. The four of us could still have an enjoyable life together, shared between North Balwyn and Ferntree Gully. As Bill sagely reminded us, we were very privileged to have comfortable homes, when so many people, even in Australia, did not.

Nevertheless, our life never seemed to remain peaceful for long! One Friday evening not long after our meeting with the builder, Bill drove to the shop to do the weekly accounts. He turned into Maroondah Highway and had just passed the Box Hill Town Hall when, in the midwinter darkness, two moving black shapes loomed in front of his windscreen. He had to swerve so violently to avoid them that his car spun 180 degrees and mounted the grassed strip between the main highway and the service road, crashing head-on into a tree. He managed to apply the brakes, so the crash was not a serious one. He was very shocked but physically unhurt; miraculously, so was the elderly couple who'd been trying to cross a major highway in the dark, obviously without looking. Through sheer luck there had been no oncoming traffic when Bill's car did its wild U-turn or the results would have been tragic.

Bill's car was a write-off. To most of us, providing we were insured and no-one had been hurt, as was the case here, this would not be a major catastrophe. But his car was more than just a car to him—it provided his independence, constituted almost entirely his mobility; it was Bill's 'legs'.

Before the crash Bill had been discussing with his younger brother Grant the possibility of buying Grant's car, an '84 Commodore, and installing hand controls, because Bill's old Kingswood was getting 'clapped out'. Bill had put off this decision because the Commodore had bucket seats, as opposed to the bench seat in the Kingswood, which would make it a lot harder to pull himself into the car with his one good arm across the central console, and then drag the wheelchair in after him. Considerations like this rule the lives of those with a physical disability.

Over the next week, in the Commodore parked in our driveway, Grant and Bill practised the precise physical manoeuvres that Bill would need to learn in order to cope with the car's bucket seats. For several days it was touch and go if they'd succeed, but eventually, through Bill's legendary perseverance and Grant's lateral thinking and great physical coaching skills, they got there. The final step was to take the car to Frank's Engineering in Coburg to have the hand controls fitted.

We both loved the new car; it was much smarter than the old Kingswood, which I'd secretly thought looked like a 'hoon's' car, despite Bill's staid and careful driving. And of course, I found the bucket seat of the Commodore much more comfortable than the Kingswood's bench seat.

This wasn't the end of the problems caused by the crash, though. Bill was anxious about a court case he thought might ensue, and which could result in his losing his driver's license. If this were to happen, he said, he didn't think he could go on. How calmly he said this, without self-pity, as if discussing a work issue. He explained to me that some years ago he had made himself the vow that if the quality of his life were to deteriorate, he would simply end it. I asked him what he meant by 'deteriorate'. He replied, 'I mean ill-health, or not being able to drive. Driving equals having legs.' It seemed quite matter-of-fact, but he spoke with a sense of finality and conviction. I found it hard to accept; the consequences of losing his licence seemed absurdly and brutally disproportionate. With head-in-the-sand naivety I reasoned that surely neither of these things was likely to happen to Bill, any more than to anyone else. I promptly made myself forget about his vow, but Bill never did. It was the very basis of his philosophy and essential to his life, as I would be reminded years later.

The court case did take place. Bill represented himself, as he had a good knowledge of the legal system through teaching VCE Legal Studies. He explained to the magistrate how the elderly couple had been jaywalking across a four-lane highway on a dark winter's night, instead of walking fifty metres up the road to the pedestrian crossing. In avoiding the pair, he said, he'd risked his own life. Not a single person argued against him.

Later that winter, in the middle of the AFL football season, Bill (a very keen Essendon supporter), asked me if he could invite Alex, who was nine and very sensible, to go with him on his usual Friday evening visit to the still-for-sale fish and chip shop, then stay overnight at Bill's place; the plan was for the two of them to go to the football game the following day. Neither of my boys had yet been to an AFL match and I knew Alex would be ecstatic. He also loved the idea of going to the shop and eating Dave's fish and chips for dinner. Once there he was even allowed to serve a couple of customers, under supervision, which made him feel very grown up.

Both boys loved spending time with Bill, one-to-one; activities like the footy were the biggest treat imaginable. It allowed me to spend time with the one who remained at home, precious time often hard to find during those years of work, study, and driving the kids around to their numerous friends and activities. Reading my diary entries, I'm incredulous at the pace of my life back then. Trying to pack so much in, did I think I was Superwoman? I made light of how frenetic and demanding my life was, never asking for help nor cutting back my activities. I never wanted to waste a second. As soon as I'd completed my master's degree in mid-1992, I straightaway enrolled for the PhD in the English Department at La Trobe University. I don't know what impelled me to fill up the boys' childhood with my own demanding study, especially during the several years when I was a single mother. The truth is, it was just something I felt driven to do.

I'd been earning my own living since the age of 16 and studying simultaneously. Having qualified as a teacher in my early twenties, I now wanted to advance in the area of tertiary teaching; my long-term goal was to teach in the university sector. I knew that to do this, I needed a doctorate. It was about more than a career goal; I'd always believed that every adult should earn their own living right through life, which means working for around 40 years. Given that this is the case, it's best if you love what you do, and I wanted to ensure I always would! Learning was as important to me as work. I'd been teaching writing for some years and knew I'd do it better if I could research it more deeply. The next logical step for me was to start a doctorate.

Crazily, to the madcap schedule of my study and work, the boys' numerous extra-curricular activities and Bill's demanding job, we added even more. Urged on by a couple of friends, especially his close friend Matthew, another politics junkie, Bill decided to take some direct action in the arena of his main passion—politics. He nominated himself as an independent candidate in the Victorian State election, contesting the seat in his district of Knox. He chose to run as an independent candidate because, as he wrote in a letter to the newspaper at the time, 'Independents represent democratic ideals; independent candidates form part of a true representative democracy,' noting that 'indeed political parties were not mentioned in our Constitution, only the concept of representation'.

How excited the boys and I were to witness at first-hand the workings of politics. I even helped Bill design his flyers. Computers were coming into vogue in the professional writing course in which I taught, and I ran a 'desktop publishing' class, so was able to produce professional looking leaflets. On weekends Bill went out campaigning, often with Grant's help, setting up in local shopping centres with a poster and a small folding table. One Sunday, when he planned to spend an afternoon at a local community fair in Ferntree Gully, the children and I went with him. Passers-by would stop to talk to Bill, and we were spellbound listening to him talk to people about how he believed more resources should be put into education and public transport in the outer suburban areas, and how an independent member, not being bound by party lines, could better represent his constituency.

The students in Bill's VCE Politics class followed the process avidly, many volunteering to hand out leaflets on election day along with several friends and even his secretary, Larraine. On 3 October we were up with the sparrows, as it were, since Bill wanted to visit as many polling booths in his electorate as possible. With Grant and the two boys, we made the rounds, proffering leaflets and how-to-vote slips as voters were entering the polling places. The day finished with all of us, now joined by the rest of Bill's family, as well as his friend Matthew, back at his house in Ferntree Gully eagerly watching the election results.

Bill didn't win; I don't believe he really thought he would. But he scored a respectable 5% of the vote, enough to secure the refund of the mandatory deposit.

As the end of our first year together approached, we couldn't believe how much we'd packed in to the twelve months. And somehow I'd even managed to carve out some time for the initial reading for my PhD. Alex turned ten in late October, celebrated with a birthday lunch at Bill's house attended by the whole Johnson clan. Bill's parents now treated my boys like their own grandchildren, and Merrilyn and Dave's four children considered my two as their cousins. The boys couldn't have been happier. As for me, Bill was my best friend and lover. We'd discerned each other's strengths and failings and managed to talk about them. Bill had made a portentous but principled statement about the limits of life, albeit one which I had willed into oblivion, and had demonstrated through merely living it, by engaging with community and family, how powerful and certain his principles were.

The one uncertainty, it seemed, was our still not knowing when we could live together, as a buyer had not yet been found for the shop. But we'd kept the drawings for the renovations to my house, ready for an instant re-launch at the first opportunity.

1971: A Place of Love

Bill arrived at the Yooralla Hospital School for Crippled Children, in February 1971. Yooralla was an Aboriginal word, chosen by the original founder back in 1918, meaning 'a place of love'. Bill would have known about Yooralla—in common with most Melburnians—from its yearly telethon, which ran for two decades in the second half of the twentieth century. Two Victorian television stations ran telethons during that time, each championing different charities held annually at different times. The Channel 7 Telethon had started in 1957 and was held on Good Friday, raising money for the Royal Children's Hospital.

A couple of years later Channel 9, not wanting to be outdone by its rival, was looking for a 'worthy cause' and decided to partner with the Yooralla charity, which had just launched an appeal to construct a new hospital school in Balwyn. The first Yooralla school in Carlton had been overcrowded for some time. While the Education Department was going to pay for the new school and its teachers, the considerable costs of the 'hospital' section, serving the medical needs of the students, had to be raised by the Yooralla Society charity.

With the Channel 9 launch of the Yooralla Telethon, the coupling of charity with disability, and the representation of people with disabilities as the passive recipients of assistance and welfare, as had been the case for most of the 20th century, was reinforced by a mass media television event, along with prominent reporting of the results in the newspapers. The charity money was an absolute necessity, of course, because federal and state governments were not providing anything like adequate resources for this segment of citizens.

As well as numerous ordinary television viewers donating small sums, and many auxiliary groups conducting fundraising, a number of businesses donated larger amounts in return for extensive media exposure, sponsoring—with prizes of cars, furs and air travel—quests such as 'Miss Sports Girl' and 'Mrs Victoria', 'Mrs Golden Dollar', and 'Mrs Personality'. So successful was all this fundraising that from 1971 the Yooralla Society set up a dedicated Public Relations and Appeals department to coordinate fundraising with Channel 9 and other organisations, disseminating videos and 'action shots of disabled children',[11] designed to maintain yearlong pressure on potential donors.

A student of the time, who attended Yooralla from the age of 5 to 15 and later studied and qualified to be a social worker, recalls how these 'action shots' were obtained. 'We were paraded around the basketball court,' she told me, 'like penguins on parade, and they would take photos of us children to show our various disabilities, and these photos would be used in the media'. The student's mother in fact refused permission for her daughter to be photographed, so any photos of children that were used were at least done so with parents' permission. Nevertheless, this anecdote shows that some children, at least, disliked the practice, and it provides a sense of the world Bill was entering.

None of this is to deny that the Telethons and all the fundraising groups were well-meaning, nor that this was just 'how things were' before equal rights were extended to people with disabilities. But one can imagine how the Yooralla children who were old enough to think reflectively would have felt about being charity recipients, about necessitating such valiant 24-hour efforts, complete with celebrities exhorting hundreds of thousands of ordinary Victorian viewers to phone in and pledge their contributions. And all because the government did not organise or fund mainstream schools in a way that enabled children with disabilities to fully participate, meaning they had to be segregated.

In addition to segregation there were the various therapies considered necessary under the medical model prevalent until the late twentieth century; all the resources dedicated to the therapies—the treatment centre, nursing staff, equipment like wheelchairs, typewriters, and vehicles for transporting children, and the students' boarding hostel itself—were contingent upon charity. Former students believe that many of the children disliked the charity aspect very much; Bill certainly saw it as demeaning.

Students felt they were being objectified and effectively forced to earn the means for their own treatment. One memorable example was the reaction of some students to the groups of people who were regularly shown around the school prior to their making donations. The classrooms had large windows about a metre off the ground, enabling the groups of visitors to look in at the children. Some children made signs to put in the windows, bearing the words, 'Five cents a look' (for which the perpetrators would later be reprimanded). The visitors were hugely disruptive as there could be as many as thirty of them peering in, yet the children and their teachers were expected simply to ignore them.

Social research conducted in Ireland,[12] where telethons commonly raised money for needy people and services, found that this type of fundraising emerged when the state was providing insufficiently, and that such voluntarism was encouraged as a solution to a social need while not attempting to change the status quo. In Australia, and very likely most countries, the status quo was that mainstream education excluded children with disabilities, making institutions like Yooralla necessary.

The situation for disabled children had of course been a great deal worse before the founding of Yooralla, and a quick look at the institution's history helps provide some context. It was founded in 1918 by Sister Faith, (real name, Evangeline Ireland), a Methodist missionary at the Fitzroy Methodist Church. At this time, the nineteenth-century view of people with disabilities was still predominant: they should be kept out of sight, at home, the responsibility of their families and certainly not the state, with no possibility of attending mainstream school. While working in the slums of Melbourne, Sister Faith came across many children with physical disabilities and long-term illnesses, including one child who was said to have been left tied under a chicken coop while her parents went to work. Initially, the 'hospital school'—for the children that Sister Faith brought in clearly needed care—was a charitable kindergarten for very young children with disabilities known as 'The Free Kindergarten for Physical Weaklings' (this was of course well before any public health care system).

The children's disabilities comprised—as well as spina bifida and cerebral palsy—muscular diseases including polio, the result of several outbreaks in the first half of the twentieth century, of which the most recent had been in 1917. Without a place like Yooralla the majority of these children were indeed hidden away in homes, and doubly disadvantaged if they were from impoverished families, the very demographic that Sister Faith and her church were helping.

A century later, in 2018, Sister Faith was still being invoked as the central character of the well-known and oft-cited 'origin story' in the area of provision for people with a disability. She has appeared as recently as 9 February 2018 in a 'small feature' on Channel 9's The Today Show, to mark the 100th anniversary of Yooralla, now a disability service provider. In this feature, an abridged version of the founding story is told, complete with a sepia photo of Sister Faith. Stills from Channel 9's Telethons in the 1960s and 70s are shown, after which the current Chief Executive Officer of Yooralla speaks of the twenty years of Telethons as something that 'raised Yooralla's profile' among influential people, that is, its benefactors, and was therefore 'a really good thing which has brought Yooralla to where it is now'.[13] The televised segment features many 'action shots' of people with disabilities, evoking the advertising in the 1970s which used similar pictures of the Yooralla schoolchildren.

Yooralla had been forced to function, then, as charity right from the start, an aspect that persisted into the late 20th century. From its inception it had a committee devoted to fundraising. In the 1920s a horse-drawn ambulance was donated by the 'Whiting Sympathy Fund'; in 1932 Melbourne Rotary donated an ambulance van.

Gradually the school became extended to children of all ages with disabilities, and was run in houses obtained in Fitzroy and then Carlton, with an increasing staff of nurses, teachers, and volunteers. The state government began providing money for the educational side of Yooralla in 1942, when the Carlton premises became State School number 4599.

For its entire existence Yooralla frequently appealed to the government for extra money, but the results were piecemeal, never lessening the need for fundraising. An example of government parsimony was when the new principal began an integration program with nearby schools in the mid-1970s, requiring a Yooralla nurse to visit the schools to assist the integrated children daily at lunchtime; the Education Department opposed this initiative as it didn't want to have to provide transport for the nurse. Fortunately, Yooralla decided to pay for it,[14] which meant the Department could no longer withhold permission for the program.

Much earlier, in 1959, before the Balwyn school was even built, the first Yooralla Telethon raised over $157,000, almost double its goal, representing a financial turning point for Yooralla. The money was needed to build a new accommodation hostel, the medical treatment centre, nurses' home, kitchen and dining hall, all of which would cost $250,000. The following year the Victorian Education Department financed construction of the school, the first in the state to be planned and built to cater for the needs of children with physical disabilities.

Special School no. 4675, Yooralla Balwyn, opened at the start of the school year in 1962. At that time, almost no one questioned the principle of segregation, even for children with no intellectual disability, as was the case with these Yooralla students.[15] This segregation can be seen as a form of 'unremarked apartheid', according to the argument in the book *Disability in Australia: Exposing a Social Apartheid* (in which the authors examine contemporary early 21st-century disablism, not even that of the 1970s).[16] Yet, apart from the Yooralla school and the then Spastic Society (which merged with Yooralla in 1977), up until the mid-1970s there was almost nowhere else for children with physical disabilities to go for their education. While government schools in that era did not in general refuse the small number of children with polio whose parents demanded that they attend (although most of those parents were strongly encouraged to send their children to schools such as Yooralla), such schools could refuse students with other disabilities, especially those who used wheelchairs, arguing that they lacked sufficient staff and facilities, especially wheelchair-accessible toilets; in addition, even many of the newer school buildings at the time were multi-storey, with no lifts, and steps at most entrances.

For Bill in 1971, there was no alternative school to Yooralla. The place had specially designed ramps and sliding doors which made it easier for children in wheelchairs or on crutches to move around. Corridors were extra wide, and flooring was a special smooth, non-slip material. There were also accessible toilets adjacent to classrooms and the playground. The hostel block was set up with four-bed 'wards', complete with accessible bathrooms and toilet facilities.

Of Bill's three roommates in the hostel, one was his own age, the other two boys a few years younger. They got along well, with Bill and the older boy, Rob, becoming very close friends. In their final two years at Yooralla, studying the Higher School Certificate[17] subjects by correspondence, the two elder boys would discuss their goals of leaving Yooralla after the final exams. Bill's goal was to enrol at university, Rob's to obtain a position in an accounting firm. In the evenings the secondary students did their homework in a large common room, but as the only two boarders undertaking final-year subjects at that time, Bill and Rob needed a quieter space in which to work; they were given a small room of their own in which to study.

In 1972 a young woman of around their age, Margaret, began working as a nursing assistant in the hostel. She remembers regularly listening to, and sometimes joining Bill and Rob in deep discussion in the evenings, about their studies, politics, or sport, and sometimes even weightier subjects like mortality. But equally there was a lot of joking around by the three of them. Perhaps the two boys had some intimation that their lives would be short, and humour was a powerful antidote to such knowledge.

One of Bill's practical jokes was to stand up his artificial leg, now rarely used, in a cupboard, and ask a new nurse to get something out of the cupboard for him. He'd position the leg so it would fall out as soon as the door was opened by the unsuspecting victim. On another occasion, in the school dining hall, one of the older nurses became impatient with the amount of food spilled on the tables. None of the children spilled food deliberately, but some disabilities made the handling of food a challenge. The nurse announced she'd give a prize at the end of the week to the children with the 'cleanest table'. At this patronising treatment, Bill and Rob looked at each other in defiant disbelief. After quickly conferring in whispers, Rob said in a loud clear voice, 'Well, Bill and I will be offering a much better prize for the messiest table!' The younger children erupted in laughter, and no more was heard about prizes of any sort in the dining room.

Bill and his room-mates, and several of the other boys, were all crazy about 'Aussie rules' football. Bill, who'd been the star of Croydon High School's under 16s football team, understood the game particularly well, and also attended Victorian Football League matches every weekend with his father, long before the VFL became the Australian Football League (AFL). Some of the senior boys already played Paralympic basketball so there was no reason they couldn't play football in a similar way, adapted for players using wheelchairs.

There were two teams: Morden ('The Lions') and Casper ('The Hawks'). Bill himself couldn't play due to the partial paralysis in his right arm, so he became the umpire. Other boys had roles such as commentating or serving on the tribunal. The tribunal was badly needed since the players could get very rough with each other; during one season eight players were suspended for periods of up to four weeks! The senior boys all put enormous energy into the organisation of the season, and Bill even donated the 'best and fairest' medals out of his own money.

A former Yooralla student, still in the primary section at the time, remembers the football seasons as being 'huge', dominating everything else at Yooralla. 'All the other students were involved too, either as cheer squad or spectators. Parents would attend the matches, and nurses would come in specially to watch a match even if it happened to coincide with their day off. Bill and the other boys took it very seriously,' I was told. 'They modelled it on the VFL, even managing to get VFL footballers involved.' A well-known footballer of the time, Don Scott, who played for Hawthorn, is shown in a newspaper clipping from 1973, presenting the best and fairest medal to one of Bill's roommates. Bill, also in the photograph, is described in the article as the 'leading light' in Yooralla's football competition.

The facilities for physical activity were an aspect for which Yooralla couldn't be faulted. At the Balwyn school there was a swimming pool, and a gym where senior boys who used wheelchairs had been introduced to Paralympic-type sports, such as basketball and table tennis. In addition to this was the treatment centre, built in the 1960s, which had sections for each of the different therapies, the rationale being that if these services weren't available on-site, children would have had to be taken to the children's hospital, meaning more loss of schooling time. In the 1960s the facilities at Yooralla were considered 'state of the art'.

Both Yooralla schools, in Balwyn and Carlton, were 'hospital schools', with nursing and medical staff, attendant carers, physiotherapists, occupational and speech therapists. Schooling was constantly interrupted for students requiring various treatments. For some students these medical interventions ensured that they remained well enough to attend school, but four hours' treatment per week would cause the students to fall behind in their studies. In any classroom there's usually a spread of ability and skills of up to several years; at Yooralla, this wide range was exacerbated by time lost to medical treatment and therapy. Some students were frequently unwell due to chronic infections (especially urinary tract or serious respiratory infections). Teaching in such circumstances required tremendous skill in encouraging each student to progress at his or her own pace. Sometimes an inexperienced or less-skilled teacher would end up teaching to the 'lowest common denominator'. One former student states that in year six she was doing grade three work. On the whole, however, former students remember the teachers as very careful to ensure students' learning pace was congruent with their capacity.

That said, Yooralla did not have a good reputation for education. Rhonda Galbally, well-known CEO and chair of many progressive organisations in health, disability, and social policy and most recently Principal Member of the National Disability Insurance Agency (NDIA) Independent Advisory Council, contracted polio as an infant. It was recommended she attend Yooralla for her schooling in the mid-1950s; but she tells in her autobiography, *Just Passions*, how her parents 'stood up to the medical profession … unheard-of courage in those days', insisting she go to an ordinary state school,

> in the face of awful warnings [that she should go to Yooralla] … where I would have been stretched, pummelled, and poked throughout day and night, getting little education, the likelihood of working in the sheltered workshop, living and dying within the Yooralla beneficence. But my mother was a teacher. And she knew that anything that diverted me from education would endanger my future. My Mum strongly suspected that in Yooralla my education would be sacrificed to a daily regime of working on my body to make it 'normal' …[18]

Bill had been desperate to resume his education after eighteen months in hospital doing only small amounts of study by correspondence when his health permitted, but he was far from happy about his new school. As a boy who had been deemed academically above average, he regarded the education offered at Yooralla to be substandard. His antipathy had somehow been conveyed to Yooralla staff even before he arrived although, as a former nurse recalls, Bill never behaved in any other way than with quiet dignity.

This view of him is seconded by Annie, a Yooralla student a few years younger than Bill, who remembers him as '… sensible, whereas we were little larrikins, naughty as typical kids are, but Bill had an air about him that made us respect him'. She adds, 'Do you remember what it was like to look at the school prefect? Well, that's how I saw Bill. He was wise, very reflective, but had a good sense of humour and would always laugh at jokes.'

Despite his sense of humour Bill saw his years at Yooralla as something to be endured, although he acknowledged he had some good friends there, especially Rob. No doubt he also acknowledged that most of the nursing staff and teachers were very caring and did their best in a highly regimented setting. Bill was most critical of the standard of education for the secondary level students. He told me that all the teachers were primary trained, albeit with Special Education qualifications, and so didn't 'teach' the secondary students, merely supervised them while they studied materials provided by the Education Department Correspondence School. As any secondary teacher knows, the dynamic nature of a classroom, with discussions, peer interaction, and group work, is crucial, especially in the final two years leading to the demanding HSC examinations.

Many children with disabilities found it difficult to write, and the only technological assistance was a manual typewriter. Bill had to use his non-dominant left hand for writing; but a student such as Rob, with muscular dystrophy, would find it difficult to write at all. This situation was not fair for either the students or the teachers, and is an example of insufficient resourcing by the Education Department of the senior student cohort there. With personal computers being a good twenty years in the future, students with difficulty writing ideally required an aide to take notes for them. This began happening some years later in many secondary schools, TAFE Institutes and universities, with disability support teams providing targeted educational support according to students' needs.

In 1971 there were around fifteen students in the 'Senior Secondary' group at Yooralla, aged from fifteen years upwards, each studying their own choice of subjects. The physical sciences that required laboratory work, languages, and the more difficult maths subjects would have been almost impossible to study effectively by correspondence at that time, so choices would have been very limited. This was well before digital technology, the internet, laptops and smartphones, advances that have certainly enhanced correspondence study since then. Audio-visual resources, such as TV sets and video and audio players, existed in most schools, but they had to be shared among many teachers, booked in advance, and moved around the school on heavy, wonky trolleys. Even duplicating a sheet to give to each child in a class required cumbersome machines (for example a 'spirit duplicator') that took up valuable time and would frequently break down.

A photograph of the 'Senior Secondary' cohort, taken a few months after Bill first arrived at Yooralla, shows only four of the fifteen smiling—two girls and two boys. Most of the students had had a disability since birth, with a small number acquiring disabilities from accidents, like Bill. Two of the students in the group were siblings, Frank and Lesley Hall-Bentick, who both went on to become lifelong and highly-respected activists and advocates in disability politics, with Lesley first becoming involved in feminist politics only a few years after the Yooralla photograph was taken.

In a 2010 publication, when she was the CEO for the Australian Federation of Disability Organisations, a position she held until her too early death in 2013, Lesley Hall (as she was later known) wrote that her political evolution started from the process of being segregated and institutionalised as a teenager in Yooralla. She saw 'special schools' as limiting and harmful, arguing that 'not only was the education sub-standard, it was socially inadequate'.[19] Thanks to people like her and the many other early activists, by the mid-1980s at least, children with physical disabilities, especially secondary students, were being integrated into mainstream schools wherever possible, a move formalized in Ministerial policy in 1984. It's therefore logical to assume that disability rights were already being discussed by some of the older Yooralla students when Bill arrived, although the disability activist movement didn't start in Melbourne until the late 1970s.

Not long after that school photograph was taken Bill contracted a serious respiratory infection and had to return to the Spinal Unit at the Austin Hospital, where he remained for two months being treated for broncho-pneumonia. He would spend most of the next year in hospital too, not returning to Yooralla until late August 1972. During that year he underwent a major operation that for the rest of his life he regarded as the worst thing he had ever endured.

1993–95: Happiness and Happenstance

Our first piece of good fortune in the early months of 1993 came in the form of a couple who bought the shop. The sale of the business enabled Bill and I to go ahead with our project of making my house wheelchair-accessible, although we pared back our original plans to what was absolutely essential—independent access to the house, and an accessible ensuite bathroom. Even the pared-back plan involved extensive work. For Bill to be able to park his car and then come into the house unaided, a portion of the front garden had to be levelled and concreted. The existing small front balcony had to be raised to eliminate the step at the front door, and had to be linked to the parking area by the construction of a wooden walkway. Bill would then be able to move from the house to his car without needing any assistance. We had to create the new bathroom by taking space from a small adjacent room, which was the most expensive part of the work.

Bill's brother-in-law, Dave, who was skilled at renovations, kindly stepped in and offered to direct and help with much of the renovation, dispensing with the need for an external builder to supervise the various tradespeople. This meant the cost would be less, and we could return to our original idea of adding a family room and an extra bedroom so that the boys could each have their own room. We planned for the work to be finished by November, when Bill would move in, and then rent out his own house to help pay his mortgage. Everything seemed to be coming together. Over the Easter break Bill and I had time to reflect and talk. We asked ourselves, if we were going to live together why not get married? I wasn't too keen; I'd already been married, and divorced, and didn't feel marriage was qualitatively different from living together. The latter was just as serious a commitment, in my view. Bill agreed, but said that as he'd never been married he didn't have any negative feelings about it.

The most decisive factor for us was his increasing involvement in the boys' lives; he wanted to be able to attend parent-teacher interviews and other events without there being any ambiguity about his role. If we were married he would be legally the children's step-father. We both thought this was important and we knew the children would too. So we decided to get married on Bill's 38th birthday, nine months away, on 19 December. With that date, Bill said, there'd be no risk of his ever forgetting our anniversary.

As with most renovations, ours didn't run on schedule. A whole range of tradespeople were involved—plasterers, carpenters, painters, tilers—and for a few weeks in November and early December I anxiously feared that the house wouldn't be ready in time for our wedding, part of which was to be held at home. But with only three days to go, the final slate tile was laid on the floor of the new family room, and Bill moved in.

We were married in our lounge-room, the ceremony conducted by a local civil celebrant, followed by dinner at our Institute's restaurant. Our immediate families were there, including my brother, mother, father and stepmother with their twins, who had all come across from Perth. The oldest guest was Bill's grandmother, Little Nan, now 92. She was almost completely deaf, so wouldn't have heard our speeches, but June later told us how much it had meant to Nan seeing Bill get married. I wore a long silk dress the colour of Dutch irises, matching the colour of Bill's eyes as well as his bow-tie. The day was fine but cool, so I was able to wear the matching blue chiffon wrap I'd bought to go with my dress.

Alex stood behind Bill's wheelchair and Patrick sat in front of us, alongside his little cousin Erin (Merrilyn and Dave's daughter) in her deep pink dress. On Bill's right sat Wayne, the best man, and on my left my friend Penny, my bridesmaid. I felt I had never been so happy, and I knew Bill and the boys felt the same way.

My father, step-mother Helen, and their twins Lucy and Stewart, aged 16, stayed on for Christmas with us. On Christmas morning Bill's younger brother Grant arrived. As a surprise he'd hired a stretch limousine for the day to take our children to see their cousins in Lilydale before Christmas lunch.

Three days after Christmas it was my fortieth birthday. In the evening Bill and I went to a nearby Greek restaurant for dinner, while Dad and Helen looked after the boys. Life hadn't felt this good for a long time. The anxiety and depression that had plagued me intermittently for over a decade seemed to have receded. It was a golden time for the four of us, one of the happiest periods of our lives. But what I didn't know, or didn't want to know, was how fragile happiness is, how easily it can be destroyed by pain or illness, or any number of misfortunes, and by our human limitations in dealing with adversity. Looking back, I can see how lucky we were to have these first few years, because such happiness is almost always happenstance—an accidental alignment of factors, a house of cards that can be blown down in an instant. For some reason I felt absolutely entitled to this happiness, saw it as my 'right', almost, after a long period of depression and difficult circumstances. Why did I think we were so special? Why did I think Adrienne Rich's poem, that I'd read to Bill on my 38th birthday, didn't apply to us? With hindsight I'm certain Bill knew it applied very well; but he didn't want my happiness shattered any earlier than necessary.

As the start of the 1994 school year approached, Bill asked Alex—now starting his final year of primary school—if he'd like to join a local cricket team. I can still recall the mix of joy and excitement on Alex's face in response to this question. He loved playing cricket in the street with his friends, and enjoyed watching it on television. Bill made a few phone calls and the two of them started what was to be a long involvement with the North Balwyn Cricket Club, with Bill the 'team manager' of Alex's team, doing all the necessary organising of the team and players, including the scoring at the weekly matches. From then on, the matches, awards nights, and fundraising events were a big part of our life, and the source of long-lasting friendships for the four of us.

Patrick wanted his own sporting activity over the summer months, so we enrolled him in the local group of 'Little Athletics'. This involved parents helping to oversee the various events that each group of children undertook in rotation each week, a responsibility that fell to me, since Bill was busy with the cricket team. Along with many of their friends, both boys also belonged to basketball teams; and on Saturday mornings in winter they participated in the Auskick football program for under 12s. And once they turned twelve, they joined local football teams for their respective age groups.

On top of the sport, the boys were learning musical instruments. I thought this was important for every child, so I'd enrolled each in turn, when he was seven, with private instrumental teachers. To my mind, music and languages were just as important as literacy and numeracy. As each of my children had approached his seventh birthday, I'd asked him which instrument he'd like to learn. Alex wasn't sure, but the music teacher at his primary school said she believed he was musically talented and recommended the violin, possibly because she herself was a violinist. Alex seemed to like this idea and when he turned seven we bought him a half-size instrument and enrolled him with a private teacher.

When it was Patrick's turn he chose the piano. Music lessons were in the late afternoon or early evening and entailed my driving the boys to their teachers' homes, and staying there for the thirty- or forty-minute lesson.

Much of my lesson planning and marking was done during music lessons or basketball matches. There was simply no other way, short of staying up till 1am. I was teaching three days a week, trying to complete a PhD part-time, and doing the majority of the physical work in the house and garden. The boys were very helpful, considering they were only 8 and 11 when Bill and I got married, making their own breakfasts and preparing sandwiches for their school lunch. They also made their beds and kept their rooms in order, although their definition of 'in order' was somewhat different from mine!

Although Bill managed by himself almost everything to do with his own personal needs, it simply wasn't physically possible for him to assist with cooking or housework. I resented the time spent cooking, and the results suffered accordingly. Bill and the boys never complained, but I was a mediocre cook; it was impossible to be otherwise. There was no time for poring over recipes or lovingly selecting and sourcing ingredients. Instead, we'd race in from a violin lesson or basketball match, I'd supervise homework, music practice, and the shower-and-pyjamas routine, before throwing some meat under the grill and then sitting down to finish my marking or read a few pages of an academic article for my PhD. I was often roused from this activity by the kitchen smoke alarm going off! Once a week we'd buy a cooked chicken, roast potatoes and prepared coleslaw at the local 'barbecue chicken' shop: the culinary highlight of the week for me, and the day could never come around soon enough.

Despite the hastily thrown-together meals, family dinners were a lively affair. Bill would arrive home about 7.30, full of interesting stories about his day: students who'd done something crazy; students he'd had to discipline; those making unexpected progress; a disgruntled staff member or two; or a funny joke someone had told him. If we got into too much in-depth 'talking shop', the boys would tell us to stop, but we always asked them about their day: the lessons they'd had; their test results; something new or interesting, even their conflicts.

About this last topic Bill taught us an invaluable lesson. If Patrick, say, had been having a conflict with a classmate, he'd naturally tell us his side of the story. Bill would ask what he thought the classmate's version of events would be, and Patrick would think about it, and come up with something plausible. 'Now,' said Bill. 'I want you to think of a position somewhere in the middle of these two versions. That's most likely where the truth lies.' This is still one of my guiding principles.

As 1994 began both Bill and I took on new projects. Bill began a Graduate Diploma in Educational Administration at the University of Melbourne, attending lectures one evening a week, something he very much enjoyed. At the same time I had the idea of creating a 'literature tour' and persuaded a friend who was a travel agent to come into business with me; together we led a tour of a dozen people, mostly elderly, to the UK for a few weeks in the English summers of 1994 and 1995. I loved visiting the homes of the great writers, giving talks, and conducting writing workshops for our tour participants. The visits to writers' homes were moments of euphoria for me: John Keats' house in Hampstead; Monks House, the country home of Virginia Woolf; and the thatched-roof cottage where Thomas Hardy was born near Dorchester. Equally pleasurable was encouraging our venerable group to embark on their own creative writing on the lawn outside Wordsworth's house, and other inspirational settings.

Bill made this possible by looking after the boys for the few weeks I was away, with help from his parents and his brother Grant. I'd not returned to the UK since leaving it as an adolescent in 1969 when my family migrated to Australia, so it was an immensely emotional return. I was able to reflect on my childhood in England, thinking about the transformation of my life brought about by emigration, and to visit Hawarden in north Wales, where I was born. In the few 'days off' during the tour I reconnected with some aunts, uncles and cousins. But I missed Bill and the children terribly; the second tour became my last, and I told my friend she could take over the business.

I don't know how we did it but, during those years, Bill and I made time to discuss our academic work with each other, see films and plays, and often go out to dinner. We talked about the big things, but I could also confide the trivial, like the dress I'd seen in a shop window. He'd always say, 'Yeah, get it; why not?' He believed in living in the moment, not delaying desires for some future that one might never see.

I look at our photo albums of 1994 and 1995: Alex in a school play or playing the violin on stage; in his cricket whites, too, waiting to bat in pads and helmet; Patrick performing in a piano concert; or the three of them around a table at Papa Gino's in Carlton, waiting for their pizza. But there aren't many photos with me in them as I took most of them with my little Canon. Bill's always there, at the cricket or the concerts, or school fundraising barbecues, sometimes with Patrick on his lap. So much was happening there was little time to reflect. My diary entries bring back memories of the many hectic pleasures, and also of my exhaustion.

By the end of 1995, I see now, Bill and I were living at an unsustainable pace. My week consisted of teaching for several days, then on Saturday afternoon attending a concert or sports event in which one or other of the children was participating, preparing all the meals, and often hosting an extended family dinner and cleaning up afterwards. On Sundays in summer it was up at 7.30am for four hours duty at Little Athletics, followed by garden maintenance and lawn moving until Alex became old enough to take this over. Bill too, was stretched to the limit, without the advantage of a fully-functioning body and reliable physical health. His week involved ten or eleven-hour high stress working days, followed by Friday evenings with Alex at his cricket match, scoring the game and helping coach the boys, a role he loved no matter how tired he felt.

I became as physically exhausted as I'd been when the children were very young; my sense of well-being had declined. I barely found time to work on my thesis. Women I knew in a similar situation often had mothers who'd assist on a regular basis. I looked on, jealously; my mother was on the other side of the continent. The normal exuberance and 'naughtiness' of boys their age were often too much for me; at times anxiety made me a monster, yelling angrily at the three males in my life.

If Bill had led a quiet, more secluded life, without a demanding career and rambunctious little tribe at home, would his health have held out longer? It's a pointless question, really, because he'd never have wanted it otherwise. His career was everything to him; so were the boys and me. He'd been plagued continually by infections since his accident, so his relatively good health in our four years together had been assuredly serendipitous, and lured us into a false sense of security; when misfortune struck we were ill-prepared.

In November Bill fell ill with a kidney infection, an ever-present risk for people with paraplegia or quadriplegia. He'd suffered a few minor infections over the past year, but this seemed much worse. He continued working, typically, but he'd come in the door at night, face drained and ashen, almost unable to speak. He spoke very little when he was ill, something I found very hard to cope with. He'd barely utter monosyllables, but would make a supreme effort for the children. Worse, he'd refuse to see a doctor. He had his own cache of antibiotics in case the infection became very severe, but rarely took them, believing they'd only weaken his immunity and make him more susceptible in future. I know now that this runs completely counter to the medical advice for kidney infections.

Many years later, reading Jane Hawking's memoir of her ex-husband Stephen, I learned that the great physicist in his younger years, after contracting motor neurone disease, would similarly avoid medication; he'd lapse into morose silences when ill yet continue to work, refusing to see doctors until the situation was critical, behaviour that is very punishing on one's partner.[20]

That November, after ten days of illness, scarcely eating or talking but insisting on working most days, Bill relented, agreeing to an outpatient consultation at the Spinal Unit. The doctor prescribed antibiotics, did a renal ultrasound and X-ray, and wanted him to have a more exploratory procedure in the new year, referring him to the Austin's urologist.

Bill began the antibiotics and slowly the infection retreated, but almost immediately he felt severe pain in his right shoulder. With hindsight I presume it was a random arthritic condition. Bill had limited use of his right arm, relying on it only for balance and operating the hand controls (accelerator and brake) of his car. Severe pain alone is enough to bring anyone to despair, so Bill agreed to take paracetamol, but as usual refused to see the doctor.

A week later the shoulder pain disappeared as mysteriously as it had appeared. But the ill winds of misfortune continued to batter us in the form of searing pain in Bill's left wrist. He depended on this limb for everything: pulling himself in and out of the car, and the bed; pulling the wheelchair into the car after him; washing and dressing; every aspect of living. Quite likely it was his very dependence on the wrist which caused the inflammation. During a brief bout of wrist pain a year earlier, my father and stepmother, Helen, had very kindly flown over from Perth for a couple of weeks, helping out with the house and the children so I could be free to assist Bill. They couldn't come this time as they were expecting us for Christmas, although that plan itself was now in jeopardy.

Perhaps you must live with a person severely incapacitated by illness to really understand what it's like when you have to help the other to wash, toilet, dress, eat, drink, fetch, lift, drive. A couple may find themselves transformed into patient and carer, no matter how hard each fights against it. The loss of independence for the 'patient' is dehumanizing and debilitating, and I struggled desperately to understand how Bill must have felt, although I don't know how successful I was. He surely sensed my struggle to understand. In the middle of this difficult period, apropos of nothing in particular, Bill said to me, 'You must have realised before we got married that my health and independence wouldn't last forever, and that they'd diminish as I got older'.

I was shattered. I'd never thought about it. And he'd certainly never raised it. But it was logical enough, and I suppose I'd been deluding myself. I felt angry with him for never having mentioned it, but I wouldn't allow myself to express my anger to him; he had enough to bear already. He hated being dependent on me. Since we'd first met, I'd never consciously thought of Bill as anything but independent. And he was; but it was a precarious independence. When his one good arm became even temporarily incapacitated, that independence was lost. With hindsight I see it would have been sensible to employ some help, but early in our marriage we had two large mortgages and couldn't afford outside help. And because Bill worked full-time he wasn't eligible for much financial aid with the expensive, specialised equipment he needed.

Bill and I tried to hide from the children how low we were both feeling, but they seemed to sense it, and went to some effort to behave as well as possible. I worked hard at controlling my temper when things weren't done as quickly or as well as I'd like. Somehow we got through it; Bill's wrist healed, and a semblance of normality returned. Fortunately Bill had agreed to contact an occupational therapist experienced in working with disabled people. She recommended that we buy a wheelchair lift which could be fitted to the roof of the car. The beneficial impact of this on our lives was inestimable. Not only did it save Bill from tugging the full weight of the wheelchair into the front seat of the car, but when we went out together I no longer had to lift the 20-kilogram folded wheelchair into the boot. At the press of the button the metal arm of the lift would descend and hoist the wheelchair up on to the roof of the car, removing the worst of the strains on Bill's good wrist. The therapist also recommended a lever-drive wheelchair, much more suitable for people who need to propel themselves with one arm; we quickly followed this advice, somehow finding the several thousand dollars required for all this new equipment.

Bill recovered from all his ailments just in time for his 40th birthday. 19 December 1995 was a work day, and Bill's secretary Larraine had tied helium balloons to his desk, and put up a sparkly blue banner that said 'Happy 40th'. She'd also ordered a cake, which Bill shared with his staff at morning tea. The following weekend Bill's brother Grant and his partner Fran hosted a magnificent sit-down lunch for the immediate family on their back patio, beneath a pergola covered with trailing vines, and surrounded by ferns. It was a mild early-summer day, everyone had brought delicious salads and sides, and Grant cooked steaks, marinated chicken, and prawns on the barbecue. Our world was resuming its more benign normal shape; the house of cards was again standing straight and strong, and we tried to forget the previous couple of months as quickly as possible.

1971–72: Surviving Medieval Torture

With my forefinger I traced the long white scar that ran almost the whole length of Bill's spine, starting just below the nape of his neck. 'Was this from your accident?' I asked.

'No,' he replied, 'it was from the spinal fusion operation I had to have two years later. The paralysis was causing my spine to curve, and to fix it they put in a steel rod. I had to lie in bed for nine months while the metal fused with my backbone. It was even worse than recovering from the accident! If I'd known what it would be like, I don't think I'd have agreed to have it done. Still, then I wouldn't have been around to meet you!'

This was followed by a burst of laughter, the usual tactic when he wanted to downplay physical hardship. It also signalled he didn't want to go into any more detail. Bill always felt there were far more interesting things to talk about—the politics of the day, or the quotidian challenges with our classes or colleagues, and especially the antics and activities of the two boys. As someone who's always been very squeamish, I never sought to learn more details of his medical procedures, anyway, preferring the brief summaries he occasionally offered. But as I found out much later, this spinal surgery had given Bill several decades of life that he almost certainly wouldn't have otherwise had.

Bill hadn't been happy to be sent to Yooralla after his discharge from hospital; but seven months later, when back in hospital with broncho-pneumonia, he'd have been even less happy, ironically, if he'd known that he wouldn't be returning to Yooralla until late the following year for the final school term of 1972. In the intervening period he would undergo an immensely invasive surgical procedure, the recovery from which would be so painful and difficult, so traumatic, that at age 16 he made a promise to himself that contributed to his decision, thirty years later, to end his life.

During Bill's long stay at the Austin the previous year, the spinal doctors had noted how the partial paralysis of his right side—known as hemiplegia—and the paralysis of his intercostal muscles, combined with the rapid growth of adolescence, were causing his spine to curve forwards as well as sideways towards the right. This curvature—scoliosis—is common in paralysed children and is frequently life-threatening, as it deforms the rib cage and greatly restricts and impairs lung function, a condition compounded when all waking hours are spent seated in a wheelchair. When lungs can't expand correctly, they become highly susceptible to respiratory diseases, a condition that worsens over time. Since his accident Bill had been experiencing frequent life-threatening respiratory problems.

Dr Cheshire, seeing how much the curvature had worsened in only eight months, consulted with the hospital's thoracic and orthopaedic surgeons, to work out a plan of action. He summoned Bill's parents and brother Wayne to a meeting and told them that without functioning muscles to hold it up, Bill's spine was collapsing. If nothing was done, it was unlikely he'd survive much beyond his early twenties, as the curvature would eventually constrict the rib cage and crush his lungs, in particular the right lung; Bill would almost certainly die of respiratory failure unless his spine could be straightened and repaired.

Bill and his parents had absolute trust in Dr Cheshire's judgement. After all, it was the doctor's expertise in spinal medicine that only 18 months earlier had set Bill on the path to rehabilitation after much misdiagnosis elsewhere. Now Cheshire and the other specialists wanted to perform what was known as a spinal fusion operation, in which a steel rod would be inserted alongside Bill's spine, to be fused with bone grafts. Prior to this, his spine would need to be held straight by an apparatus known as halo-pelvic traction, a relatively new procedure in Australia. Wayne recalls being told that Bill could die from the operation. Faced with the prospect of Bill's certain death in a few years' time if the operation did not go ahead, Mr and Mrs Johnson agreed to it.

At that time there were a number of procedures for attempting to straighten curved spines, from various braces through to very complicated and invasive surgery for people with severe curvature, whether caused by paralysis or by poliomyelitis, spina bifida, or other conditions. In the early 1970s, spine-straightening surgery was still somewhat experimental. A small number of orthopaedic surgeons around the world were performing this surgery, and had been refining techniques and treatments for a few years. By December 1971, when Bill's operation was performed, surgeons were using a combination of procedures and equipment, building up their knowledge as they did so and publishing their results, permitting other doctors to benefit from them.

It's from these publications that at long last, many years after Bill's death, I've been able to learn something of the procedure, to gain at least some idea of how it was performed in the 1970s. Bill never talked to me about it, and probably knew little of the details in any case. It's highly complex surgery and, despite my researching it extensively, it's almost impossible for a person without medical training to properly comprehend it; even more of a challenge to try and explain it in ordinary language, but I'll do my best.

In the 1970s there were many complications from this operation. Certainly, some patients died, although it would seem only a minority. Sometimes the instruments used would break or become dislodged; where the metal rod was in contact with the spine, the bone could become eroded, or infection could develop around the steel inserts; and sometimes the curve returned. There were also documented cases of neurological impairment and damage to the spinal cord. It was thought to be even more dangerous when performed on paraplegic and quadriplegic patients. Apart from the serious potential complications, one of the cruellest aspects of spinal surgery of this type, especially for children or young people, was that the patient had to be kept immobile for a long period, often several months. For Bill, aged fifteen at the time, it would be nine months.

The first part of the process, the halo-pelvic traction, not only kept the patient's torso immobile but, as the word traction implies, exerted pressure to straighten the spine. This device had only recently been developed by Dr Arthur Hodgson at the University of Hong Kong, in response to severe spinal deformities in that region since the 1950s, caused by poliomyelitis and tuberculosis of the spine. Similar traction devices were also being developed in some parts of the United States. The Austin hospital didn't have this equipment in 1971, as it was relatively new to Australia. The hospital couldn't even afford to buy it, so the manufacturers agreed to lend it to the hospital for Bill's operation.

The apparatus itself and the method by which it was attached to the body evoke accounts of medieval torture devices; to think of a fifteen-year-old boy undergoing it is almost too much to bear. Thankfully, this type of apparatus is rarely used today, and treatments for scoliosis have been greatly refined in the past 50 years.

The halo-pelvic traction apparatus consisted of a stainless-steel ring—the 'halo'—fixed around the patient's head; at the other end two long 'pins' inserted into and right across the pelvis, crossed over each other towards the patient's back before emerging through the skin. Here the risks were perforation of the intestines, nerve injuries, injury to the spine, and infection of the pins. A metal ring was also fastened around the pelvis to keep the pins in place.

Under general anaesthetic the 'halo', which had holes at regular intervals, was fixed into the skull with four screws, or pins, one each side of the forehead, and one each side of the back of the head. According to the pictures accompanying medical articles, the pins resembled sharp-pointed screws which were hand-screwed into the outer layer of the skull. The pins had 'shoulders' to prevent them penetrating further into the skull. A potential complication was damage to cranial nerves, or to the eyes.

Once the metal ring and the pelvic pins and circle were fixed to the patient's body, four long vertical rods (that is, vertical if the patient were standing upright) were attached, two at the front and two at the back, each running from the 'halo' down to the pelvic ring. The rods had devices on them, like locking nuts; when turned, they gradually lengthened the rods a few millimetres a day, progressively straightening the spine.

Patients in halo-pelvic traction needed 24-hour monitoring by nurses, checking for infection, dressing the wounds, and watching out for any nerve damage caused by the daily tightening. The apparatus was also checked each day to ensure all fixtures were tight, as looseness could cause pain and infection. On top of the discomfort for the head and pelvis, the apparatus weighed at least three kilograms. The value of this device, as one of the spinal doctors noted in a report, was that not only did it straighten the spine to the correct position, but it could be left in place during the spinal fusion operation, afterwards functioning like a plaster cast to keep the spine immobile.

On Remembrance Day, 11 November 1971, Bill underwent the operation to attach the halo-pelvic apparatus. Later, back in the spinal ward, he awoke in agony, with drainage tubes attached to the sutures where the pins fixed the metal rings to his head and pelvis. Nurses turned him every two hours to prevent pressure sores from developing.

Over the next three weeks, sutures leaked regularly, and pins would become dislodged from the circular frame around his head; the two-hourly turnings made this more likely to happen, and Bill had to return to theatre several times to have the pins reinserted under local anaesthetic. His head ached remorselessly, and each pin site caused near-constant pain for which he was given paracetamol, pethidine, and a combination of sedatives and anti-anxiety medication; these alone made life bearable, almost. Nurses' notes unsurprisingly described his mood as 'miserable' or 'unhappy', during this drawn-out period of suffering.

How could any teenager keep his or her spirits up, maintain an interest in life, lying in bed for weeks on end, heavily medicated yet in continual pain, knowing the situation would continue well beyond the long and frightening spine-straightening operation that lay ahead? The nurses' logs note Bill's reluctance to eat or drink, almost as if he didn't care whether he survived or not. Bill's sister Merrilyn, then aged about 13, remembers visiting him during this time. Her parents would drop her at the hospital entrance, before going on to find a parking spot, so she'd be the first to arrive at Bill's bedside. She clearly recalls his terrible distress, both before and after the operation, and his saying to her, 'Just get me out of this. Tell them to get me out of it, I don't care if my spine isn't straightened.' The strange thing is that in his medical notes there's no evidence he expressed this to anyone else apart from his family; certainly not to the nurses and doctors.

I try to imagine what it must have felt like, having to lie in a bed for nine months, with a metal band held to my skull by four screws, another metal band attached to my pelvis with two metal pins passing right through from one side to the other. The two spinal doctors understood very well Bill's suffering, and in their reports from that period they referred to what he was going through as 'terrible', in 'this ghastly piece of traction apparatus'. But in reports written towards the end of Bill's nine months in traction, they described him as having a good morale, and retaining 'through all this adversity' his sense of humour, aspects they rightly said were crucial to Bill's recovery.

It's likely that those closest to Bill—the nurses, his sister, and other family members—were the people with whom he could let down his defences; he couldn't maintain a brave exterior all the time, and he let them see him at his lowest. But with the doctors he made determined efforts not to show his distress or depression. I'm reminded of the periods in the last couple of years of Bill's life when he was very ill; it was only to me that he showed how really wretched he felt, but at work or with the children he made superhuman efforts to behave as if nothing were wrong.

From the little that Bill told me, he certainly saw the spinal operation and its aftermath as the worst period of his long rehabilitation following the accident. I often wonder how many of us could endure it and retain our sanity, or even our will to live. I doubt that I could; just trying to imagine and describe what he went through is deeply distressing. But endure it Bill did, and it was his endurance in the face of such a consuming challenge—the physical suffering, the mental anguish, his fears for the future—that formed his particular personality, the depth of his character, and gave him the strength, the will, that served him well for the rest of his life. The psychological quality of resilience, the key component of 'wholeheartedness', can only be formed in response to enormous adversity. It was precisely this quality that had drawn me to Bill in the first place, and the one which drew mention from all who knew him well. But even Bill had limits; he made a secret promise to himself that he would never undergo such surgery again.

But the procedures that the doctors had set in motion were beginning to show results. After only two weeks in the traction, the curvature of Bill's spine was almost completely corrected, albeit temporarily, according to notes made by Dr Burke. The tightening of the rods by only a couple of millimetres a day had made a dramatic difference. Due to the absence of muscle function, though, and the already collapsed nature of his spine, the doctors knew that the curvature would quickly return once the halo-pelvic traction was removed. That was why they'd decided from the outset to follow the traction with the complex and lengthy spinal fusion operation, a procedure that would brace the now-straightened spine from the inside.

A fortnight after the halo-pelvic attachment, Bill's doctors planned several times to commence the operation. Each time it had to be cancelled because he was feverish, or his wounds had healed insufficiently, or there was infection at the pelvic pin sites. After waiting a month, the doctors decided to go ahead, even though Bill was still in a lot of pain, with the wounds from the pins requiring constant drainage.

Nine days before his sixteenth birthday, at 8.00 am on 10 December, Bill was taken into the operating theatre. The six-and-a-half-hour operation was performed by a team led by surgeon Mr John Critchley, head of one of the orthopaedic units at the Austin Hospital, assisted by Dr Cheshire.

I've found very little in the way of detailed notes about Bill's actual operation. My primary information comes from the few details Bill told me over the years, the doctors' medical reports on his progress after the operation, the daily nursing notes in the following months, and my own research into such operations performed at around that time. For the last, I've read a range of medical articles, some written by the very doctors who had pioneered or developed the procedures. I can't claim that my account of the operation is identical to the one Bill underwent and anyway my lack of expertise precludes me from providing much detail. What I'll describe instead is a simplified generic version of the operation, interspersed with any more precise information I've gleaned from the sources mentioned above.

In a 'spinal fusion' operation the section of spine to be reinforced with a steel rod, and then fused, must first be surgically exposed. Bill was cut from high between his shoulder blades, as the fusion was to extend from the fourth thoracic vertebra (roughly chest-level) to the sacrum—the five conjoined bones forming the lower part of the spine—just above the coccyx.

Next, the surgeon removed the vertebral discs from the section of the spine to be fused to make space for the steel rod to lie close beside the vertebrae. At least one rib was also removed to give access to the vertebrae. The vertebrae are separated by spinal discs that act like shock absorbers, and provide pivot points for the spine. Providing the muscles are working optimally, the discs are what give a normal spine its mobility. But the discs would have no further function in cases where the spine is to be fused to a metal rod.

Once the spinal discs were removed, the surgeon drove metal hooks into the vertebrae at intervals. My research indicates two to four or more hooks were used. The hooks had holes, into which was screwed the steel rod. In those days, the most common type of rod was a 'Harrington' rod, which Bill's surgeons used. Paul Harrington, an American spinal surgeon, had invented this instrument in 1953, initially for curvature of the spine in poliomyelitis patients. In Australia in 1971 the surgery to insert the rod was considered pioneering if not experimental. The Harrington method remained the most common way to straighten and stabilise curved spines until it was superseded by a different instrument, invented by French surgeons in the 1980s.

Harrington in his own writings referred to a second, smaller but more flexible rod attached to part of the length of the primary rod; its purpose was to exert pressure on the primary rod in order to keep everything straight, for spines can begin to curve again, even after fusion, causing serious damage to the vertebrae in the process and necessitating another major operation. Given Bill's very marked and dangerous spinal curvature, which had been only temporarily straightened by the halo-pelvic traction, and which without further surgery would have returned very quickly once the traction apparatus was removed, it's highly likely the surgeons inserted a secondary rod to exert pressure on the main rod. Harrington explained in one of his articles that paralysed spines needed 'more extensive instrumentation' than non-paralysed. Once the rods were in place next to the spine, the surgeons then placed small pieces of bone—either from the removed rib, or from the patient's hip—around the rod now in its fixed position against the vertebrae. In time, these small pieces fused the metal to the vertebrae.

Bill always referred to the steel rod in his spine in the singular, but it's almost certain that the precise details of the operation weren't given either to him or to his parents, perhaps because of the traumatic nature of the procedure. Even today this withholding of details happens, especially with uncommon or pioneering surgery. But most of us now have access to the internet and can easily find highly graphic details of all types of surgical procedures and explanatory notes, often to our own discomfort! Or we can search for and gain access to articles in medical journals, as I've done. Before the internet, more specifically before effective search engines and searchable databases, these articles were rarely available to people not working in the medical field. Before the early 2000s, even finding out what articles existed on what topics involved specialised knowledge about searching medical indexes, and even once the titles and authors of the articles were identified, these articles could only be accessed in paper journals in university or medical libraries. At that time this was the only way that non-medical people would have been able to see pictures of the operation and the instruments used. Most of us would have had no idea how even to begin to search for such specialised articles, much less obtain copies of them. So I think it unlikely that a 15-year-old boy would have known, or been told, anything more than that a steel rod was going to be placed next to his spine and fused to it in order to straighten his back.

After more than six hours in the operating theatre, Bill was returned to the ward. As with any mending of bones, a period of immobilisation is needed, or the internal fixation might be dislodged or broken before the spine has had a chance to fuse. Dr Harrington wrote of using a 'plaster cast', but that was in the 1960s. Bill would have perhaps been put in a cast, had the manufacturers of the halo-pelvic traction not loaned the apparatus to the Austin hospital specifically for his use.

Back in the ward, the nursing staff noted that Bill was very pale, but conscious and in some pain. They monitored him very closely for the next week. After a few days the doctors declared they were pleased with his progress, but Bill seems by all accounts to have still been in considerable pain and very miserable. A week later, on his sixteenth birthday, he was more cheerful and had lunch with a friend from another ward. He would have had to lie on his right side in order to eat, using his left hand for the fork or spoon.

For Bill, the following seven-month period was the worst time of his life. No sooner had he adjusted to the pain where the 'halo' was fixed to his head, than the skin began to wear away, causing a pressure sore on his lower back. Pressure sores are very worrying as they may become infected, frequently don't heal of their own accord, and require repair by surgery, as Bill's did several times over the next few months. Completely unable to move his body independently, except for his left hand, Bill was turned every two hours during the day by nursing staff or orderlies, and every three hours at night. Astoundingly, he still managed to sleep relatively well, at least according to the nursing notes.

All the pin sites remained open and raw and would frequently become infected, despite the daily dressings. The pelvic part of the apparatus had to be tightened periodically to maintain the pressure on his spine so it would stay straight. Bill also suffered periodic chest infections, although not as severe as those before the operation. But one of the most bothersome afflictions was that scourge of adolescence, acne, which attacked his skin severely; the long days lying in bed and the lack of fresh air probably worsened it. Dr Cheshire referred him to a dermatologist who prescribed various creams and some time outdoors, where he was wheeled on a trolley. It's remarkable that Bill did not succumb to semi-permanent depression, at least not outwardly, for nursing notes describe him as 'rude and cheeky', behaviour that might well have been his survival mechanism.

Despite Bill's grim memories of the months after the surgery, at the start of the new school year, in February 1972, he was able to resume his studies in Year 10 of the Victorian secondary syllabus, which must have helped him focus on life beyond the hospital. When he felt well enough he went to the hospital's school room, to which Education Department teachers came to supervise the correspondence study of the children who were long-term patients. Bill's immobility meant he had to be transported to the room on a trolley. As he couldn't write while in the halo-pelvic traction, schoolwork was conducted orally, although he could hold a book in his left hand when lying on his right side.

Reading while lying down and immobile isn't easy, especially with the use of only one arm. To help Bill with this, an ingenious device was provided for him. It had been invented and constructed by a man named Stuart Sanderson for his son Blair, whom Bill met in hospital. Seeing Bill's difficulties, Mr Sanderson kindly made a second device for him. It worked ingeniously: the open book was placed face down on a sheet of glass within a wooden frame mounted on an arm attached to the bedhead, so that the frame was positioned directly above the reader's head. The page of the book was then reflected twice by way of a bent metallic mirror sheet, so that it was the right way around when viewed by the person below when lying on his side. I've no knowledge of how the pages were turned; perhaps Bill was able to do it himself, or else nurses or visitors could have done it when they were nearby.

Bill shared a two-bed ward with Blair Sanderson in the Austin Hospital's Spinal Unit for some weeks in early 1972. At 19, three years older than Bill, Blair had become paralysed in a diving accident a few months earlier. The two teenagers required more intensive nursing than the patients in the main 12-bed ward, and so were in a smaller room near the nurses' station. One of the few people able to recall Bill from that time, Blair remembers most of all his sense of humour, reinforcing the doctors' view of Bill's morale.

With their door open, both boys had a clear view of the nurses' station right outside, and could hear everything that was said. When the nurses did their handover at the start of each new shift, they would give a verbal report on each patient, identified by their bed number. Blair tells how Bill would listen carefully to this and, as soon as he heard his bed number called out, would interject with '... has been excellently behaved all day!' He'd also tease a nurse if she stood within range of his left arm when he was lying on his right side, shooting out his hand and grabbing her wrist tightly, refusing to let go.

After a few weeks in Bill's ward, Blair was transferred elsewhere. The two met again in the rehabilitation facility some months later, and would pass each other from time to time in the hospital corridors and in the meal room once Bill was able to use his wheelchair again.

After leaving hospital both boys became completely rehabilitated and independent, got on with their lives and never saw each other again. It was easy to lose contact with people in those days, long before the internet, email and social media. Anyone at that time trying to locate Bill or Blair in the unwieldy White Pages phone directory would have found pages and pages of Johnsons, and probably several columns of Sandersons. An effort of will was required to keep track of lost friends and acquaintances. While Blair managed to keep in touch with a few of the other patients and staff in the Spinal Unit, Bill never did. For several years after his accident he spent so much time in hospital, undergoing such deeply distressing procedures, that once discharged he just wanted to forget all about it and concentrate on rebuilding his life. Forty years later Blair read the advertisement I'd placed in various newsletters, asking if there was anyone who had known Bill when he was young, and would be prepared to provide information for the book I was writing. Blair contacted me and generously shared his memories.

For several months the doctors took regular X-rays of Bill's spine to assess the progress. Each time, Bill must have hoped to hear that the fusion of the steel rod to the bone was strong enough for the halo-pelvic apparatus to be removed. At last, at the end of May, six months after his operation, the spine was considered to be sufficiently fused for Bill to begin sitting up in bed for short periods, supported by pillows and under the supervision of a physiotherapist. After lying horizontal for so long, the human body takes a while to adjust to sitting upright, and there were the additional three kilograms of the halo apparatus to be borne by Bill's shoulder and neck muscles, already greatly weakened by the long convalescence.

Once Bill could sit up in bed for an hour without ill effects, he was able to transfer to his wheelchair. This activity too had to be managed very gradually because of neck and head pain and the risk of pressure sores. Sometimes Bill would have to return to bed after only an hour, suffering nausea and dizziness; some days he didn't even feel well enough to try it, but on most days he was able to spend a few hours in the wheelchair. By the end of June, he could go to the school room and the physiotherapist's room in his wheelchair. He was having regular physiotherapy for his arms, upper chest, shoulder and neck muscles, and to assist him to cough. Bill's right lung was no longer being crushed, but the paralysis of most of his intercostal muscles prevented him from coughing as effectively as he needed to.

On 18 July Bill's halo-pelvic traction was removed in the operating theatre. Although it was a great relief to Bill, he required a significant period of adjustment and healing, and anti-anxiety and pain medication. The sites where the pins had been inserted were raw and painful, and had to be stitched up. Bill often felt exhausted, nauseated and feverish; it was eight days before he was allowed to have the head of his bed elevated to a sitting position. He tolerated this well, and by the next day he was able to spend a few hours in his wheelchair. From then on, unless ill with an infection, Bill was up, dressed and in his wheelchair by 9am, ready to go to the school room. One of his doctors wrote in a report that Bill had stuck conscientiously to his schoolwork throughout the long healing process.

During August Bill coped so well on two outings with his parents, on 'day leave', that his doctors decided they'd discharge him at the end of that month, and he'd return to Yooralla a few weeks later. Dr Burke, now the head of the Spinal Unit since Dr Cheshire's departure to take up a position in the USA, drew up a full report on Bill for the Yooralla doctor. The spinal fusion operation had been deemed a success, Dr Burke wrote. He continued: 'Bill has grown up a lot in the past year, and I think he is going to develop into quite a fine young man. Certainly he is one of the most courageous young fellows I have ever met'.

1995–97: Travels with a Wheelchair

Christmas Eve, 1995: Grant drove Bill and me to the airport for our flight to Perth. We'd driven twice to South Australia to visit Wayne and his family, but this was our first plane trip together. If it went well we thought we'd plan a holiday further afield. Bill and Wayne had travelled overseas when they were in their twenties, but Wayne was very strong and could do any lifting required; I couldn't!

Boarding a plane is complicated for a wheelchair-user; normal wheelchairs are too wide for an aircraft aisle, so airline companies use special narrow wheelchairs for disabled passengers. But even an average sized adult would find these small wheelchairs uncomfortable after a few minutes. Fortunately, Qantas procedure at that time permitted Bill to remain in his own chair right up to the door of the plane, when an employee and I helped him transfer to the aircraft wheelchair; this was reversed when we disembarked after waiting for the other passengers to leave, and his own chair was retrieved from a storage compartment.

Earlier in the year, my father and stepmother had decided to install an ensuite bathroom connected to the master bedroom in their Perth home. While this was still in the planning stage, Dad rang us, saying, 'Helen and I are thinking of making the new bathroom wheelchair-accessible, if you'd like to come and stay with us for Christmas'.

We were overwhelmed by this kindness, as bathrooms were the bane of our lives if we ventured very far, and a major impediment to travel. We gratefully accepted the invitation. Our two boys had already left

Melbourne ten days earlier with their father, stepmother, and half-siblings, to drive across to Western Australia, camping along the way; we planned to meet up with them in Perth, where they'd stay with us at my father's place.

Dad and Helen, my brother Graham and his wife Sharon, and their blended family of six children, were at the airport to meet us. We couldn't have felt more welcome. The sense of belonging we felt with Bill's extended family didn't happen so often on my side as they all lived so far away. I appreciated their occasional visits as I knew the cost of a return airfare for a whole family was prohibitive. But there wasn't much alternative; I knew the three-day journey by car was an arduous affair as I'd made the trip numerous times before the children were born.

Once settled into Dad and Helen's house in Padbury, a northern beach suburb of Perth, I stuffed the turkey, as promised, with my special recipe of dried fruit, nuts, bacon and sage. I wasn't the world's best cook, but Alex and I had perfected roasting a stuffed Christmas turkey in a charcoal-fired 'kettle' barbecue, so for once I knew what I was doing!

On Christmas morning I put the turkey in the oven and helped Bill get up and shower. Dad and Helen had hired a bathroom commode chair for Bill to use, but in unfamiliar rooms I had to help him with his transfers, bathroom use, and many other things. For doing such manoeuvres at home he had a varnished wooden 'slide board' of about 30 x 50 centimetres. A piece was cut out so that it sat on the top of the right wheel. With the right armrest removed Bill could slide on to the board, and with his left hand supporting him on the other armrest he could work his way across to a seat, bed or commode. This was difficult if the target surface was a different height from the wheelchair seat, so in Dad and Helen's house I had to provide plenty of assistance.

With Bill up and dressed and able to keep an eye on the turkey, I nicked off to the beach for an hour. A typical Perth summer's day: blue sky, cloudless, no chance of rain, a perfect maximum of 29 degrees. There were few people about. I swam briefly then lay on the silver-white sand. How I treasured those fleeting, solitary moments—much-needed respite from the constant busy-ness of my life—in which I could savour my many blessings: a husband who was my best friend, two lovely, bright, healthy children, a wider family who cared about me, a career, and a comfortable home in a safe society.

After this brief period of restfulness with Bill and the boys, we raced around Perth for days in Helen's little car, visiting cousins, dining in restaurants with Graham and Sharon, visiting my mother and stepfather, and showing Bill all the sights as he'd not visited Perth before. On New Year's Day, I packed our bags—a mammoth task with all Bill's equipment—before farewelling the boys, who'd be staying on in Perth for a fortnight with their father, and Bill and I caught the plane home.

We made the most of our child-free weeks to catch up on studies, dine out, and see a couple of films we'd been looking forward to. We knew Bill's appointments with the nephrology doctors at the Austin Hospital were looming but tried to keep them out of our minds until the last moment by making plans for the following year when we'd both have three months long service leave due. Bill had coped well with the trip to Perth, so why not a longer one to England? Bill and Alex were crazy about cricket, so if we arrived in May they might be able to attend some of the Ashes test matches.

In mid-January Bill attended the Austin Hospital for appointments with the urologist and the nephrology team. He was familiar with this team, he told me, having had yearly tests of kidney function for some years after leaving hospital. Like many people who are paraplegic or quadriplegic, Bill was in a high-risk group for kidney disease and had suffered repeated urinary tract and kidney infections for many years after his accident, although I hadn't been aware of any in our time together, oblivious to such things as I was. Neither could I recall his having had a test.

'Why haven't you been having the tests in the past few years?' I asked him. He mumbled something about being 'too busy,' or 'forgetting', but wasn't very convincing. In my ignorance I hadn't realised to what extent the kidneys function as waste filters for the body, cleansing our blood twelve times an hour, nor was I aware that if they're not functioning well, the consequences are serious: fluid builds up, particularly in the lungs, impeding breathing; toxins accumulate in the blood; and chemicals such as potassium can cause the heart to stop. Yet kidney disease is described as 'silent' because there are few clear symptoms, and sufferers can lose up to 90% of kidney function before becoming aware of any symptoms. On hearing Bill's dissembling, I made a mental note to strongly encourage him to have regular tests from now on.

This was 1996, pre-Google times, the internet itself still in its infancy; in any case there was only a fraction of the information that's now available and easily accessible. When I Google 'symptoms of kidney failure' today, the top link returned by the search is Kidney Health Australia, with lists of symptoms such as blood in the urine, tiredness, general feelings of being unwell, loss of appetite, nausea and vomiting, and shortness of breath. Bill displayed all of these during periods of illness, although not always simultaneously. Other health problems can also cause these symptoms, so I hadn't realised they were probably due to his kidneys; if such information had been easily accessible then, I would have better grasped the precarious state of Bill's health.

The first tests in January revealed Bill's left kidney was functioning poorly and blood flow into both kidneys was slow. At least that was all he told me. I asked Bill to explain, but he typically made light of it, saying that he'd had similar results to this in routine renal tests in the past, and assuring me this was nothing to worry about. But the urologist wanted him back in three weeks for more tests that would help them see more precisely how damaged his kidneys were. Because of Bill's unwillingness to discuss it and my own ignorance of renal disease, I failed to grasp that his health was starting to plummet dramatically. With hindsight, I'm sure Bill understood only too well that he'd entered either the moderate or severe stage of kidney disease.

Little wonder he started drinking much more than was good for his damaged kidneys. Alcohol affects people in different ways; Bill never became aggressive or unpleasant, he just lost the ability to do anything for himself. Returning home after an evening out, often dead tired myself, I'd have to help him with absolutely everything. Already, during his periods of illness, our relationship had seemed one of patient and carer; although I made a point of never complaining, we both knew it did not have a positive effect on our marriage. So I was devastated that he'd willingly bring on this helplessness at times when it wasn't even necessary.

One evening, back home after dinner in Lygon Street, I helped Bill to undress, use the bathroom, get into bed. As I got ready for bed, I recalled longingly the evenings of lively intellectual conversation that had been the norm until quite recently. By halfway through this evening, as soon as the effect of several glasses of wine had kicked in, he'd barely been able to talk. There was no point saying anything to him about it at this hour, so I went to sleep.

The next morning Bill seemed contrite and asked me if I'd like to go out for dinner again that evening, to the Red Emperor, my favourite restaurant. I immediately declined, ungraciously, saying I felt too tired to dine out two nights in a row, which was the truth. For two days we hardly spoke. I tried to do some PhD reading before the boys returned, but I found myself reading the same paragraphs over and over. Inside, I felt shrivelled with misery.

During the weekend I took a deep breath and confronted him. 'When I have to help you with everything and put you to bed, when you're not ill and shouldn't need that, I feel like your carer, not your wife, and I hate that. I'm scared it's going to drive us apart.' Surprising me, he quickly said he understood my feelings, and would try to avoid it happening again. He didn't apologise, though; he was certainly no saint!

On the Monday Bill went back to work and the boys returned from Perth, while I set about getting organised for the new school year, checking the boys' uniforms to see which items needed to be replaced or mended, buying new textbooks for Alex who was now in the second year of high school.

Towards the end of January Bill received a letter from his urologist, proposing an overnight stay in the hospital for further tests; depending on their findings, they might need him to remain in hospital for surgery. On a bright, scorching February morning ten days later Bill drove us both to the Austin hospital. After helping him settle into the Spinal Unit, I drove his car home. First, he'd undergo an IVP (Intravenous Pyelogram), an X-ray of his kidneys and urinary system, after having a dye injected into his veins. If the IVP revealed anything conclusive, the next test would be a cystoscopy, requiring a general anaesthetic.

Back home, everything felt wrong. It was the first time we'd been apart since our marriage over three years ago. I tried to busy myself with my PhD work, and tending to the children, but everything jarred my jangled nerves. I had a perpetual headache and could barely eat. Two days later, Bill rang to say the hospital was discharging him. They'd aborted the cystoscopy because his blood pressure was dangerously low and he'd become feverish; he was still feverish when I brought him home with enough antibiotics for five days. Fortunately, the symptoms soon subsided.

The usual routine reasserted itself: the teaching year began for Bill and me, the boys were busy with homework, sports, and musical instruments. Bill and I continued juggling work, studies, and parenting. The two boys were always fully occupied, both doing well at school and seeming to thrive on the busy-ness; each had a wide circle of friends whom they'd frequently visit, and who in turn would come to our house.

In April the boys' stepmother, Lyn, turned forty; she and their father wanted to host a party at their house, so we agreed to look after their two small children, the boys' half-brother and half-sister, aged four and three. The two little ones knew us very well as our two families saw each other often, mainly thanks to Bill and Lyn's shared passion for the Essendon Football Club, and to their idea that we all get together to watch the matches on television. Our boys, themselves only fourteen and eleven, loved this idea, and happily did most of the work—the bathing, reading stories, putting the little ones to bed—feeling very grown up and responsible.

In the middle of the year Bill and I applied to take our three months of long service leave the following year, and began planning to spend most of that time in England. This was before most travel could be organised via the internet, but through published networks and guides we contacted various English people who had paraplegia or quadriplegia to see if they'd like to swap houses with us. We felt this would be the best strategy, as then the houses would be wheelchair-accessible, and set up with all the correct equipment.

Throughout the year, Bill's minor bouts of kidney disease responded each time to antibiotics. In December he turned forty-one; I wrote in his card, 'To my darling Bill, my best friend, partner, co-parent'. Our house of cards seemed stronger than I'd thought; it had weathered the storms of the past year and was standing firm.

The following May the four of us flew to England. We'd arranged a house swap with a couple in Wraysbury, a village just outside London, not far from Windsor Castle. Once there we spent a lot of time with my Aunt Ruth and Uncle Mike who lived not far away; they were like walking guidebooks for us. Ruth was my youngest aunt, only 17 years older than me, and we were good friends. With them we visited Lord Nelson's HMS Victory at Portsmouth and the 'Bat and Ball' public house in rural Hampshire, where it's claimed cricket was invented. Alex was enchanted to be on such hallowed turf.

Patrick practised piano in the village church, and Alex played cricket with a local team. Patrick even asked if he could attend a local school, where he befriended a boy whose father was one of the royal chauffeurs at nearby Windsor Castle.

My uncle Mike was a Londoner and knew the city intimately. One day he took Bill and Alex to see all the sights in town, while my aunt Ruth and I spent time in the beautiful Savill Garden in the Windsor Great Park. It was late spring, and every day the foliage in the parks and gardens and bordering the country roads grew more lush; in the garden of the house where we were staying a new plant or bush burst into flower each day.

Beside the door was a climbing rose bush bearing overblown yellow flowers, its branches like long arms stretching out in all directions.

Before leaving Melbourne, Bill and I had researched the forthcoming Ashes cricket series between England and Australia; it was Bill's main reason for wanting to make the trip at this time. There was some information on the internet, but we had to make the bookings by international telephone. We'd managed to book tickets for Bill and Alex for three of the five test matches: at Edgbaston in Birmingham, Lords in London, and Old Trafford in Manchester. We'd decided to stay in picturesque locations in the Cotswolds or the Lake District, each location only a train ride away from Edgbaston and Old Trafford. Patrick and I weren't particularly interested in cricket, so Bill and Alex would travel to see the tests together. Now fourteen, Alex was very tall and strong and could push Bill's wheelchair quite long distances and help him on and off trains.

Our short stay in the small Cotswold town of Newent was challenging; the accommodation had been advertised as wheelchair-accessible but the usual problems of unfamiliar equipment came into play. The unit—looking out on to a large lawn bordered by garden beds full of late spring flowers—was lovely, with wooden floors, and stylish, comfortable furniture, but there was no accessible shower, only a bath with a plastic chair in it and a handheld shower attachment! This would have been fine if I'd been strong enough to lift Bill into the bath and on to the chair, but of course I wasn't. Fortunately, we'd brought with us from Wraysbury a commode chair, and somehow I managed to help him shower on that, with large towels placed on the floor all around the chair.

Bill and Alex would catch the morning train to the cricket ground, leaving Patrick and me to explore. I especially loved the Gloucestershire countryside as this was where I'd spent much of my childhood before migrating to Australia. Driving back from the station on the first morning, in early June, all I could see around me were misty green hedgerows and fields, and wild spreading oaks under a chiffon sky. In the afternoon Patrick and I visited nearby Goodrich castle, where we learned not only that King

Charles the First took refuge there, but that Cromwell's army had taken him hostage on this very day in 1647.

Although Alex and Bill enjoyed watching the four-day test match, the final result made them miserable: England won by nine wickets. The next day I drove us all to Stratford-upon-Avon for a performance of Hamlet at the Royal Shakespeare Theatre. We all loved it; Bill and I had already familiarised the boys to some extent with Shakespeare's language by taking them to plays in Melbourne. They didn't seem to have any problem comprehending Hamlet. The next day I packed up our rented Volvo station wagon and drove us all back to our 'base camp' in Wraysbury.

We combined London sightseeing with learning opportunities, seeing the boys were missing many weeks of school. At Madame Tussaud's Bill—always the Politics teacher—directed us to various world leaders and recounted some of the stories about such figures as Churchill, Bill Clinton, Nelson Mandela.

On Bill's wish list was theatre in the West End, and we saw Barry Humphries play the role of Fagin in a performance of Oliver. For Patrick (then only twelve) it initiated a great interest in Dickens' work that has continued for more than two decades. Alex already loved all forms of literature: from Shakespeare to science fiction.

Taking the train into Waterloo Station was my favoured mode of transport as I found the driving very tiring. It had become apparent I'd made a huge mistake in this regard. When planning the trip, I hadn't enquired about hiring a car with hand controls. Although Bill felt very safe driving in Melbourne, the roads were familiar to him. On the much busier English road system, with its numerous giant roundabouts—a traffic feature he found challenging even in Australia, thanks to having only one hand with which to steer—I wasn't confident it was safe for him to drive. I'd expressed this fear to him and he'd not sought to change my mind about my doing all the driving, so I'd booked an ordinary car. For Bill, driving provided much greater mobility and freedom than merely using his wheelchair. Deprived of driving for our three-month trip, Bill felt wretched. Stupidly, we didn't fully realise the cause of his depression until weeks into our trip, by which time it was too late to change anything.

We weren't to feel down about the driving for too long, though. Bill's hero was Winston Churchill, and one day when Patrick was at school, Bill, Alex and I visited Churchill's home at Chartwell, run by the National Trust. With many of the rooms still as they were when the Churchills and their children lived there, including Churchill's study, we were spellbound by this glimpse into history.

It was at this time that the stereotypical English summer seemed to have arrived. The first day of the next Test match at Lords was rained out, and only an hour and a half's play was possible on the second; the match drifted towards an inevitable draw, played out over the last three days. Bill and Alex were despondent.

The next short trip was to Hest Bank in Lancashire, to take us closer to the Old Trafford test, where we'd booked a house on Morecambe Bay; from the rear windows we could see in the distance across the water the slopes of the Cartmel and Furness peninsulas, the southernmost parts of the Lake District. For two days before the cricket started, we explored the dramatic countryside, taking the car ferry across Windermere, and driving home down the other side of the lake.

Once the cricket resumed, Bill and Alex took the train from Lancaster into Manchester each day. The rain held off, and Australia won by 268 runs; Alex and Bill were in high spirits. I have a fond memory of a picnic in Fellfoot Park on our last day in the Lake District. The boys hired a rowboat and took it out in a sheltered part of the lake. Bill and I watched, laughing, as the boat zigzagged slowly in the calm water, while the boys argued loudly with each other about who was or was not using correct oar techniques. It had been a week to remember.

Back in Wraysbury, Bill and Alex excitedly prepared for a visit to the British Parliament. Bill had telephoned the Australian High Commission in London, explained he was an Australian politics teacher, and managed to convince the person on the other end of the phone to issue passes for himself and Alex to attend the Prime Minister's Question Time in the House of Commons. The highlight for the two of them was seeing then Prime Minister Tony Blair addressing the parliament. Bill used this episode as a springboard—as he so often did—to teach Alex the features of the Westminster system of government, on which our Australian one is based. It was no surprise to us a few years later when Alex chose Political Studies as one of his VCE subjects, nor when he chose to major in Political Science at University.

We returned to Melbourne at the end of July. The trip had been nothing less than epic, and settling back into our ordinary life required real effort. I'd taken leave from my PhD, and now had to resurrect my research.

Within a week of our return, Bill became ill. A long, uncomfortable flight—27 hours with a short stop in Kuala Lumpur—is hard on anyone, but Bill's body must have really taken a battering, especially given the precarious state of his kidneys. He was aching all over, feeling nauseous, not eating. His skin took on a greyish tinge. He even had to delay his return to work, a rare and uncharacteristic concession to illness for Bill. A few days after our arrival back home, Bill sat slumped in his wheelchair in the lounge, shivering, refusing to let me call the doctor. We had antibiotics in the house, but he rejected them, accepting only Panadol. I'd never seen him so ill. I wondered now if a busy three-month trip to the other side of the world had been a big mistake.

1972–74: A Place He Hated

By the time Bill returned to Yooralla in September 1972 after his spinal fusion operation, society's views towards people with disabilities were slowly starting to change. Segregation as the default, particularly for children who wanted to study the mainstream educational curriculum, was approaching its last decade, and was already gradually being phased out. This doesn't seem to have been unequivocally supported by everyone concerned. We can see evidence of this ambivalence—perhaps a natural enough human reaction in the face of social change—in the 1972/73 Yooralla Annual Report, where the Medical Advisory Committee notes, in a less than positive tone, that 'the greater acceptance of children with minor problems into normal schools'[21] has resulted in 'the pattern of physical handicap in the Special Schools … tending to be more severe …'

Surely if the children's progress were a high priority, those with 'minor problems' now attending 'normal schools', instead of coming to Yooralla, would be a development to celebrate? In purely ethical terms, in my view the children should always have been in ordinary schools.

Two pages later, the Chief Medical Officer feels compelled to give his views on integration:

> There are those who advocate the total integration of disabled children into normal classes throughout the school community and clearly this is highly desirable for those who can cope … However, it is clear that there are those whose level of disability is so grave or complex that they can only be

> adequately helped within a special environment designed to provide the support and services they need. To incorporate these children in a normal school system can be medically inappropriate, impose considerable hardship on them, and *would be highly wasteful of personnel trained to fulfil their special needs* (emphasis added).[22]

Nowhere in these reports have I read about the waste of potential of the children with disabilities due to their not being accepted in ordinary schools, or their not having sufficient resources provided for them in special schools, such as fully-qualified secondary teachers which the state government did not provide for Yooralla.

It would seem that in the early to mid-1970s, Yooralla Hospital School for Crippled Children was somewhat stuck in the past, especially when viewed from today's perspective. By this time, there had been the Civil Rights movement in the United States, second wave feminism in many western countries and, since badly injured Vietnam veterans had started returning home, the demand for equal rights for the disabled. All of these movements were gradually changing society, in Australia, as in many other countries during the 1960s and 70s.

Yooralla students and staff from the 1970s tell how the first real change began to occur when Mr Len James took over as school principal in early 1973. I won't enter into the very complex debates about inclusive education, but change was certainly required at Yooralla, as the world was now quite different from the one in which Sister Faith's kindergarten had been badly needed in 1918.

What was needed in the 1970s, among other things, was an improvement in the integration rate of Yooralla students. This seems to have been the belief of Len James and certain members of his teaching staff, who began to set up programs with cooperating local schools, starting in 1976 with the nearby Balwyn High School and one or two others. So far small numbers of students each year (although less than 10%) had transferred from Yooralla to mainstream schools, but the initiative in 1976 was Yooralla's first systematic attempt at integration; it relied very much on the student's teacher believing the child had sufficient ability, and championing the student at the 'School Leaving Panel'. The panel was something before which each student, and usually one or both parents had to appear yearly once they turned 16, or earlier if they wanted to transfer, until the time that they left Yooralla, something which supposedly could only happen with the panel's permission.

Everyone believed that 'the panel decided our future,' recalls a former student. Legally, any parent was free to take their child elsewhere at any time (although there were few educational alternatives), but this was not how things were viewed back then. Most students and parents did not challenge the panel, which comprised the student's own teacher, the principal, the senior physiotherapist and senior occupational therapist, as well as a doctor. There were very likely also representatives from the Education Department and from Commonwealth Social Services. Most significantly there was a representative from the Yooralla 'supported employment' or sheltered workshops, into which a sizeable percentage of senior students would be encouraged to move each year. A much smaller percentage, thanks to integration, went on to become successful employed people. Were there ever any representatives of this latter group, with all their experience of overcoming enormous physical difficulties, as well as discriminatory attitudes, on the panel? Or even among the sizeable ranks of the Yooralla management? I doubt it. How about today? A look at the website doesn't suggest so, although certainly there are now advisory panels comprising former students, such as the Independent Advocacy Advisory Group which provides recommendations and advice to the Yooralla Board.

Mary Henley, who was fifteen in 1976, was strongly recommended by her teacher Myles Stanmore for integration, and was among the group of students who transferred to Balwyn High School as part of the new integration initiative. But there was no transport for the first few months, so Mr Stanmore took Mary each day from her home in Box Hill to

Balwyn High School and back again in the afternoons, until a bus for the integration students was organised by Yooralla. In the interim, Mary changed to an ordinary wheelchair—instead of her usual motorised one—which was non-foldable, and very heavy. Mr Stanmore would push her into school, but very quickly the other children took over this task. Mary loved Balwyn High and never looked back. She did her HSC there and went on to university. Of Mr Stanmore, Mary says, 'I owed my future to him'. Balwyn High School also deserves some credit for being one of the first schools to embrace integration. Not quite twenty years later, my own two children undertook their secondary education there as well.

Two years before Mary left Yooralla for Balwyn High, Bill, now approaching 19, had asked the yearly School Leaving Panel for permission to transfer to an ordinary school to complete his HSC. His friend Rob appeared before the panel too, as his goal was to leave Yooralla and obtain a position in an accounting firm, having studied HSC Accounting by correspondence and doing well in the exam, like Bill.

It was Bill's third appearance before the panel over the four years he attended Yooralla. The first time, when he was almost 17, he'd asked to transfer to an ordinary school and had been refused. The second time, a year later, he and Rob decided to have some fun. Bill told the panel he wanted to leave and train to become a brain surgeon, while Rob, suffering from Muscular Dystrophy, told them he wanted to become a body-builder.

The third time, though, they were serious. It was Bill's interview with the panel that dominated his narrative when he told me about Yooralla years later. He related how his plan for integration had been opposed, but he didn't elaborate on the reasons he was given. On what could this opposition have been based? Despite my having written requests (under Freedom of Information laws) to all relevant bodies, I've been advised that there are no longer any records available of what transpired, so all I have is guesswork. Could the panel have suggested that if Bill wanted to go to an ordinary school he should go to Balwyn High—although the integration program was not yet in place—as it was the nearest to Yooralla? Balwyn

High wouldn't have suited Bill, in any case, as there was no transport from his parents' home in distant Croydon. He couldn't return to his former high school due to lack of wheelchair access there, but he had in mind the recently built and accessible Pembroke High School at Mooroolbark, a short drive from Croydon. Perhaps the panel found it too hard to provide the visiting nurse—support that they saw as essential—to a school further afield. Was the panel perhaps concerned about his health, as he'd spent most of 1972 in hospital, and had been readmitted for short stays once or twice each year?

The panel was notoriously conservative and emphasised over and over that they did not want a student to leave and then 'fail', with Yooralla subsequently being blamed for the failure. Was there no teacher who recognised Bill's ability, as there would be two years later for Mary Henley, to explain to them that he was not going to fail? By all accounts, the teacher who supervised Bill and Rob's correspondence study, Mrs Clough, believed in their ability. What about the elaborate football competition that Bill and the other senior boys had organised? Surely this showed self-motivation and team-building skills. This 19-year-old would go on to earn three university degrees and run a department in a TAFE institute with over 50 staff. Yet in 1974 no one believed in him, or no one powerful enough to convince the whole panel, at any rate.

The School Leaving Panel, as stated in various Yooralla annual reports, 'is a team devoted to achieving the maximum opportunity for each physically handicapped student'. At the conclusion of the interview, the panel would make its recommendation of a placement for each student. How did students feel about their placements? The previous principal Miss Baglin noted that, 'Sometimes there is some dissatisfaction in the placement, this is usually because of an unrealistic attitude adopted by the pupil or his parents of the child's capabilities. We feel that we must all strive *to have these children accept their disabilities and be realistic in their goals* (emphasis added)'.[23] Bill's goal was to obtain high enough marks in his HSC to enable him to go on to university. The panel clearly did not think his goal was 'realistic'. Bill said to me once that the members had ridiculed his goals. But this time he and his mother insisted on the transfer—he was almost 19 after all—and he left Yooralla at the end of the 1974 school year, starting at Pembroke High School the following year. Rob left too and began working, combining this with further study in accounting.

In the absence of any records it's impossible to know where the panel members actually thought the two boys *should* go. Surely not into the Yooralla sheltered workshops? Perhaps they expected them to remain in the school and hostel for another few years, as students did in fact have the option of staying until they were 22. What I do know is that Bill maintained his rage at the panel's treatment of him for the rest of his life. His view of the four years he spent at Yooralla was completely coloured by the panel's failure of judgement. In my view, the Education Department should also be answerable, for the inadequate provision of secondary education during that time at the Yooralla School, for which the Department alone was responsible.

For Bill, when he spoke about Yooralla, it was as a place he hated.

1997–99: Guerrilla Warfare

In the two years following our return from England, Bill's kidney infections flared up again and again, in escalating degrees of severity. To him they were like continuous attacks by guerrilla rebels, each new onslaught ambushing him just as he thought himself recovered. The attackers, the bacteria, would do their damage and then retreat for a while before returning, stronger than ever. He now almost always took antibiotics when ill, but the bacteria would be back, sabotaging his work, his family life, his state of mind and certainly mine too.

Bill's doctors told him he'd be lucky if his kidneys lasted another two years. There was talk of a kidney transplant, once his kidneys failed altogether, or of dialysis. The word 'despair' doesn't come close to how we felt. We deliberately didn't talk about a third d-word, death, but it was there from now on, flapping its dark wings over our shoulders. Bill may have had an idea of his state of health for some time, but I had been kept in the dark. Or maybe I hadn't wanted to know, had placed my head firmly in the sand.

Most people in our circle of family and friends thought that dialysis would be a solution, a lifesaver even, that would quite simply annul the death sentence, and we didn't try to contradict them. In reality, most patients have dialysis only for short periods while waiting for a transplant, although many transplants have only a low success rate beyond a few years, and haemodialysis for end stage renal disease has a poor prognosis (haemodialysis is the more common of the two types of dialysis, the other being peritoneal dialysis). But we didn't know too much about all this in

1997, or at least I didn't; so I too desperately grasped at the idea of dialysis as the thing that would 'save' Bill once his kidneys failed altogether.

Many of us have trouble facing the concept of our own death, and that of our loved ones; we live our lives as if we'll go on forever. This fear of death is understandable, but it's a fear that is psychologically repressed, at least in our modern urban culture. To a certain extent, this repression is justified, since a full apprehension of our mortality could drive us insane, as Ernest Becker explained in his ground-breaking book *The Denial of Death*.[24] Bill had faced up to the prospect of death more than most of us. During the long years in hospital and at Yooralla he'd been surrounded by people with serious injuries or terminal illnesses; and his close friend Rob had died at 23. Yet even Bill could not help but be deeply affected by the imminent failure of one of his own major organs.

He'd achieved so much, but his work wasn't finished, not by a long shot. His department was expanding, there were ever more students seeking the type of education it offered, and he was considering a wider range of courses to cater for their needs. Most of all he wanted to stay with the children and me, wanted to see the boys grow up and make their way in the world. He'd already lived many more years since his last scrap with death, but there was now even more to lose; he was approaching 42, and although he'd survived much longer than first predicted, it was still barely half a life when compared to the average. The worst thing was not really knowing how long he had.

All I knew was that the husband whom I'd always regarded as independent and invincible (hadn't he come back to life from that terrible accident?) was seriously ill, but somehow he would get through it. Perhaps this was my survival mechanism, the only one available to me. We couldn't both be facing the awful truth, especially not with two adolescents to finish raising. Through all this Bill remained a committed and active father to the children. On the days they played sport, if he had only the smallest vestige of energy left, he'd drive them to the sports ground and stay to watch them. In the cold winter months he'd get up at 8am to take Patrick to his football games, and then cheer him on from the sidelines. But sometimes, during the worst bouts of illness, he'd have to stay in bed, bitterly disappointed with himself.

Our life during this period was lived in cycles: there were intervals of 'normality', with the bacteria more or less in abeyance, when Bill was well enough to converse, resume his independence, work eleven-hour days, and generally lead what looked at least from the outside to be a normal life. By some tacit agreement, instigated by Bill, we did not discuss his illness, or the future. If he didn't want to discuss it, how could I insist when he was taking the brunt of it all? In any case, Bill could be incredibly stubborn and if he didn't want to talk, that was it.

These 'normal' cycles alternated with periods when he would arrive home from work so depleted that he could barely talk or eat, when his urine would be various abnormal shades, from pink-tinged to bright red, and when he needed a lot of nursing care from me. In between these two extremes there were times when he certainly wasn't himself, but in the absence of overt signs of illness he must have been trying to hide from me that he felt another onslaught of the guerrilla warfare was about to hit him. This meant I had to try to gauge for myself the state of his physical and mental health.

On weekend evenings he now drank more than he had before, first beer then wine, until he couldn't move, let alone do anything for himself. It didn't take a great deal of alcohol for him to become incapacitated, since he only weighed about 65 kilos. If he drank less than his usual amount, I'd read this as a sign that he was ill. Why didn't he simply tell me each time? I guess it was because he didn't want me calling the doctor, or pressing him to take antibiotics; he would decide these things for himself, although never early enough for my liking. On weekday evenings he often returned home from work so exhausted that he had energy for nothing at all, could barely eat his dinner. With a superhuman struggle he would manage to exchange a few words with the children, and that was it.

Yet he wouldn't miss a day of work unless he couldn't move his left arm to propel the wheelchair. I was deeply anxious about his long days in his office, especially since I knew that after one glass of grapefruit juice for breakfast Bill didn't eat all day—he thought lunch breaks were a waste of time—and wouldn't be home until after 7pm. This lack of food would only make him more susceptible to the next onslaught, I believed. In desperation, I discussed this with Larraine, a wonderful, supportive woman who'd worked for Bill for years. She offered to buy an extra sandwich when she bought her own from a nearby café, and to give it to him with his coffee at midday without saying anything. He would be unlikely to refuse it, as he was always scrupulously polite with her. This plan worked well, and we continued with it until Larraine retired, after which I organised a nearby café to make and deliver Bill's lunch.

Meanwhile, to the outside world, our life must have looked relatively cheerful. Bill and I went to extraordinary lengths to keep it looking that way. As soon as we'd returned from England, in addition to my three days of teaching each week, I resumed working part-time on my PhD. Bill had greatly encouraged me in this endeavour, right from the start. I was determined to finish my thesis before he needed any major surgical intervention that would inevitably be followed by sustained nursing from me. So I now had to spend even more time in my study; in any case Bill was too weak to do much beyond collapse in front of the television when he was at home. I bitterly mourned the loss of the discussions Bill and I had had until recently; we'd talked about all manner of things, especially my research and writing. But he was mourning the loss of far more, so I pushed my selfish feelings aside.

If the children had an event he needed to attend, or if there was a family party, Bill would make a superhuman effort, would almost will the bacteria into a truce for the duration, so we could present our 'cheerful family' face to the world.

Just before Christmas 1997, Bill turned 42, and it was our fourth wedding anniversary. Crazily, we'd decided to renovate our kitchen, and at the start of the week the old kitchen had been ripped out. Its entire contents were packed into boxes; workmen arrived at the house early every morning, and I had to do industrial clean-ups in the evenings. That same week Patrick graduated from the local primary school. The night before there had been a concert, with all the grade six children performing group skits or song-and-dance routines. On Bill's birthday, coincidentally the primary school final assembly was held, and as Patrick was School Captain, both Bill and I were keen to attend. Bill didn't seem too well, but I didn't know whether it was his illness returning, or the result of over-indulging at his end-of-year staff dinner the previous night.

A few days later Bill's younger brother Grant and his partner Fran took us for dinner to one of the restaurants at the casino to celebrate Bill's birthday. We loved seeing Grant and Fran as they were such good company, full of conversation. After the meal, we decided to go and have a brief play on the poker machines. Once inside, Fran (who was studying marketing at university) drew our attention to the contrast between the advertisements for the casino featuring radiant happy people, apparently enjoying each other's company, and the people we could see in front of each machine, solitary and grim, focused only on the brightly-coloured reels spinning endlessly in front of them. The observation dissuaded us from staying very long, so we didn't waste any money that evening!

In the new year, major family events came one after the other, requiring our scarce resources of energy but providing welcome distraction. At the end of January, Patrick started secondary school. A month later, Bill's sister Merrilyn held her 40th birthday party in her large garden at their home in the hills. Grant set up his DJ booth and ensured a continuous stream of seventies music that had been popular during Merrilyn's teenage years. Bill made the main speech, a memorable one, as entertaining as usual, full of jokes, but sincere in his deep appreciation of his sister. I loved listening to him on these occasions. He took speech-making so seriously that he wouldn't touch an alcoholic drink beforehand, as he believed even one drop marred a speaker's performance. I didn't argue with that.

The following Saturday I arrived home from several hours' duty at

Patrick's athletics meeting to find a box on the doorstep. Inside was a bouquet of a dozen deep red roses. A small card bore the words 'From your admirer'. I swear I felt my heart jumping around with joy in my chest. I certainly cried a few tears. I hadn't even remembered it was Valentine's Day. I put them in my best crystal vase. I knew this was Bill's way of showing the appreciation that he couldn't express verbally. He was out somewhere, and this was before mobile phones. I'd thank him later.

The cyclical nature of our life, swinging wildly from happiness to despair, and back again, was psychologically hard on both of us. Bill's health loomed large, assumed prime importance in our lives, a bit like a third, unwanted person in a relationship. This perspective has been termed the 'focusing illusion' by Nobel Prize winning psychologist Daniel Kahneman, in which nothing else in life is as important as whatever we're focusing on. So when a person thinks about their illness, or that of a close family member, they become depressed and dwell on their depression, quickly launching a self-reinforcing vicious circle of miserable thoughts. But of course I didn't read about Daniel Kahneman until many years later.

I still sometimes ask myself what we should or could have done differently. We might have paid for some nursing assistance during Bill's sick periods so that I wouldn't have to be on duty twenty-four/seven; I might then have been a less exhausted and happier companion. During the interludes when Bill was relatively well, I might have booked more outings to the theatre, to concerts, and many more dinners with our friends, travelled to Norway to see the Northern Lights; even taken the children to Disneyland; anywhere, anything, to stop us focusing on his poor sick kidneys.

But retrospective speculation is pointless. Back then, Bill self-medicated by drowning his despair in alcohol, at least on the weekends. And I, also caught in the focusing illusion, became reacquainted with my old foes—anxiety and depression. This made me an erratic and irascible companion and mother. I complained long and bitterly to my journal, reinforcing the misery. There was nothing and no one else in whom I could confide, as I didn't want to burden friends and family with something so personal. Seeing my depression, Bill must have felt even worse. For much of the time we each inhabited our own private hell.

For the sake of the children, though, we would pull ourselves together as much as possible. To help Alex with his Political Studies subject, Bill started the habit of watching the '7.30 Report' each night on the ABC with him, often discussing various political issues afterwards. If Patrick had obtained good marks for his schoolwork, he'd bring it to show Bill, and would often tell him all about his day, as secondary school was still a new experience for him. When Bill was so ill that talking was an effort, the children seemed instinctively to know and wouldn't expect anything of him.

To try and preserve some sanity, I joined the gym at work, where I attended aerobics classes for the first time in my life. At first I found it difficult to perform the steps and to keep up with the pace of the class, but I made huge efforts to improve. I suppose this must have helped generate endorphins and dopamine, and mitigated my feelings of absolute despair. As well as caring for Bill when he was sick, I was also trying desperately to finish my doctoral thesis. I grumbled endlessly into my diary about exhaustion. I wonder now if all this activity may well have been a safeguard against complete collapse. To finish a chapter draft, discuss it with my supervisor, and hear her pronounce that it was well done, was a potent if temporary distraction from the nightmarish progression of Bill's illness.

In May 1998, Patrick turned thirteen, and we allowed him to have a party with 15 of his schoolfriends. He'd wanted 30, but we thought 15 was sufficient and could be fitted more or less comfortably into our family room.

Throughout the winter, whenever he could, Bill would drive the boys to their football matches on the weekends, and stay to watch them. In June Alex and I flew to Perth for a week to attend my father's 70th birthday, which was also a large family reunion, organised by my stepmother. It was a welcome break in routine, and I was glad to get away.

In October of that year Alex turned 16, and we held a small family party. The children's father brought along their little half-brother and sister, aged 6 and 4, who always liked an excuse to visit their two older brothers. Suddenly it was December, and Bill and I attended the end-of-year school concerts and the high school presentation night, held at the Concert Hall in the city. Both boys seemed happy and thriving, doing well at school, with several good, close friends each. I clung to these fortunate facets of my life as if to a life-raft.

The guerrilla warfare continued its ravages against Bill on into 1999, each onslaught leaving him weaker, and both of us more miserable. Bill's resilience, which had developed when he was a gravely ill adolescent and helped him reconstruct a successful life, seemed more and more to be going AWOL. Although I did a great deal in assisting Bill in his daily activities, I was so depressed I must have been little help with morale. It seemed to me that the more he required assistance and even nursing from me, the more vulnerable he felt, for no one wants to saddle their partner with those duties. And the more vulnerable he felt, the more emotionally withdrawn he became, and the more I reacted in a like manner. This is my assessment with hindsight, though. At the time, I was so mired in our joint misery I couldn't see clearly at all. When he barked commands at me, instead of asking me politely, I refused to get him what he wanted, unless it was a serious nursing situation, in which case I had no choice. If I 'crossed' him, he would look at me with hatred, and not speak to me for two weeks, except to say he was going to leave. During much of that difficult period, neither of us seemed capable of communicating honestly to the other. But he didn't leave. Neither did I.

In August 1999 Bill became sick with what we assumed was bronchitis, which may have been caused by the build-up of excess fluid in his lungs due to his failing kidneys. We were only guessing because he refused to see his doctor. He took first one, then two courses of antibiotics from his stash but there seemed to be no improvement, and he had to spend several days in bed. Finally he got up, and said he was going to work. I noticed he was down to his penultimate tablet, and said I wanted to call his doctor. With what little breath he had left, he growled at me, 'Don't you fucking dare do that,' before wheeling slowly out to his car. He reversed out of the driveway but was too weak to control the car and mounted the opposite kerb before knocking into the wall of the garden across the road. Fortunately our close friends lived there, and in any case not much damage was done to either the car or the wall. But he realised he shouldn't try to drive the few kilometres to work, and pulled back into our driveway. He saw this as one more blow to his independence and mobility. A couple of hours later he asked me to drive him to work. But when he got there he was too ill to do much, so I had to return and bring him home.

The next day, unable to get out of bed, his lungs filled with fluid, he said I could call his doctor, who arrived that afternoon. After an examination, he ordered Bill straight into the Spinal Unit at the Austin Hospital. By this stage Bill was too weak to argue. In hospital he was diagnosed with renal failure: one kidney was not functioning, the other only poorly. The doctors wanted to insert a tube into a vein in his chest (a central venous catheter) so he could have dialysis straightaway, but he refused. When I visited him the next day he could barely talk, but between gasps for breath he said dialysis would be a huge drag that he couldn't bear and he just wanted to be allowed to die. I told him he was being ridiculous, that he should at least give dialysis a chance.

At home I reported Bill's words to Alex. He replied, 'Well I'm going to tell him that not having him around would be a much bigger drag!' He did tell Bill when we visited him in hospital the next day. In response, Bill managed a little grimace of a smile.

The reality was that if his kidneys had completely failed, he would have slipped into unconsciousness and the medical staff would have given him dialysis through an emergency tube into a vein in his neck. For now, they gave him antibiotics intravenously, and blood transfusions, because they found he had a dangerously low volume of blood, a condition known as hypovolemia. After a couple of weeks, Bill agreed to prepare for the procedure whereby a vein and an artery in his arm would be joined using a small plastic tube under the skin; this would enable all the blood in his body to be transferred via needles into the dialysis machine where it would be cleaned before being returned to his bloodstream, a process taking several hours. This small artificial 'communication' channel is known as a fistula, and is essential for long-term dialysis as a normal blood vessel isn't strong enough to have needles inserted several times a week over a long period.

Although Bill had agreed to have the procedure to create the fistula, scheduled to take place in a few weeks' time, he was far from happy about it. The next day was Father's Day, and the boys and I took presents and cards to the hospital for him. By the end of the visit we began to see small glimpses of the old Bill but it was clear he was as low as it was possible to be. The following week Bill was discharged. His depression seemed to lift a little once he was at home and, although not well enough to return to work, he was able to read and to talk to us.

Two weeks later—it was now late October 1999—Bill was back in hospital, this time with septicaemia. His diseased kidneys were poisoning him. He was given more antibiotics, more blood transfusions. After three weeks he was once again discharged. This time Bill lasted only 48 hours at home. By the second day, his urine was bright red, like the bags of blood that hung next to his bed when he was receiving transfusions. The doctor I had rung came to the house and, after examining Bill, told me to call an ambulance to take him to hospital. I felt there were wide bands of steel around my head, being gradually tightened by the hour. The pain was excruciating. I knew Bill suffered terrible headaches during his kidney infections, so perhaps I was emotionally identifying with him. I didn't tell him. It doesn't do to mention one's own headaches to someone who is gravely ill.

The septicaemia was back, the doctors told us, and Bill's kidneys were about to fail at any moment. The next day, they started him on emergency dialysis, using a vein in his neck as he'd not yet had the procedure to create the fistula in his arm. Two days later he had his second dialysis session, and

I drove to the hospital so I could stay with him for the whole four hours of the process. He asked me to read aloud some articles from the newspaper, which I was happy to do, and then we chatted a little about work, about what the children were doing. Bill received another four-hourly session two days later, and by the end of the week he was looking and feeling a lot better. The doctors hadn't yet told us whether dialysis was going to continue regularly or not. The renal team was planning to meet to discuss the best course of action.

Somehow during this period, I managed to finish my thesis, and submitted it to the university on 19 November. The next day, I fulfilled a longstanding promise to Patrick—that he could have a dog once my PhD was finished. Being the younger of the two boys, he'd been especially distressed by Bill's lengthy illness and hospitalisation, and I felt that a dog would give him something positive to focus on. We went to the RSPCA, where Patrick was permitted to go into the pens where the dogs were housed in order to make his choice. In the first pen was a tiny Maltese Shi-Tzu, barely the size of an average cat, with her hair shaved very short. She immediately stood on her hind legs and held out her paws. As Patrick knelt down in front of her, she very gently placed a paw on each of his shoulders, standing on her back legs. He turned to me and said, 'Mum, I must have this one'. So we adopted her and named her Jessie. We found out that she'd been rescued in an appalling condition a few months earlier from a puppy farm with a number of other breeding dogs that had simply been abandoned once they were no longer the optimal age for producing litters.

Bill had only reluctantly agreed to our adopting a dog; like many other people who've been bitten by a dog at some point in their lives, he had a dog phobia. But Jessie was so tiny she was barely able to reach up beyond the footplate on Bill's wheelchair, so we hoped he'd be able to cope with her presence once he returned home.

Bill had now been having regular haemodialysis for about two weeks. The fistula had been created in his arm, but there was a wait of between four and eight weeks to allow the surrounding skin and tissue to heal before it could be used for dialysis. In the interim his doctors had inserted a catheter into an artery in his upper chest which was easier to manage and less uncomfortable than using the artery in his neck.

Amidst these procedures came Grant and Fran's wedding, on 21 November, for which Bill was jointly best man with his brother Wayne, an original and lovely idea of Grant's. The hospital gave Bill leave to attend and both his brothers brought his outfit into the ward to help him get ready. Grant tied a white scarf creatively around Bill's neck to hide the bandaged artery opening. The small plastic tube leading into the chest artery had been covered by sticking plaster before Bill put on his shirt.

The wedding, at a venue in the Dandenongs surrounded by rain forest, was a beautiful interlude in this difficult time. Bill made a great speech as usual. The well-known Melbourne singer Debbie Byrne sang magnificently. We didn't manage to get Bill back to the hospital until 2 am.

A couple of days later I attended Balwyn High School's presentation night, the first without Bill. Patrick received two awards, and Alex played beautifully in the first violin section in the school's senior string orchestra and symphony orchestra. My pride in the children helped offset my anxiety about Bill, but my disappointment that he couldn't be with us was acute.

On the last day of November Bill's doctors, spinal specialists and urologists, held a meeting and decided that the only way to prevent further episodes of septicaemia was to remove his kidneys. They believed it was better to do this while he was relatively well, before a strain of the bacteria became resistant to the antibiotics, in which case he would die. After the removal of his kidneys, dialysis would be the only way that he could remain alive, while a kidney transplant would be an option further on, they said.

Bill agreed to the operation—there really wasn't any other choice—and the 'bilateral nephrectomy' was scheduled for a week later, on 8 December. We knew the operation was a major one which would take around five to six hours. Although the chance of death during the operation is low, only 2–3%, the possibility of post-operative complications is much higher, at 20%. Afterwards, there would be no turning back, and to stay alive Bill would be totally reliant on dialysis.

In the meantime, Bill's doctors allowed him to come home for several days, returning to the hospital for his scheduled dialysis treatments. I drove to the hospital to collect him, and as it was nearly 3.30 on our way home, we stopped at the High School to give the boys a lift; they were overjoyed at the prospect of having Bill at home for nearly a week.

Those few days before the operation had an unreality that is hard to describe; it was of course quite literally 'borrowed time'. Yes, he was still alive, but could so easily not have been, and could also be taken from us at any moment. If all went well with the operation he would live on, thanks only to a process that was barely thirty years old—the use of indefinite dialysis by way of a fistula for patients who had suffered end-stage renal disease, first invented by a Dutch doctor, Willem Kollf.

I vividly recall the first morning of that week. After breakfast Bill wheeled into the lounge, passing through shafts of bright yellow summer sunlight streaming through the large floor-to-ceiling windows, illuminating the room like floodlights on a stage. Bill and I must have been thinking the same thing, as we often did, and he proposed we go to see a play that night, with dinner in town beforehand; it sounded like a great idea to me.

For some reason my memory insists we saw Julius Caesar, though I've no actual recollection of the play, nor the theatre. But it could well have been that particular tragedy, as we saw many Shakespeare plays during the years we were together. Julius Caesar isn't even one of my favourites, so I don't know why I feel so strongly it was that one, although Marc Antony's speech at Caesar's funeral is one I later returned to again and again in teaching Rhetoric. Other lines that are lodged in my mind are the famous ones spoken by Julius Caesar when his wife is trying to talk him into staying at home because she's had a premonition of his murder: 'Cowards die many times before their deaths; The valiant never taste of death but once. Of all the wonders that I yet have heard, it seems to me most strange that men should fear, seeing that death, a necessary end, Will come when it will come.'

After seeing a play we always discussed it on the drive home. It's possible we talked about how Shakespeare never stops being relevant. The power play and betrayals of ancient Rome seem to function as a template for all subsequent struggles, and our workplace was certainly not exempt. I doubt that we discussed death, as we never did, or at least not yet, mainly because Bill wanted to shield me from it for as long as possible. I was in denial, an attitude I would soon have to change.

Now, nearly twenty years after I was forced dramatically to abandon that denial, I can see that Bill was one of Shakespeare's 'valiant' in his attitude towards his own death: he faced up to it with a bold courage. Bill knew he would not have a full lifespan, and this knowledge made him concentrate on the value and quality of life more than most other people I've known.

The following evening, Bill wanted to have dinner at an Italian restaurant in Southgate, and this time we wanted the boys to come with us. I noticed Bill was eating well, with more appetite than he'd had for a long time, something he believed was stimulated by the dialysis. Another unexpected effect of dialysis was that Bill was absolutely not allowed to consume more than one litre of liquid per day, of any type. Once his morning glass of juice and a couple of cups of tea or coffee were subtracted, that left room for only two small glasses of wine in the evenings. Given this small quantity, Bill said he now wanted to drink only the best wine, not the cheap stuff he admitted, rather sheepishly, he'd been drinking until recently, 'just to get pissed'. We both managed to see the funny side of this, and made a point of visiting our local bottle shop so Bill could carefully select his new, 'high quality' supply.

On the Saturday night Bill felt well enough to attend the Institute Management Dinner, a twice-yearly event for heads of department and senior managers and their partners. I didn't particularly want to go, but Bill's identity was strongly based on his professional role, and it was important to him to maintain his involvement with work, despite being on sick leave.

On Sunday Wayne made the six-hour drive from South Australia especially to see Bill before his operation, and we had a barbecue lunch cooked by Alex. I took a photo of the two brothers. Bill looks almost jubilant; it's Wayne, standing next to Bill's wheelchair, whose forehead is creased in anxiety.

For me, this happy interlude recalled our early years together, before illness had struck and robbed us of so much. Although the operation was a huge and drastic intervention for which there was absolutely no alternative, I saw it as something of a watershed. Once the cause of Bill's illness was removed, we could go back to how we'd been: best friends, endlessly discussing everything, going out together; no more silent treatment, no anaesthetising himself with alcohol, no anxiety and depression and neurotic raging from me. I was determined to remain positive.

I drove Bill back to hospital on Monday morning, 6 December. He was scheduled to have the operation the following day. On Tuesday afternoon, I phoned the hospital, and was told the operation had been a success and Bill was recovering in the Intensive Care Unit. Later I read the full report which stated Bill had had 'chronic long-term kidney disease, which had caused both kidneys to be blocked, acute inflammation of the whole area, and sepsis'. It was clear that, if not removed, his kidneys would have killed him very quickly.

After four days in Intensive Care Bill was transferred back to the spinal ward and soon began attempting short periods out of bed, sitting in his wheelchair. His goal was to be home in time for Christmas, an objective that the boys and I were desperately hoping he'd achieve.

1975: Out of Gaol

'It felt like getting out of gaol.' That was how Bill saw his new, post-Yooralla life. Deprived of a real education since he was 13, he relished everything about attending an ordinary secondary school, especially having teachers trained to teach specific subjects. Although Bill had been an above-average student before his accident, his goal back then—like many a young teenage boy—had been to become a footballer or cricketer. As soon as these goals were snatched away, he'd resolved to complete the Higher School Certificate and go on to university. As Bill would tell a journalist who interviewed him some years later, 'When I knew I would never walk again, I decided that it wouldn't stop me from making something of myself'.

Bill knew that if he were accepted into university, he'd be the first member of his extended family to have a tertiary education. In the 1970s only around 35% of students pursued secondary education to year 12, and less than a third of those went on to complete a university degree. Very, very few university students had a physical disability, especially one involving a wheelchair, because most of those students would not have been able to attend ordinary secondary schools which lacked wheelchair accessibility, thereby depriving them of the all-important university entrance requirement—a high HSC score. The statistics quoted above might explain the incredulity expressed by the School Leaving Panel at Yooralla when Bill told them his goals, but it doesn't excuse their scepticism and derision.

The statistics are significant, though, and Bill always kept track of them as they changed dramatically throughout the 1980s and 90s. He'd be very happy to see that in Australia today, two decades into the 21st century,

85% of students complete year 12, with around 36% of 20-year-olds in tertiary education.

The main generator of these developments was the Labor government of 1972–1975, under Prime Minister Gough Whitlam, Bill's all-time hero. As Bill liked to point out, along with implementing many other reforms, by 1975 Whitlam had abolished the onerous university fees in order to increase participation rates for the children of families who couldn't afford to pay; this included Bill's family (although fees were reintroduced in 1992).

Bill followed zealously the controversial actions of the Whitlam government during its three years in power, a government intent on rapidly reforming a great many aspects of Australian society after 23 years of being in opposition to a conservative government. Gough Whitlam was a politician whom Bill revered all his life, devouring books by and about him as soon as they appeared in bookshops. Like many people in 1975, Bill was incensed when the opposition in the Senate blocked supply on 11 November, leading to Governor General John Kerr's dismissal of the elected government.

In early 1975, though, Bill's principal preoccupation was to do well enough in the HSC exams to qualify for a place in a Bachelor of Arts course at one of the Victorian universities. After four and a half years with only intermittent study, it wasn't going to be easy. He had, however, already passed the subjects of English and Accounting at HSC level at Yooralla at the end of the previous year, thanks to his correspondence studies. He needed to pass three more subjects in order to obtain the HSC and qualify for a university place.

He'd made up his mind he would succeed. It wasn't a matter of 'if I go to university', but 'when …' His goals for when he finished university were not so clear. But he thought he'd possibly seek a graduate position in the public service in an administrative role, or perhaps do further study and go into social work; teaching was also very likely another possibility in the back of his mind.

Bill enrolled at Pembroke High School[25] at the start of the academic year, February 1975, which had been his goal since hearing about the school a few years earlier when he and his mother had read about the school's official opening by the Governor of Victoria. Bill had also heard that some of the teachers from Croydon High had transferred to the new school, guaranteeing some familiar faces.

Before the Yooralla panel meeting, June Johnson hadn't been one hundred percent sure that leaving the institution was the best thing for Bill. But she knew how much he hungered to complete his secondary education, and she'd said to him, 'If you're sure this is what you want, I'll support you'. And this she did, from then onwards.

Bill now lived back at home with his parents in their small three-bedroom house in Croydon. Wayne had moved out five years earlier, leaving Merrilyn who was now 16, and Grant aged 9. Bill and Grant shared a bedroom. Bill could now do almost everything independently, but as the bathroom was not wheelchair accessible he needed assistance from his father. He also needed help getting into and out of the house as there were steps at the doors. But he could transfer from his wheelchair to bed, get dressed, wheel around the streets of Croydon by himself, and go in and out of most shops. The one thing he couldn't do independently was travel to school. A half-hour walk from home, it took much longer in a wheelchair, especially with that suburb's hilly roads. In a car it took less than ten minutes, but his father used the family car to go to work each day, and June didn't drive. So Bill used a local taxi company to travel to and from school each day. To help with the cost, which at that time was around $20 per week, he'd successfully applied for a government subsidy.

After five and a half years of correspondence school, interrupted many times by ill health, Bill now had to work very hard to bring himself up to year 12 standard in his three subjects. As he could no longer write with his right hand, he'd had to re-learn, using his left; all note-taking had to be done by hand in those days. I only have to try to write my name with my non-dominant hand to see how laborious it can be. The pen won't submit to my awkward grip, and seems to have a mind of its own; the eight letters of my name that I must have written tens of thousands of times in my life, now squash and slip into an untidy scrawl. Bill had used typewriters on and off, but in the 1970s they were still mechanical models, not electric, requiring effort to press the keys, and typing one-handed wouldn't have been much quicker or easier than writing with his left hand.

Bill's motivation more than made up for the disadvantages, summed up by his Legal Studies teacher who wrote on his half-year report: 'Bill has the right attitude towards the subject'. He noted that in the mid-year exam Bill's answers had been a little too brief, so he advised him to try to write more on exam questions. Perhaps the brevity was at least partly the result of Bill's difficulty in using his left hand. At any rate, in September the head of the senior school wrote to the Examination Board requesting that Bill have an extra hour and a half for each examination, a request that was granted.

The Social Studies teacher remarked that Bill's contributions to class discussions were excellent and his knowledge and grasp of key concepts was good, but once again he needed to write more in-depth answers to exam questions. The teachers of these two subjects helped Bill develop his essay-writing skills during the four months remaining before the final exams. Bill always spoke highly of the teachers at Pembroke and credited them with providing the skills and encouragement he needed to perform well in the HSC.

Economics was Bill's strongest subject, in which he scored 77% in the mid-year exam. His teacher noted that Bill had worked 'with intense thoroughness and confidence, showing sound knowledge and understanding of concepts', and that if he continued this way he would do very well indeed in the final examination. He took the time to add to his report that Bill was an extremely pleasant and co-operative student, who 'has been a most welcome addition to the cohort, and I feel that his presence, attitude and approach is of great benefit to his fellow students'. I'm guessing that the teacher is referring not only to Bill's positive attitude but to the inclusiveness that Bill's presence in the school represented. Indeed, it's very likely that Bill was the only disabled student with whom the other students would have come into contact during their school years, given the educational segregation that had been widespread and would continue to be until the following decade.

Although successfully completing his HSC was Bill's priority in 1975, he didn't neglect his friends. His closest friend Rob had also left Yooralla at the end of the previous year, as well as their friend Margaret, who'd been a nursing assistant there; she and Rob got married in 1975 and bought a house in Croydon. Rob worked for an accounting company, and Margaret in aged care, but the three friends managed to spend a lot of time together. Margaret had a car, and she recalls frequently lifting the two wheelchairs in and out of the boot. All three supported the Essendon football club and often took the train to the games. During the journeys, as Margaret remembered them, the two young men would be having such intense conversations—usually about the merits of different football players, or coaches, or the politics of the Melbourne football scene—that other footy fans in the carriage would join in. By the time they arrived at the station the three friends had 'collected' a small crowd, who volunteered to help Bill and Rob off the train and into the football ground.

Once, during a walk in a park, some children asked Bill and Rob what it was like to be in a wheelchair. Rob asked Margaret to help him out of his motorised chair and he sat on a bench while the children took turns to whizz around the park. 'This was their way of educating people about disability, of breaking down barriers,' Margaret recalled. She believes their determination to leave Yooralla to pursue their own goals and live independently was 'trailblazing', inspiring other students with disabilities and perhaps even influencing the Yooralla School-Leaving Panel to be more open to students' plans for the future.

Clearly, there was a need for attitudinal change towards people with disabilities, and the following year the United Nations declared there would be an International Year of Disabled Persons, to be held in 1981. The Australian campaign, designed by well-known media figure Phillip Adams, was called 'Breaking down the barriers'. The central principle of the IYDP was that people with disabilities had the right to full and equal participation in society, which was not a widespread view at the time, and had not been put into practice at all in the design of public facilities and buildings. The main aim was therefore to change attitudes in the community generally, and especially among decision makers in government, private enterprise, and other institutions.

Everyone at Pembroke High School was very supportive of Bill, but he encountered discrimination elsewhere. He was very philosophical about it, rarely angered, believing that more knowledge about disability would change attitudes. But according to a newspaper clipping I have from this time, Bill's patience was to be severely tested towards the end of the school year when a problem arose with the taxi company he used for transport. The waiting periods began extending out to half an hour, and then an hour, suggesting that a number of the taxi drivers were refusing to take the call. With the exam period approaching, Bill was becoming anxious. His mother was furious; he'd come so far, only to have his plans derailed by discrimination! June contacted the local newspaper, saying that the taxi drivers were shunning her son. Knowing that this sort of human-interest story would help sell papers, a reporter came and interviewed her.

June always had a dramatic way of telling stories, a trait she possessed until her death at age 83. Her whole family knew of her powers of exaggeration and dramatisation. The reporter wasn't spared the dramatics. 'The taxi drivers are shunning my son because he's paraplegic,' she told the reporter. She made sure she also gave the backstory of Bill's accident, adding that of all his limbs he now only had use of his left arm. Explaining that her son's Higher School Certificate studies were now at a critical stage, she related how he relied on taxis to take him to and from school: 'A taxi is his only method of transport. His father leaves for work early and I don't drive,' she exclaimed vehemently. 'I usually order the taxi about an hour before he's due to leave for school, but quite often I have to make four or five calls before a taxi arrives.'

June thought some drivers believed they would have to lift Bill into the car, which was incorrect as he had a 'slide board' to transfer from the wheelchair into another seat. The only extra work required was to fold the wheelchair and put it in the boot. 'This naturally takes a little time', she said, 'but the meter is switched on as soon as the taxi arrives at the house'. The article was soon published, under the three-centimetre high headline, 'Taxi men shun my son'.

The head of the senior school at Pembroke High, Mr Michael Freeman, also a Croydon City Councillor, was quoted in the article, saying that on some afternoons the school had had to phone the taxi company up to ten times before a taxi arrived. 'I'm incensed about the matter,' he said, 'and have asked the Transport Regulation Board to investigate'. In his letter he wrote that he believed the company's treatment of Bill was callous and finished by saying that on behalf of the school he would 'appreciate some action to ensure that this man, who has overcome a grave handicap to return to school and study, is treated with the consideration and compassion he deserves'. Alongside the article was a large photo of Bill at his desk, looking as calm and composed as ever.

A week later, in early November, with the exams about to start, the Croydon Mail published another article, 'Wheelchair youth gets taxi pledge'. It stated that following the complaint to the Transport Regulation Board by Councillor Michael Freeman, the taxi company had assured Bill that a permanent booking would be made to get him to and from his examinations.

It was a promise that must have been kept because just before Christmas Bill received a yellow-hued certificate with a patterned border, headed 'The Victorian Universities and Schools Examination Board, Higher School Certificate Examination', underneath which was the list of subjects he'd passed. I never saw the certificate, so I don't know the exact details but, together with the two subjects he'd already passed, he now had the marks to apply to enter a Bachelor of Arts program. He chose Swinburne College of Technology, as it had just opened its new Arts building, which was much more wheelchair-accessible than the buildings of the older universities.

When he started his degree in early March 1976, Bill was one of only around 10% of Australian students of his age cohort to go to university, and the first member of his family to do so. It was a remarkable achievement. He felt justly proud of it, and his family shared that pride.

1999–2000: A Delicate Balance

Bill arrived home from hospital on 18 December, with three sessions of dialysis now a non-negotiable part of his week. He was very thin, weighing only around 57 kilos, not much more than me yet he was over six feet tall. He may have lacked a vital organ, but emotionally he seemed whole again. The months in and out of hospital had shown him only too clearly how much he loved his home and us, and he returned lively and animated. The children couldn't leave him alone and hung around him, discussing anything and everything. Bill seemed full of energy and ideas, always laughing and making jokes. With his diseased kidneys dispatched and his blood now being regularly cleaned thoroughly for the first time in several years, he was a new man, or rather once again the man with all the qualities I'd loved so much when I first met him. In response, my own spirits lifted, and I too tried to return to being the person he'd married, forgetting the misery of the past few years in the same way I always tried to forget bad dreams.

The following day was Bill's 44th birthday and our sixth wedding anniversary. Bill's family came for lunch—his parents; Merrilyn and Dave and their children; and Grant and Fran—although we'd all agreed it would be strictly for two hours as Bill was still supposed to be convalescing. Alex had assigned himself the role of head chef, in charge of preparing the meat; Dave would bring his home-made coleslaw, for which he was justly famous; this left me with only the bread rolls to buy and the potato salad to make.

We'd always ordered takeaway food at these gatherings, but Bill's haemodialysis meant he had to follow a strict diet, with 'junk food' at the top of the banned list. I can't say I was sorry about that.

Shortly before Bill was to leave the Austin, a dietician provided us with guidance on the nutritional changes I'd have to make to our meals. Because under dialysis the blood can only be cleaned of its waste products (known as urea) three times per week, instead of continually, as it is with healthy kidneys, the levels of certain minerals and chemicals can't be optimally controlled and will build up to dangerous levels over the days in between dialysis sessions. Salt had to be restricted, but the most dangerous mineral was potassium. Under normal conditions potassium is of great benefit to the human body, controlling nerve and muscle function, and in particular enabling the heartbeat; our bodies can't function without it. But when the potassium level is too high, which could more easily happen to a person without kidneys, the heartbeat will start to become weak. If the potassium level keeps rising, the heart will stop within one to two weeks. Although I didn't realise it at the time, Bill took particular note of this information.

Most foods contain potassium, but now the challenge was to eat low-potassium foods, guaranteeing enough of it to keep Bill's heart beating, but not too much, which would shut it down. Unfortunately for Bill, most of his favourite snacks and drinks were high in potassium or salt: orange juice, Coca-Cola, potato chips, and all tomato-based foods. With the information and recipes supplied by the dietitian, I thought I'd be able to devise meals that would satisfy Bill's needs, and which we could all eat. He also needed more protein, especially on the dialysis days.

After our meeting with the dietician it was the turn of the social worker. She asked Bill how he felt about the four-hour dialysis sessions three times a week, and whether he had any ideas about how to pass the time. Given that Bill had only one good arm which, until the leg fistula was created, was being used to connect him to the dialysis machine, he didn't have a lot of options. But he'd be able to read, he said, either work-related material or books. And he aimed to find some voice-recognition software so he could write emails on his laptop.

She then turned to me, this earnest young woman in her twenties, asking, 'And how do you feel? How are you coping with all this?'

I was dumbfounded. I'd never asked myself this, nor had anyone else. I began to think that maybe I should consider how I was feeling; but what I said to her was, 'I'm okay, thanks, I'm coping'. Later, home on my own, since Bill was still at the Austin and the boys were with their other father, I sat at the desk in my study, and asked myself the same question, before writing a response to it in my journal.

How did I feel? Strangely, I felt in desperate need of exercise. It was more than that, though: I felt a physical need to force my body to its limits. I wanted to push myself to the point where I was gasping for breath with my heart jumping around in my chest until I was about to drop. It was as if the stress of the past few years needed to be physically pushed out of my body.

A year earlier I'd joined the gym at work and was doing a weekly aerobics class. I frequently ran on the treadmill or did a session with weights, but it was nowhere near enough; I knew that if I was going to exorcise my anxiety, I needed to be outdoors, and away from the Institute and from our house.

I explained some of this to Bill the day he came home. I hadn't planned to mention it straightaway, but one of the first things he said was, 'I know I haven't been able to give you much support over the past few years, and I want to make up for that'.

A tsunami of love for him washed over me. I told him he'd been an enormous support to me in bringing up the boys, that I couldn't have imagined coping alone, especially during their teenage years. But it was also true that Bill's illness had eclipsed a great deal of our needs as a couple, and my needs; it was typical of him that he could recognise this and want to atone for it.

He suggested I choose a bicycle for my anniversary present, and he'd buy it for me. I was overjoyed. I hadn't really considered this form of exercise, but it was the perfect solution. I could do it at any spare moment, and close to the house there was an entry to the many kilometres of bike path that ran through parkland abutting the Eastern Freeway, part of the much larger metropolitan network.

It was ideal cycling weather, warm and dry. The first time I set off, I rode until my legs were like jelly and I could pedal no more. I had to get off the bike and walk slowly home. Later, looking at the map, I calculated I'd ridden only 6 kilometres, but over time the distances increased.

In between bike rides, I managed my present-buying. For Bill's birthday I bought him an electric shaver. Not terribly imaginative, but something very useful if you can only use one hand for shaving. He'd been really indignant when nurses had shaved some of his full beard off to place the dialysis stent in his neck. He now sported a much smaller beard which required a shave every few days. For our anniversary I gave him a leather bag to carry his laptop, phone and a book to dialysis sessions. A new phone was his Christmas present. He bought me the huge two-volume Oxford English Dictionary that I'd long coveted. It still sits on the bookshelf beside my desk, to be consulted when the online dictionaries I use now don't yield as much etymological background as I'd like.

On Christmas morning we decided to play loud music in the family room to wake the boys up. Bill went through his CD collection and suggested John Lennon's 'So this is Christmas'. At 9.30 we turned the volume turned up full bore and it did the trick; after a little while the boys emerged from their rooms. I still play it every Christmas morning.

Christmas dinner was a very celebratory affair, held at Merrilyn and Dave's; we all felt a great sense of relief that Bill had survived the huge operation, and all seemed well after two weeks of convalescing. Bill was the life of the party, actually, making jokes, laughing, but talking seriously when the subject warranted it. Late in the afternoon we drove the boys to their father's place. He'd planned to take them and their two younger half-siblings to Western Australia for a month to see their grandparents, aunts and uncles.

Boxing Day dawned; it was back to dialysis. It was usually scheduled for Tuesday and Thursday afternoons, and Saturday mornings. Bill wasn't yet strong enough to drive to the hospital, so he either took a taxi or I drove him, sometimes remaining there with him for the four hours. I'd take a book or the newspaper, or we'd chat to the dialysis nurses. There was a pleasant and friendly atmosphere in the dialysis unit, and Bill got to know the nurses and other patients well.

For the haemodialysis procedure, Bill was transferred from his wheelchair into what resembled a large comfortable reclining armchair. The fistula had been put into Bill's good left arm, as it had a healthier blood flow than the right, so he couldn't do much for himself during the four hours. He'd asked his doctors if a fistula could be created in his thigh as soon as possible, so that he could then use his left arm for computer work or for writing, and this had been approved; but even the new fistula would not be operational for another couple of months.

Most of the time during dialysis sessions he wasn't in any discomfort. Only about one to two cups of blood are taken out of the body at any one time, but over the four hours all six to seven litres that the average body contains is filtered through the machine. Bill always ensured he had an interesting book with him, usually political biographies, which he was consuming at a great rate. Whenever I passed a bookshop I'd quickly check to see if a new volume on politics or on a political figure had been published. Bill's favourites were Gough Whitlam and Winston Churchill.

Although I'd accompanied Bill to dialysis a few times I'd deliberately looked away as I have trouble watching anything that involves blood, but that Boxing Day I willed myself to pay attention so that I could understand what he was experiencing. It took great willpower to curtail my nausea. The nurse rolled up Bill's sleeve, located the fistula, and inserted the two thin needles into it, each pointing in a different direction: one to slowly draw the 'dirty' blood out of the artery, the other to return it into the vein after it had been cleaned by the machine.

Each needle was connected to a plastic tube which snaked away to a large rectangular metal machine, about a metre and a half in height and covered with tubes and dials, lights and beepers, the whole contraption working as a filter in order to remove waste products and extra fluid from the blood. The machine had been set according to the dialysis doctor's specific instructions, as it is for each patient, and Bill was closely monitored throughout the four hours, with his blood pressure taken every thirty minutes. I tried not to look too closely at the long tubes of blood, but I noticed that one tube was bright red, while the other—the one returning the cleaned blood—was darker. It was scarcely comprehensible to me that the work of a major organ like the kidney could be entirely and successfully accomplished outside the body. But it was. And it was a procedure to which Bill owed his life.

The first month of Bill being back at home was peaceful and positive. The boys were still away. We'd go out for dinner with friends, or I'd meet a girlfriend for coffee or lunch while Bill was having dialysis. I rode my bike, often with our dog Jessie strapped into the padded basket on the handlebars. I could take her out of the basket and let her have a run around when I reached a park, while I sat and regained my breath.

As we were still on our summer break, I tried to spend a couple of hours at my desk most days, trying to write. Although I'd finished my PhD I now desperately wanted to return to writing for mainstream publication, something I'd had to put on hold while completing my thesis, as I also worked three days a week. But I found it very hard, if not impossible, to get back into a mainstream writing style after concentrating on academic writing for so long. I'd even been teaching a weekly class called Clear Academic Writing at the School of Graduate Studies at the University of Melbourne for the past few semesters. The person who'd engaged me for the job now encouraged me to apply for another position, as lecturer in media writing for the new Bachelor of Media and Communications degree. As part of the selection process I was asked to write a proposed outline of the new media writing subject, a task that I found daunting yet exciting, in equal parts.

For some time now I'd been applying for other jobs, something that

Bill fully supported. Following a restructure a few years earlier my course was now part of Bill's department, and I was one of his five program coordinators. A number of our colleagues seemed to resent our being a couple, and now and then some of them would snidely say that too many departmental decisions 'were being made at the North Balwyn office', referring to our home. In a way there may have been some justification for a critique, but not for the cheap shots, as Bill had always been very committed to running his department democratically. Nevertheless, because of this antipathy, and because eleven years seemed more than enough of working in the one place, I'd been looking around for a teaching position elsewhere.

I laboured painstakingly over devising the outline for this new University subject, and Bill and I spent days poring over my draft and discussing it. Bill was a great sounding board. Even though he hadn't taught at university level he knew the whole year 12 syllabus in detail, especially the humanities subjects, and could easily conceptualise the level required for first year university students.

The University's deadline arrived. I submitted the draft and was summoned to an interview. A few days later the professor who headed the department rang and offered me the job. I was to commence at the start of second semester, in late July. I'd start on a one-semester contract followed by a review, he said. I now had to research and write the weekly lectures. Being a perfectionist, I wanted most of them written well before the start of the new semester, so I immediately set to work. Again, I was able to discuss the content with Bill. His own subject area, Politics, was becoming more and more intertwined with media, as reflected in many of the books he was reading during dialysis, the latest one being political journalist Gerald Stone's book, *Compulsive Viewing*. He was a great help to me in this new work I'd taken on.

After six weeks of convalescence Bill could drive again, and he returned to the Institute at the start of February, working three and a half days per week, intending to resume full-time hours later in the year if all went well, an arrangement he'd negotiated with management. I also resumed teaching in early February; it would be my last semester at the Institute.

In March Bill's operation to have the fistula created in his left thigh was scheduled. He'd have a two-night stay in hospital, and there would be a three to four week wait for the fistula to be ready for use. The dialysis doctor had explained that leg fistulas don't last as long as arm fistulas, and would need to be reconstructed more frequently, but Bill desperately wanted to use his strong left arm for the four hours of enforced immobility during dialysis. He could do a little with his right arm, but not nearly enough for his liking, and certainly not tasks like writing emails.

Bill's health was now checked three times a week at the start of each dialysis session, so I no longer had to worry about his refusing to see a doctor when unwell. Following the fistula procedure, Bill's doctors recorded that he was 'looking well', and his weight was now 59kg. A note from this time indicates that Bill and his dialysis doctor had discussed the issue of a kidney transplant. The doctor thought Bill would be 'a suitable candidate at some point', but noted that Bill wanted 'to firmly establish himself on dialysis first and reconsider at a later date'.

From time to time Bill and I discussed the possibility of a transplant, but with fading enthusiasm; the sheer quantity of anti-immune drugs Bill would have to take, and the high risk of infection, coupled with his weakened state after five years of illness, didn't augur well. We agreed that the popularity of transplants was probably related to the view that life must be conserved at any price, including—in some circumstances—a sacrifice of the recipient's quality of life. A kidney might be rejected, for a start, and in any case a transplanted kidney has a use-by date of five years if it is from a deceased donor, although a kidney from a living donor lasts longer, especially if from a family member. None of Bill's family had, nor should have, volunteered to donate a kidney; they were not really well placed to do so. His parents were aging and none too healthy themselves, two of his siblings had children and soon-to-be grandchildren for whom they very much needed to stay alive, and the third was hoping for children in the near future. Nobody articulated this view, but I'm certain we all shared it, including Bill: those who are ill or dying should not take precedence over the living.

A donated kidney would, statistically at least, not have preserved Bill's life for much longer than dialysis would. I didn't know the statistics at the time, although I'm certain Bill did because of something he said to me much later, but dialysis patients have an extraordinarily high mortality rate with the single most prevalent cause of death being sudden cardiac arrest. Due to this and other medical conditions, average life expectancy on dialysis is five years, although some dialysis patents have lived for 20 years or more.

Before each dialysis session, Bill was required to eat a high protein meal. On Saturdays I would get up at 6.30 so I could cook poached eggs on toast for him. Sometimes I'd accompany him to the hospital if I didn't have any pressing commitments; the boys, aged 17 and 15 and fairly independent, were usually still in bed when we left the house.

After four hours of dialysis, two nurses would come to disengage Bill from the machine. One Saturday when I was there one of the nurses began talking to me, saying that I could train to operate the machine, to be Bill's 'carer', so it could all be done at home. I was shocked; Bill required hospital surveillance, with blood tests done and blood pressure taken at the start of each session, and I was already fully stretched with all the existing demands on me, as well as trying to maintain a career. Bill's drive to the Austin three times a week was a nuisance for him, but at least for weekday sessions one of us could still work; that wouldn't have been the case if I were in charge of operating the dialysis machine.

I tried to indicate my feelings to them, although feeling selfish all the while. I started by saying, 'I couldn't, I have no nursing experience and …'

'Oh, you'll get the hang of it, you'll be able to do it,' said one of the nurses, making me think they assumed my primary duty was to slot into the role of 'carer', irrespective of my own needs and professional life, not to mention the necessity of earning an income. More importantly, from long experience and observation of others I believed that the roles of 'carer' and 'wife' may be mutually exclusive. Certainly they were for me, as they must be for a great many other people. Bill and I had only recently managed to snatch back a semblance of our life as a couple, and I didn't want to lose it a second time. For the moment, though, I remained silent.

Bill and I went out for lunch afterwards and I gently raised the topic. He understood my position perfectly and said it was a ridiculous idea anyway since even experienced nurses often found it tricky to insert the needles. Once his leg fistula was ready to be used he thought he could learn to do it himself, and if it was indeed possible to have a dialysis machine at home he would manage the entire process. But he didn't think home dialysis would be happening inside six months, if that. I remember thinking that it wasn't just his body's chemicals that needed to be kept in a delicate balance.

1975–1977: Adult Life ... and America

'I majored in Politics, Sociology, and pub-crawling, the latter being the most taxing,' Bill would sometimes say when introducing himself to new acquaintances, not long after finishing his Bachelor of Arts. More seriously, he also described the three years he spent at Swinburne College as the most enjoyable and fulfilling of his life so far.

Bill felt that the new Arts building at Swinburne's Hawthorn campus must have been designed with wheelchairs in mind, as he was able to enter unaided all the rooms in which lectures and tutorials for his subjects were held. The one exception was the café where there were two steps, an inexplicable oversight.

A more pleasant difficulty was selecting his subjects. Bill pored for ages over the prospectus, in those days a huge paper handbook, trying to choose from among the many subjects that interested him. Politics was top of his list; it didn't exist as an HSC subject in those days, but it was the first one Bill chose in the initial year of his BA. He'd discovered he loved analysing power, human interaction, and societal and historical events, so he also enrolled in Sociology, and Asian History.

Swinburne was a long trip from Croydon, forty-five minutes each way by car. Bill desperately wanted to learn to drive but he couldn't see how it would be possible, as even with a specially adapted automatic car he'd need one hand on the steering wheel and one for the hand-operated controls. The muscles in his right hand and arm didn't yet feel sufficiently strong or responsive, so Bill made the journey by taxi, often leaving home before 8am and not missing a single day throughout the three years of his degree. The long daily commute was hard at first and he felt the usual school-leaver's fear of entering a large institution where he knew no one. On top of that, for the first week or so Bill found many of the students 'stand-offish', perhaps because a student in a wheelchair was still a rare sight in a university. But as soon as tutorials started Bill plunged into the discussions, contributing intelligently and interspersing jokes with his more serious points, which had the effect of putting everyone at ease.

In the Asian History lectures Bill befriended fellow student Greg, with whom he remained friends for the rest of his life. Greg remembers Bill as popular and well-respected at Swinburne, where he became the nucleus of a small, close-knit group of students studying the same subjects.

After lectures on Friday afternoons, this group would meet for drinks at the Governor Hotham Hotel (renamed the Hawthorn Hotel in 2001), conveniently located right next door to the campus. Greg recalls that the hotel's clientele of the time also included two other distinct demographics: the notorious waterside workers from Melbourne's docks, and members of the Hell's Angels. The students would meet in the lounge bar, where Bill would be the centre of attention with his trademark outrageous jokes, leading the dissection of the week's classes. The drinking would start mid-afternoon and continue until late, when Greg and another friend would help Bill into his taxi for his homeward journey, after which the other two would stagger off to Glenferrie Station to head home themselves.

As the end of his first year at Swinburne approached, so did Bill's twenty-first birthday. His mother who, along with the rest of the family, still called him by his childhood name of Billy, asked him what he'd like for a present. He replied, 'You can start calling me Bill. That's all I want!' June knew it would be hard to break the habit of over twenty years, but said she'd do her best. Gradually, 'Bill' became the rule in the family. For Bill himself it signified he was an adult who wanted and needed the independence appropriate for any young man of that age. He was still sharing a room with his ten-year-old brother, Grant. They adored each other, but that wasn't the point.

Bill wasn't quite ready to leave home, and in any case didn't have a salary to support the move, but he had the idea of constructing a self-contained studio in the back garden of his parents' house. To pay for this he proposed using some of the modest compensation he'd received following his accident. June and Adrian agreed to the idea, and Bill contacted a building company and explained his needs.

He needed the studio to have a large bed-sitting room and an accessible ensuite bathroom so that he could be totally independent in all aspects of life, except for cooking. Not only was cooking impossible for the moment because of Bill's weak right arm, or so he said, but he was very happy for June to continue supplying his meals! To come and go freely without any assistance, he needed the studio to be accessible from the street and driveway, with a ramp at the entrance. The studio was completed early in 1977, around the time that Bill's sister Merrilyn married her long-time boyfriend Dave, with Bill as best man. Later, Dave would joke about how he was still helping Bill put the finishing touches to the studio on the very morning of his wedding.

Bill bought a large wooden table that doubled as a study desk and dining table; a bookshelf and television set; an electric typewriter for his university work; a hi-fi stereo that included a record player, tape deck (no CDs in those days) and enormous speakers; a couple of lounge chairs for visitors, and of course, a bed. He could now perform all activities in his daily life completely independently. Before going to bed each evening, he placed the clothes for the next day within easy reach. With the bed at a certain height, he could transfer into and out of it from his wheelchair with the help of a strap attached to the bedhead. In the morning he'd put on his trousers while lying on the bed, then once in the wheelchair he put on his other clothes. The bathroom was large enough for Bill to enter easily in his wheelchair, and to use the commode chair for the wheel-in shower and adjacent toilet.

Each night as he opened his books on the large desk, amid the smell of new wood and fresh paint, he exulted in his new-found sense of privacy and independence. The distance that separated his new living space from that of his parents was only a few metres, yet it signified far more, the beginning of a normal adult life. But he wasn't finished yet, not by a long way. After university he'd find a good job and start saving for a deposit on his own house. He also needed to find a way to operate a car. He knew of people with paraplegia who could drive; surely it would somehow be possible for him too. He raised the subject with his doctors at the Austin Hospital Spinal Unit, asking if they knew anything of a 'one-hand drive' vehicle which he'd he read about in the newspaper. They didn't, but they noted on his file the fervent desire to learn to drive.

Another person who appreciated the wheelchair access to Bill's studio was his close friend Rob, who lived nearby with his wife Margaret. Now, when they visited Bill, Margaret would have a cup of tea with June in her kitchen, leaving the two men to their long, intense conversations in Bill's studio.

While the studio was still being built, in November 1976, Bill and Wayne began planning a trip to America. After losing most of their teenage years, the brothers were reconnecting as young men, their lives having gone in completely different directions from what each had expected, and from each other. Wayne had left hairdressing and was in the early period of a long and successful career in his cousin's grain export company in Mount Gambier, South Australia; he was married to Maureen, and they'd had their first child, Kate. Bill was building a life based on his intellect. Each was enormously supportive and proud of the other, and once Wayne had bought a car, he made the drive from South Australia as often as he could. The two brothers quickly became very close again, although the larrikinism and laughter of their childhood seemed gone for ever. Or almost.

Wayne and Bill planned to spend a month in the United States, in January 1977. Bill, ever the politics student, had been inspired to make the trip after Jimmy Carter, the Democratic Candidate, had won the Presidential Election in early November. It would be winter there, definitely not the best time for visiting the northern states, but Bill only had the long Australian summer academic break in which to travel for a month. It was arranged that Maureen, together with Kate, now a toddler, would stay with June and Adrian while Wayne and Bill were away.

The brothers weren't to know that North America was experiencing its coldest winter in nearly 100 years, and snowfalls had started in October. In mid-January Bill and Wayne landed in New York, where it had snowed almost every day since just after Christmas; many streets were closed to traffic, and a lot of businesses were shut. Nevertheless, they managed to find one car-hire business still open. They'd intended to travel 100 miles north to the small town of Stanford to visit a friend to whom they'd promised to take some Australian wine, but the road north was blocked by snow. Instead, they headed northwest, and just over the Canadian border to Niagara Falls, which had been frozen over for more than a month.

With Wayne at the wheel, they now headed south through Pennsylvania to Washington, DC. It snowed every day, but they still managed to see two places that were at the top of Bill's list, Capitol Hill and the White House, in which President Carter had just taken up residence after being sworn in on 20 January. They continued south to Richmond, Virginia—which Bill wanted to see as it was an important site in the American Revolutionary period—before turning due west towards Dallas, via Oklahoma, Lexington, and Louisville to see the home of the Kentucky Derby.

The next day, driving into the outskirts of St Louis, Missouri, Wayne realised they were nearly out of petrol. Through the thickly falling snow he spotted a Chevron sign over a down-and-out looking petrol station, and pulled in. The pump attendant said, 'Where you from?', and when Wayne said Australia, the man asked, 'What state that in, man?'

After filling up with petrol, they drove a hundred metres down the road to a toilet block. A few seconds after they pulled up, a scruffy, wild-looking man appeared at the passenger window and gestured for Bill to open it, which he did. The man then put a gun to Bill's head, saying 'Get out'.

Before Bill could reply, Wayne said, 'He can't,' and pointed to the wheelchair in the back. The man's face took on a slightly sympathetic look. 'Nam?' he asked.

Bill now found his tongue, and he was angry. 'It doesn't matter how I became disabled, you're a fucking predator picking on someone who can't defend themselves.' But the man's eyes were glazed, and it was clear to Wayne he wasn't taking much in. It would be best to give him the money and get out of there. Telling Bill to shut up, Wayne took out his wallet, and told Bill to do the same. The man pocketed the wallets, saying almost regretfully to Bill, 'I really don't like robbin' you, you bein' a vet an' all, but …'

Fortunately, this was before international credit cards came into vogue and most people used travellers' cheques, which were useless for anyone other than the legal owner. The cheques were hidden in the suitcases anyway, so the robber only got away with around a hundred dollars from the wallets.

After that, all the brothers wanted was to get out of St Louis and on to Oklahoma. But suddenly the snow thickened, lashing the car with increased violence; driving was like trying to push through a white wall. They found themselves in the middle of a long traffic jam; visibility was reduced to a metre and no one could advance beyond a crawl. The car's heater was on its maximum setting, and still they were shivering.

They didn't yet know it, but they were experiencing the fringe of the blizzard that was devastating New York state, and would wreak havoc in the northeast of the country for five days from 28 January. By travelling southwest as quickly as they had, Bill and Wayne had mercifully missed the worst of it; many parts of western New York had been declared federal disaster areas by President Carter.

Somehow, travelling at only 10 miles per hour or less, they eventually got out of St Louis. It was already late, and they wouldn't make it across the state border into Oklahoma that night, but managed to get as far as Springfield in the southwest of Missouri.

Wayne wanted to depart very early the next day despite tiredness from the long days of driving. According to the television news the main roads had been cleared, and for once it wasn't snowing. Nevertheless, the journey to Dallas would take longer than the seven hours they'd planned. But when Wayne woke him in the morning, Bill didn't want to get up. He pulled the rugs up higher and shut his eyes, grumbling that he wanted at least another hour's sleep. Wayne was furious. Taking a washcloth from the bathroom, he went outside and grabbed a heap of snow, massaged it into a snowball, and carried it back inside. He lifted the bedcover and dumped the snow all over the top of Bill's chest; his yells of rage must have woken every guest in the hotel. But Bill got up. He didn't speak a word to Wayne for over a day and a half.

As they travelled southwest, then due south, bypassing Oklahoma City, the snow gradually disappeared. In the early evening they arrived in Dallas, Texas. They'd been travelling for nearly two weeks, yet Dallas was the first city they'd seen that had no snow. They checked into their motel and retired to their room; in the morning when they looked out of the window they saw it had snowed during the night.

Bill, ever the history and politics buff, wanted to visit Dealey Plaza where President Kennedy had been shot 14 years earlier, and to see the building that had been the Texas School Book Depository from which Lee Harvey Oswald had fired. Bill still wasn't speaking to Wayne, but by the afternoon he was so overwhelmed at being in these places where historical events of global significance had taken place that he couldn't help but break his silent sulk.

They drove west from Dallas, their destination El Paso on the Mexican border. Crossing the Rio Grande, that forms the border at that point, they drove into the Mexican city of Ciudad Juarez, site of the first battle of the Mexican Revolution in May 1911.

Next stop was Phoenix, Arizona to visit Bill's former spinal doctor, David Cheshire. Dr Cheshire had resigned from the Spinal Unit at the Austin Hospital a few years earlier to accept a position heading the Southwest Regional System for Treatment of Spinal Injury at the Good

Samaritan Hospital (it's now the Banner University Medical Centre) in Phoenix. Dr Cheshire showed them around his section, introducing Bill to the other spinal doctors with the words, 'This is the young man I told you about … my miracle boy!' Bill was overwhelmed at seeing the doctor who had been so crucial in his rehabilitation and who, in encouraging Bill to have the spinal fusion operation, had effectively given him many more years of life.

The brothers now travelled northwest to Las Vegas, both eager to see the fabled casinos, of even more mythical fascination to Australians in those days, when we had only one legal casino, Wrest Point in Tasmania. In Las Vegas they spent two hedonistic nights of drinking and gambling. One evening, after returning to their room, Bill wanted to use the toilet, something he needed Wayne's assistance to do as they had not brought along a commode chair. Wayne helped him on to the toilet, but very soon passed out on the bed, thanks to their wild evening. With his wheelchair some distance away, Bill could not get off the toilet by himself. Despite Bill's shouting, Wayne did not awake until 6am. Neither of them reported the words that were then exchanged, but from my knowledge of Bill, the next day in the car would have been a very silent one. Bill may well have broken his silence, though, as they drove through the Grand Canyon National Park, the immensity of this natural wonder demonstrating the smallness of human concerns. After this detour, they doubled back east to Tennessee via Albuquerque and Oklahoma City.

In Memphis, Tennessee, as with many of the cities they visited, Bill had a mental list of important sites to see. The city had played a prominent role in America's civil rights movement and was where Martin Luther King had been assassinated only nine years earlier, in the Lorraine Motel. It was still a functioning motel when Bill and Wayne saw it, although the owner had turned the room where King had been killed into a memorial. Nearly 15 years later the motel building would become part of the Lorraine Civil Rights Museum.

Only a few hours to the east, Nashville also held historical and political interest for Bill, as it was the first city captured by Union troops in the Civil War. But the brothers mainly wanted to see the Grand Ole Opry House, the 4000-seat venue that had made country and western music famous, and its adjacent theme park. There's no record of which singers were in the Grand Ole Opry show that night in mid-February 1977. It may well have included Tammy Wynette, Dolly Parton, the Gatlin Brothers, Barbara Mandrell, Johnny Cash, and very likely Minnie Pearl, who performed there for fifty years. Regardless, attending the show was what mattered, and is that all Wayne remembers of it more than thirty-five years later.

One thing Bill always remarked on later, when he spoke of this trip, was how there was rarely a problem with wheelchair accessibility: from the smallest motel to the Grand Ole Opry House. And this was back in 1977. By then America had a very large number of disabled veterans from the Second World War, the Korean War and the Vietnam War, the latter conflict having ended only a few years earlier. Accessibility for the many citizens with a disability was ensured by strong legislation for government and commercial buildings of any kind, especially those providing accommodation.

Bill and Wayne concluded their heroic road trip with the drive up to Washington DC, from where they would fly home. The difficulties and joys of the journey, the month-long closeness and camaraderie, went some way towards making up for the shared adolescence so brutally cut short only eight years earlier.

2000–2001: Reading the Signs

Bill's dialysis slowly became normalised and our family life resumed its usual pattern. Most teenagers find those last few years of living at home to be a challenge, but I understand now that we unwittingly demanded of Alex and Patrick a resilience and flexibility that few of their peers would have been required to demonstrate. Their father had moved on from his second marriage and had a new partner with two sons of her own. Alex and Patrick were having to cope with a second stepmother and two new step-brothers of around their own ages, in addition to their two younger half-siblings to whom they were devoted. It was hardly surprising that occasionally one or other of the boys would be unsettled and difficult to talk to. Bill never did much discipline; discipline was down to me. But what a great stabilizing influence he was; I certainly couldn't have coped with the boys on my own during those years.

My diary records a lot of good times. The four of us often went out together. I recall our seeing the newly-released film, 'Looking for Alibrandi', based on the novel which Patrick was reading in year 9 English. Afterwards, over dinner at the Nataraj restaurant, that had long been one of our favourites, we discussed the film. 'You see, Mum,' said Patrick, 'we're no worse than other teenagers'. He was referring to the histrionics the main character inflicted on her mother when she returned home from school in the afternoons. I grudgingly had to agree.

At the start of August I began teaching my new undergraduate subject, one of the two compulsory subjects in the new Bachelor of Media and Communications at the University of Melbourne. This type of degree was still quite new in these more traditional universities and many of my students were among the most motivated and enthusiastic I'd ever taught. The twelve weeks of the semester seemed incredibly short compared to the sixteen I was used to in TAFE. I worked extremely hard in delivering the lectures and conducting the several practical writing workshops or tutorials each week, and found this new job used up most of my energy. At home we now employed cleaners once a fortnight for the housework and the ironing of Bill's shirts, but there was still a lot for me to do.

Wheelchair maintenance was one of the skills I'd developed over the past seven years. Punctured tyres had to be mended like bike tyres. Sometimes the tyre valves would need to be sent off for professional repairs and we'd get one of Bill's old wheelchairs out of a cupboard where it had been kept folded flat. Alex had also become very capable with these chores and was a great help.

At the end of August, I bumped into the professor at the photocopier in my department, and he said, 'I hear you're doing a brilliant job'. This made my day, as I'd been very anxious about this new teaching at university level, despite having taught for over twenty years. I couldn't wait to get home and tell Bill and the boys. A few weeks later the course manager asked me if I'd be interested in a new contract for both semesters of the following year. My reply was instant, and again I raced home to tell Bill.

September, and the school holidays arrived. Alex said he wanted to study from 10am until 4pm every day of the fortnight, to prepare for his VCE exams in November. I needed to write two remaining lectures, so I told him I'd keep him company and work at my desk for the same hours. Patrick had to be very quiet at home or else go out and leave us in peace. Alex and I worked as planned for the two weeks, but perhaps he was the more efficient because he was motivated to watch the Sydney Olympics when his study period was over. I continued my bicycle rides, and one day a week would ride for three hours with a friend, stopping for coffee in the middle. It was the most peaceful and enjoyable school holiday we'd ever had.

After the two-week break I resumed teaching, and at the end of the first tutorial, several students told me my subject was their favourite. I'd always loved teaching, but now I loved this job so much I felt almost guilty being paid for it! From my office, I looked out over the trees to the South Lawn and beyond to the sandstone Old Arts building, feeling I'd never been so happy.

I was forty-seven and noticing changes in myself. My periods were extremely heavy and painful; I had sleeping problems, abdominal pains and headaches; more worrying were wild mood swings. There was no reason for this latter problem really, given that Bill's health seemed more stable than it had for years, although it was always a day-by-day proposition. I never liked to tell him too much about my health. I wasn't surprised when my doctor told me I was very likely experiencing the 'perimenopause', a transition period that can occur up to ten years prior to the menopause proper. The body reduces its production of oestrogen, causing sleep disturbances, mood swings, anxiety and irritability. Afraid of my depression returning, I started seeing a psychologist, to Bill's great relief, since he'd been recommending this for some time. Pouring out all my joys and sorrows to a sympathetic older woman did me a power of good as I normally never confided in anyone, having few close friends during that time. Bill had been my best friend for nearly a decade and due to our hectic life I'd neglected most other close friendships. The psychologist had teenage children, and occasionally when I told her of something rude or irritating uttered by one of my sons, she'd say with a sigh of resignation, 'Oh yes, I get that too'. I found this very affirming.

Bill had started experiencing a new health problem a few months into dialysis. Naturally, he made light of it, so I never knew of its seriousness until reading his medical records years later. Small lesions began appearing on his lower leg, one or two at a time, soon becoming infected; they would heal eventually after many months, only to break out again a few weeks later. When the first one appeared, he was prescribed antibiotics, and the wounds were dressed by a nurse each time he went for dialysis. After a week there was no improvement, and the dialysis doctor wanted to admit Bill to a ward overnight to administer a large dose of antibiotics intravenously. Bill of course refused. The doctor noted that he'd 'explained the risks and the necessity of intravenous antibiotics', but that Bill wanted to wait until his next dialysis in three days' time to see if there was any improvement, promising to come to casualty if he felt unwell or if the wound worsened. Bill told me only that he had a superficial wound on his leg, of unknown cause, which was being dealt with by the nurses and doctors in the dialysis unit.

On Bill's medical records, which I read for the first time only recently, next to the first mention of the leg wound are the words 'S.aureus'. Known by its simpler name, 'golden staph', this is the bacterium staphylococcus aureus. Common enough in healthy humans, it will often invade damaged skin. Lesions on the lower legs can occur in a small percentage of dialysis patients when the level of calcium in the blood is too high, accumulating in small blood vessels and causing the death of skin cells because of inadequate blood flow. This condition, poorly understood even today, judging by the medical literature, can be fatal. Bill was spared the associated pain because of the paralysis in his leg. But when there's pain in a paralysed part of the body it's often referred elsewhere. The pain is exacerbated by the infection, which manifests throughout the whole body as alternating shivers and overheating, blinding headaches, nausea, and weakness.

Ironically, and sadly, the vitamin which can inhibit calcification, Vitamin K, is found in potassium and sodium, both restricted for dialysis patients who are therefore usually low in this vitamin. This alone illustrates how dialysis is a delicate balancing act that can never adequately replace healthy kidney function. From that time onward, one or more leg or ankle wounds were almost always present, with only a few weeks of respite now and again. If Bill knew the seriousness of this condition, he kept it to himself.

By now Bill must have been reading the signs inscribed on his body, and absorbing the information they revealed. He'd long been aware, I know now, that he would not have a full life span, but he'd always lacked precise knowledge of how long he had. Until now. Five years' survival on dialysis was the average; some people last twenty years, some two. Now the potentially fatal leg wounds had to be factored in.

Another sign, more serious still, had revealed itself in an X-ray even before he'd had his kidneys removed, in November 1999. The steel rod that had been fused the length of his spine to save his life when he was 15 was revealed to be fractured. I first heard about it only a week before Bill died; that Bill had known two years earlier I only discovered upon reading his medical records, 15 years after his death. The fracture was a time-bomb. It could be likened to having a broken spine, and would soon require extensive surgery, if indeed the rod could even be mended or replaced.

Facing these realities, Bill must have been dealing with an emotional undercurrent that was gradually moving him towards a private awareness and acceptance of impending death, perhaps as soon as in the next few years. It must have been at this time that he set out his personal parameters: if his mutinous body robbed him of his work and family life, he'd take matters into his own hands; he'd be the one calling time, no one else. His dependency on dialysis paradoxically put him in control of his own death. This very control enabled him, no doubt, still to enjoy life, his pleasure derived from the two roles that meant everything to him. In running his department there was a constant stream of students to advise and encourage, staff to mentor and manage. And in our little tribe at home there was always drama and delight in varying measures.

I've pieced a lot of this together only in hindsight, in which one always has perfect vision. But as the euphoric period after starting dialysis passed, I witnessed the necessary journeys into his emotional interior coming closer together. He wasn't morose exactly, more preoccupied, as he made the visceral and valiant efforts needed to face death. It wasn't something he could see any point in sharing with me; I believe he knew I wasn't even up to sharing in it. Few would be. And he wouldn't have wanted to take my energies away from the two things that he valued just as much as I did: two teenage boys to finish parenting, the elder one doing his VCE that year, and a new direction in my career that needed enormous efforts to nail. Bill's silence, his secrecy, was not duplicitous, but stemmed from love. He was of necessity on a solitary journey, and he'd inform us only once he knew the date of departure.

In the meantime, he decided he needed a new TV set; he would give the boys his old one. I knew I should have gone with him, but somehow got distracted by another commitment. Instead, Patrick accompanied him. A few days later the biggest TV set I'd ever seen was delivered to the house and installed in the living room. I'd never liked television much at the best of times, but Bill now spent a lot more time in front of his new set; he needed to rest, and he'd decided he was going to do it in style. He did wear headphones, which meant I could still continue my work peacefully in the next room.

Alex began his VCE exams at the end of October, two days before his 18th birthday. The previous day I'd asked him what he'd like for breakfast. For years both boys had prepared their own, but I thought that VCE exams warranted something special. I prepared the requested two poached eggs on English muffins, pineapple juice and strong tea. He was quiet and focused, and read the newspaper while eating. He wanted to arrive early so I drove him to school a good half hour before the first exam was to begin. Because Alex's birthday fell right in the middle of his exams, he'd agreed to put off his party for two weeks. But we still wanted to mark the real date in some way, so we asked him to choose a restaurant for dinner. He chose Planet Hollywood in the Crown Complex.

Ten days later Alex came home from his last exam, saying he felt he'd put in a 'solid but not exceptional effort', and then proceeded to party with his friends until his money ran out. Bill had been giving Alex driving lessons in his automatic car for some months, and now we paid for lessons with a driving school to prepare him properly for his driving test. He passed it on the first attempt.

On 14 December Alex's VCE results arrived. He'd scored in the top

7% in the state, and was very happy. It was more than enough to gain him entry to his degree of choice—the Bachelor of Arts in Political Science at the University of Melbourne. He'd been aiming for it ever since visiting the British House of Commons one Wednesday afternoon with Bill four years earlier, and seeing Tony Blair walk in and speak at Prime Minister's Question Time. We celebrated his results at the Plane Tree restaurant in the Hyatt in the city; photos show Alex wearing a blue shirt and a huge surreal grin. Bill and I felt so proud of him.

Soon Christmas was upon us. None of us knew that it would be Bill's last, except maybe Bill himself. He'd suggested we go to Singapore for a week's holiday in late January, so we immediately started planning. Most of my students at the university at that time were from Singapore. I regretted that I knew so little about the country and I'd been avidly reading about it, when Bill had the idea on Christmas Eve. We bought guide books, and Bill contacted a hospital there with a dialysis unit to arrange for his three sessions.

We loved Singapore right from the taxi ride from the airport, peering out of the car windows like excited children at the lush vegetation and tropical flowers. Although the weather there is always very warm, January is the coolest month, with monsoonal downpours most afternoons.

Because we needed a wheelchair-accessible bedroom and bathroom Bill had chosen the five-star InterContinental hotel. I'd never experienced such glittering, vast expanses of marble and chrome, and huge displays of orchids, Singapore's national flower.

On our first day Bill visited the Institute's agent in Orange Grove Road, something managers from the TAFE often did if they were in a country from which the Institute attracted students. Most days we ate our lunch in traditional food courts, and on the second day I discovered Singaporean writers' books in an immense bookshop nearby. We visited a factory where we watched traditional Ming and Qing reproduction pottery being made by hand. I fell in love with a small pale blue vase, bulb-shaped, decorated with a line drawing of an orchid and its long leaves, in a darker blue on one side. The vase sits on my desk, all these years later, reminding me of that sultry Singapore day and our last holiday together.

On our second day we had to get up at six for an early breakfast before taking a taxi to the Singapore General Hospital in Outram Park for Bill's eight o'clock dialysis appointment. I took the underground railway (known as the MRT) back into town and visited Arab Street, famous for its traditional fabric stores. The mosque at the end of the road was encircled by scaffolding for repairs, but as I walked past the Muezzin began his haunting call, the plaintive stream of sound in a minor key that I always find so beautiful. Reluctantly I left Arab Street and took the MRT back to Outram Park to meet Bill. After lunch near Chinatown, we set off down a side street where all manner of Lunar New Year trinkets could be bought—red good-luck money packets and charms, wind chime bells, tiny Buddhas, Chinese 'health balls', New Year edible treats and snacks like pineapple tarts, spicy yam chips, and Sichuan chilli broad beans. We also found 'love letters': crispy rolled wafers etched with Chinese symbols that lovers sent to each other. Once received in this way, eating them signified that the message was kept private and close to the heart, showing, too, that it had been taken to heart. I bought samples of all of these, some for Bill and me, some for the boys.

The next day we visited the resort island of Sentosa, attached to the southern part of Singapore by road and rail, as well as a cable car, as Bill was very keen to see the historical museum. We were both moved to read about the many deaths that had occurred on the island when it had been a prisoner of war camp during the Japanese occupation.

Bill explained to me, when nobody was within earshot, how Singapore's political system worked. Although calling itself a 'parliamentary representative democracy', the ruling party ensured through a variety of means that the opposition only ever gained a fraction of the seats. The then Prime Minister had only a few years earlier made it very clear that constituencies that voted for opposition MPs would not be prioritised for housing upgrades. He'd justified this quite openly by saying, 'we focus the minds of voters on the link between [housing] upgrading and the people whose policies make it happen'. The Singapore political system could only be classified as 'authoritarian', Bill explained. I must have been very naïve, but I was dumbfounded to learn that a country would call itself a democracy while openly behaving in anything but a democratic way. Bill's fascination with the political and historical backdrop to absolutely everything was rubbing off on me, but I still lacked his knowledgeable framework to make sense of complex political situations.

We returned to Melbourne refreshed and renewed and I hoped we'd make other trips like this. Bill's dialysis in Singapore had gone well, which gave us confidence that we could still have short holidays. He needed my assistance in using unfamiliar bathrooms, and in getting up and down a couple of steps at various places, although passers-by almost always stopped to help. Overall, it was achievable, we could see that.

Back in Melbourne, Alex's cricket resumed on Friday nights, which Bill never missed unless he was in hospital. In early March he was told he needed a small operation to repair his leg fistula, which had somehow become blocked, and his dialysis doctor wanted him to go to hospital the following Friday. Bill talked the doctor into allowing him to be admitted on Saturday afternoon immediately after dialysis, so he wouldn't have to miss Alex's cricket game, nor a day at work.

Bill's medical records from that stay in hospital show he was unwell with chills by day, followed by night sweats. A new leg wound was also noted, but he came home a few days later and straightaway returned to work. A month later Bill began vomiting, and we had no idea why. Twenty-four hours later he allowed me to drive him to the hospital. There, after I'd left to return home, among other tests he had an X-ray, although no one mentioned it to me. The results of the X-ray revealed that the 'spinal fixation rod is broken in its mid part'. If this was below Bill's paralysis line, as it undoubtedly was, and doing damage to surrounding tissue, the pain and effects of the damage would be referred, causing at least a temperature, and probably accounting for the vomiting. Other effects were noted, including high blood pressure, diarrhoea, and sepsis of the leg wound. A week later, these symptoms seemed to have subsided and he was discharged from hospital.

Bill would have known from his X-ray result that his time, always borrowed, was nearing payback day. Today I ask myself how he managed not to share this knowledge with me. Only by a superhuman effort, surely? Yet if he'd shared it with me, what would have changed? Not the outcome, certainly, but I and the rest of his family would have had longer to try and talk him out of what he was planning. Our pleas would have made no difference to his decision, of that I'm sure; it would just have made life almost intolerable for us all, and made Bill's last few months more miserable. As it was, we continued with a kind of normality, which was almost certainly what he wanted. He remained deeply involved in the boys' activities, with Patrick now in year 10 and Alex in first year university, and continued to be immersed in his job. I was the same with my new job at the University. This was how our life had long been; it was the only life Bill wanted. A life in a hospital bed, or even a life confined to the home, too incapacitated to work, was simply unacceptable to him. He'd made the vow to himself at the age of fifteen, when he'd lain in hospital for nearly a year following the procedure to fuse the rod to his spine. Ever since then, he'd fought continually to create a certain quality of life, a quality he wanted and needed; for him, anything less was intolerable. It was absolutely his choice, as it should be for each of us, to decide how we are meant to be, and as a result, 'how we are meant to act', in the words of playwright Aidan Fennessy.[26]

In the middle of the year my dear half-brother Stewart, just starting his career as an accountant with a major firm in Perth, visited us while he was over in Melbourne on a work trip. None of us could know that fourteen years later he too would die far too young, from leukaemia, aged only 36.

For the time being, life continued; a kind of normality prevailed.

On the last Saturday in September, when Melbourne's streets are quiet and for those of us who don't like football it's the best time in the year to go out for the afternoon, Bill and the boys and several of their friends gathered around Bill's giant television set to watch the AFL Grand Final. As I did every Grand Final day, I went into the almost-deserted city for lunch and shopping with friends.

For Alex's nineteenth birthday at the end of October, Bill insisted on taking us to the Plane Tree at the Hyatt, our favourite for special occasions. A few days later, seemingly out of the blue, Wayne and Maureen came to Melbourne for the weekend, staying nearby at Grant and Fran's house. The two couples came over to our place for dinner, and we all spent a quiet but enjoyable evening. Had Bill's two brothers sensed something was about to happen? But how could they have known that he had only six weeks to live? Unless perhaps there were already signs that I alone was unable to read.

Bill was now quieter than usual and seemed very preoccupied, almost withdrawn, although he'd talk readily enough when we spoke to him. Never one to waste his words, he now only spoke seriously; there was no longer any small talk, and very little joking. Why couldn't I see what was happening? I didn't want to see, is the truth. The knowledge would come soon enough, and then there'd be no turning away from it.

Bill had been having agonising headaches for several days each week and was almost living on Panadeine. He also had pain between his shoulder blades, but I was still in ignorance of the broken rod. Wear and tear on various parts of his body had been commonplace for years; sometimes a shoulder, another time a wrist, the pain receding after a few weeks after minor interventions or change of routine. I assumed the back pain was in the same category. What I didn't know was what the doctor wrote in the medical notes at the hospital: 'Central … back pain, radiating upwards to base of skull, constant pain. [He has a] … feeling of "crunching" in his vertebrae.' Extensive sweating was noted, evidence of a fever. The fracture of the internal spinal fixation rod was mentioned, its position unchanged from previous scans, and evidence of degeneration of the spine, the logical outcome as the rod breaks away from the vertebrae. But I wasn't to see these records nor read any of this for another 15 years.

On Saturday morning, 8 December, when Bill was at the hospital as usual for dialysis, his doctor arranged for scans to be done immediately afterwards. He would then consult colleagues, he told Bill, after which he'd talk with him again on Tuesday when he came for his next dialysis, or telephone him over the weekend if he thought it necessary.

This was the last dialysis session Bill would have.

1978–89: A First-Class Employee

After completing his Bachelor of Arts Bill set to work straightaway to find employment. Three months later he'd sent off 100 applications for graduate positions in government departments and other organisations: over seven applications each week. He was desperate to find a job. He'd worked hard for his degree and wanted to use it, to give something back to society.

Out of his 100 applications, Bill received only three replies and two interviews, which were unsuccessful. He believed that as soon as the members of the interview panel saw he was in a wheelchair, they made up their minds immediately not to employ him, either from outright discrimination, or else assuming he'd need frequent sick leave.

It's impossible to know for sure whether a similarly qualified young graduate without a disability would have met with the same results, but given that tertiary graduates constituted only about 10% of his age cohort, compared with three times that number today, it's surprising that Bill was called for only two interviews for the graduate positions for which he'd applied. The 1970s in Australia, especially the first half of the decade, certainly had more unemployment than the previous, more prosperous decade, as well as rising inflation. But even by the following year, 1980, the unemployment rate was still only 6%, and it was not until 1981 that both inflation and unemployment started to surge.

A similar experience to Bill's was encountered by Blair, the young man with whom Bill had shared a ward in 1972, when he tried to find employment at around the same time, following the completion of his bachelor's and master's degree. Forty years later, he still recalled the cold demeanour of many panel members as he wheeled into job interviews. It was precisely this sort of discrimination that the first International Year of Disabled Persons, in 1981, was set up to combat, although it wasn't until 1992 that the Disability Discrimination Act came into force, making it illegal to discriminate against people with disabilities. From then on, employers were expected to treat applicants with a disability in exactly the same way as they would a similarly qualified person without a disability; they were expected also to provide 'reasonable adjustments' to allow people with disabilities equal participation at work, assuming the employee was capable of carrying out the requirements of the job.

Given that this law has now been in force for over 25 years, a quick look at our current employment situation in Australia for people with disabilities can help to place Bill's job-seeking experiences in context. It's been found, for example, that despite discrimination being illegal, disabled people face a range of individual and structural barriers to finding work. To help address this in 2011 the Australian Department of Social Services released the National Disability Strategy 2010–2020 to ensure equal access to employment, among other things; and in 2015 the Australian Human Rights Commission conducted a major inquiry into employment discrimination. The inquiry found that only 52.8% of people with a disability participate in the workforce, compared with 83.5% for people without a disability, despite most of the former group saying that they want to work and are capable of working. The inquiry also found that access to employment is one of the major human rights issues these people face. The work participation rate has apparently changed little over the past few decades so it's likely that when Bill was sending off applications in 1979, the discrimination was even worse.

As recently as 2010, Australia was ranked 21st out of 29 countries in the Organisation for Economic Cooperation and Development (OECD) in terms of the employment rate of people with disabilities. Bill's desire to enter the Public Service, although he didn't know it, was doomed from the start: while people with disabilities make up 8.8% of the wider Australian workforce, they make up only approximately 3% of Australian Public Service employees today, and likely a much smaller percentage in 1979.

There is no logical reason or economic benefit to this discrimination, quite the reverse: it has been estimated (by PricewaterhouseCoopers) that almost $50 billion in Gross Domestic Product could be added to Australia's economy by 2050 if we moved to being in the top eight OECD countries in employment of people with disability. And a study by Deloitte Access Economics found that a one-third reduction in the number of unemployed (which disproportionately includes between half and a third of those with disability) would provide a $43 billion increase to Australia's GDP over a decade.

For Bill, as with many others with a disability, the difficulty of access to employment was about a lot more than money. In most cases, as adults we all value earning our own living and gain satisfaction from being able to support ourselves financially. Even if we are not in our dream job, work forms part of our identity, bestowing self-worth, social contact, and many other important rights. After studying sociology, Bill was well aware of all these factors. He didn't become angry or bitter about his difficulty in finding a job, but he had a deep sense of the injustice of his situation.

Neither Bill nor his mother was going to quietly accept this predicament. As with the discrimination by the taxi company during Bill's HSC year, Bill and June discussed publicising the issue in the media. This time they set their sights higher than the local paper, and instead contacted one of Melbourne's two daily and widely read broadsheet newspapers, *The Herald* (merged in 1990 with the tabloid *Sun* to become *The Herald Sun*). Reporter Shaun Carney came to the Johnsons' house to interview them. June, with her flair for dramatic storytelling, told Shaun the backstory, although she didn't even need to exaggerate. Eleven years earlier, she said, Bill had been so critically injured in a road accident that doctors told her he would die. Instead, he had survived, completed his HSC and a Bachelor of Arts, but was finding it impossible to get a job. With a newly completed

BA himself, and around the same age as Bill, Shaun must have decided this was a human-interest story worth telling.

Shaun spent some time talking with Bill, and the resulting article appeared in *The Herald* on 28 May 1979, under the punning headline, 'Bill, battler of high degree'. It featured a summary of the more dramatic moments of Bill's journey of the past eleven years, from the accident through to his recent graduation, including the one hundred fruitless job applications, and Bill's strong desire to obtain work. Shaun commented in particular on the intelligence and sense of humour of his subject, and on how Bill had him laughing throughout most of the interview.

One of Bill's former doctors at the Austin Hospital, David Burke, who'd become the Director of the Spinal Unit, read the article, immediately remembered Bill, and wrote a letter to *The Herald*, which the newspaper published a few days later. Dr Burke wrote,

> I know this young man very well. I do not think the story does him full credit, and that is no criticism of the writer, because you could not possibly get to know a person in one interview. This young man is probably the most courageous fellow I have ever seen pass through the spinal unit, and that includes hundreds of people who have made amazing adjustments to severe disability. I hope he does find a job now that he has completed his Bachelor of Arts because he would make a first-class employee …

Among other readers of the article, and very likely of Dr Burke's letter, was one of Bill's former teachers from Croydon High School, Sue Allen, the librarian. She showed it to a colleague, Bryn Jones, asking if he remembered Bill Johnson. Of course Bryn remembered him. In the years following Bill's accident several teachers had kept in touch and visited him in hospital, while the whole school had held the fundraiser to pay for a television set for Bill's first hospital room.

Sue and Bryn were appalled to read of the one hundred job applications that had resulted in only two interviews, and wanted to do something to help. Perhaps if they could find him some work at the school, he would at least gain work experience to add to his curriculum vitae, which would help with future job applications, they reasoned. Bryn, a senior teacher of English and History, was now also Head of the Adult Evening School, which had its own administrative office, funded and overseen by what was then Box Hill College of TAFE (later renamed Box Hill Institute). Sue believed she could find some tasks in the library for Bill, if Bryn could organise the wage through his budget, perhaps later finding work for Bill in the Evening School as the need arose. The school installed ramps at the entrance to the main building and the library, and in September 1979 Bill started working three days a week in the Croydon High School library.

When Bryn first proposed the job to Bill, he'd eagerly accepted. But he immediately began to worry about how he was going to get there. The route was too hilly for a single-handed wheelchair, and no taxi could be expected to pick him up reliably for a five-minute trip. But he had an idea. June had been his staunchest ally in all his plans since leaving Yooralla; perhaps she'd like one more challenge. When she arrived home from work that afternoon, Bill said to her, 'How would you like to learn to drive? I'll pay for lessons. And I'll buy you a car. You can use it for yourself, as long as you can drive me to work three days a week.'

June was 45 and had had neither the time nor the money to learn to drive. She'd often regretted this, as she always had to rely on her husband or friends or on public transport. With her youngest child now 14, and only working three days a week herself, she finally had some spare time. With her own car, she knew she'd be able to go anytime she liked to visit her daughter, now living some distance away with her husband and new baby; she could visit her friends and her sister more frequently as well. She happily agreed to Bill's offer.

June took twice-weekly lessons with a local driving instructor. Bill bought her a small automatic car, and she surprised everyone by obtaining her driver's licence in ten weeks. Her driving skills reflected this hasty process, according to Grant, who recalls Bill being secretly so terrified by her driving that the following year he got his Learner's Permit and began experimenting with various hand controls.

Bill's first task in the library was to source supplementary material for the teachers, culled from the daily media—mainly the mass-circulation newspapers, *The Age*, *The Sun*, *The Herald*, and *The Australian*—to serve as real-life case studies, especially in the fields of Legal Studies, Social Studies, and Economics, the subjects with which Bill was most familiar from his own HSC. Bill familiarised himself with the wider secondary syllabus, and began to comb through each newspaper, clipping all the pertinent material he found. He indexed the clippings so the teachers could see what was available, and finally filed all this material so that it could be easily retrieved.

Bill enjoyed the interaction with the teachers, and reading all the dailies, but soon felt bored and under-utilised. A competent HSC graduate could have done the job easily. If this was the best he could expect as a job, then his Bachelor of Arts had been a complete waste of time. But he was appreciative of Sue and Bryn's efforts, and didn't want to appear ungrateful; he'd have to wait until the appropriate time to express how he felt.

The disappointment was compounded by the anguish he was experiencing as the health of his closest friend Rob, who suffered from muscular dystrophy, was fast declining. Friends since meeting at Yooralla when they were 15, they continued to see each other frequently. At the end of October Rob died. He was only 23. Bill felt there was no justice in the world at all.

Not long after, Bryn asked Bill how he was settling in. Bill saw this as the moment to tell him the truth about the work. 'I'm not really being utilised to the full,' he said. 'You'd get better value for the money you're paying me if you could give me more challenging tasks. Is there anything I could do to assist you in the Evening School?'

Bryn promised to look into it. A week later he asked Bill if he'd like to come and work with his secretary, Judy, to learn how the whole Evening School ran. He could assist by producing the monthly newsletter for the evening school students, containing information relevant to the running of the school, notification of public lectures and any other matters of interest, including student contributions. Towards the end of the year, Bryn found Bill more duties—assisting with timetabling, and then with the enrolment procedure. As Bill dealt with each new task efficiently, Bryn found him more to do, gradually but deliberately increasing his responsibilities.

Bryn was struck by Bill's dedication, his determined efforts to master new tasks quickly, and to embrace more and more responsibility. He was aware that by the time Bill arrived at work, he'd already made a huge physical effort to get himself ready every morning, before climbing in and out of June's car, unaided, particularly hard in hot weather or when it was teeming with rain. More than an hour was added to his working day by these activities which most of us carry out automatically in a few seconds. Bill never discussed this with anyone; it was obvious to all of us who cared about him. Nothing ever seemed to diminish the energy he had for his work.

The first years at the Evening School, working for Bryn, were the start of a long professional relationship that was to be crucial to Bill's success. 'Mentoring' is the best way to describe it, but that is from today's perspective. Back when Bill began his working life, formal mentoring processes in workplaces were still a decade or so in the future.

Nowadays mentoring is recognised as 'particularly effective in fostering the career development of members of equal employment opportunity (EEO) groups such as women, people with a disability, Aboriginal people, Torres Strait Islanders and members of racial, ethnic, and ethno-religious minority groups', as detailed in a recent Australian Public Service Commission document. A good mentor-mentee relationship is not just one-way. Ideally, it's a mutually beneficial relationship, and valuable for the organisation. The value can be due to the increased diversity of the workforce that mentoring can foster, and also to the targeted training from the mentor.

In the case of the Evening School the numbers of students were increasing each year, as HSC and post-secondary studies were becoming more and more required by employers. As such, this environment was an ideal training ground in grass roots educational administration during a period of swift societal changes. At the same time, Bryn was able to continue overseeing the program in the way he knew was best, while confidently delegating the day-to-day administration to Bill. Today, forty years on, Bryn agrees that his role may have been one of 'mentor', but it was not a conscious action on his part, he says, 'it just happened'. As Bryn's assistant, Bill grew with each new task—in confidence, in administrative skills, and in relationships with colleagues and students. The evening school students, most of whom began their resumption of studies with a conversation with Bill, had left school early for a number of reasons including serious problems or trauma. Bill's own experience meant he had empathy for others in the same category, and he found he had a flair for engaging people of all ages in conversation and for drawing them out.

Bryn's responsibilities were increasing at the College, away from the Evening School; midway through 1981 he decided he'd need Bill full-time from the start of 1982. Bill accepted with alacrity. Full-time work in some useful capacity had been his goal since finishing his degree. He was good at the work and loved it. With a full salary he hoped to apply for a loan to buy his own house or apartment. A more pressing need, now he'd be working every day, was to be able to drive.

His partially paralysed right arm was the problem. It could manage large motor movements, such as pulling or pushing, but the wrist was weak and unstable, and there was limited fine motor control in the fingers of Bill's right hand. But the most serious impediment was the arm's involuntary spasticity, a phenomenon that often occurs with paraplegia, and which would make driving unsafe. He'd been discussing solutions to this with the spinal doctors at the Austin, and at Bill's insistence in March 1981 they started him on a course of monthly injections, a motor nerve blocker. By the end of July, medical records show that the injections had improved the spasticity in his finger flexors, and also in his elbow and shoulder. He could now open his right hand, so a specially made wrist splint was ordered and an assessment for driving ability was organised.

During 1982 Bill learned to drive, mainly thanks to the ingenuity of the owner of the eponymous Frank's Engineering in Coburg, who'd installed specific tailored hand controls, suited to Bill's limited abilities, on the automatic Holden Kingswood that Bill bought. Wearing the new wrist splint, Bill was able to manipulate the purpose-built lever attached to the right of the steering column that enabled the accelerator and brake to be operated; he had to pull to accelerate, push to brake. He used his left hand to steer by means of a special rotating knob affixed to the steering wheel. After several months of lessons, he felt sufficiently confident to take his driving test, which he passed.

The mobility of four wheels changed his life completely; he now had total independence. With some practice he developed a way of transferring from his wheelchair on to the car's bench seat by means of a varnished wooden 'slide board'. He'd enter the car from the passenger side and slide across to the centre. From there he could reach with his left hand, fold up the wheelchair and drag it on to the bench seat. He'd then manoeuvre himself across into the driver's seat, and pull the wheelchair the rest of the way on to the seat beside him. With an elasticated 'bungee strap' fastened on to the door handle, he could pull the door to close it. For the first time since his accident, Bill could go from his studio to the car, from there to work or anywhere else, with complete independence. He spent a lot of time driving around, familiarising himself with the roads, visiting family and friends. He even made the six-hour drive to South Australia to visit Wayne and his family.

One of his great pleasures was taking his three-year old nephew Leam out for drives, strapped into the back seat. They'd always shared a close bond, and with one year-old twin brothers at home, Leam loved going out with his uncle and doing something special with him. Once the twins, Sean and Shane, were old enough, Bill would take all three boys out for a drive. Grown men now, with children of their own, they fondly remember those outings with their beloved uncle.

In 1983 Bryn promoted Bill to the position of 'Assistant to Head of Evening School'. Bill was hard-working, efficient, and got along well with everyone—students, teachers, support staff—and he'd become certain that he wanted to make his career in educational administration. But he was also developing a desire to teach, thanks to his special rapport with students. Bryn was a role model here, having a career that encompassed both administration and teaching. Bill planned to research Diploma of Education courses during the forthcoming summer holidays.

With his promotion, Bill was finally able to apply for a housing loan. He contacted a real estate agent, informed him of his budget and the geographical areas he was interested in. Bill wanted to be no more than a 15–20 minute drive from Croydon High School. To his dismay, the agent didn't fully understand the concept of accessibility, and at first took him to houses with steps at entrances or even inside, or with too-small bathrooms and toilets. After explaining patiently for the sixth time why a particular house was unsuitable, Bill lost his temper, a rare event, at least in public. 'Have you any idea what it's like,' he yelled at the man, 'to be faced with a step, any step of more than a few centimetres, and be absolutely physically unable to climb that step? Just imagine for a second what that feels like. Or to need to use the toilet, but not be able to get in and close the door and have privacy!'

The agent clearly hadn't thought about this sufficiently, but he did now. He apologised profusely, and said he'd make it his mission to find a suitable house. He would not show Bill any more houses, he said, unless he'd been right through the house himself, imagining how a person in a wheelchair would enter and move around. Two weeks later, Bill got a phone call; the agent asked him to meet him after work at an address in Ferntree Gully. It was a house owned by a couple in their fifties who often had one or more of their elderly parents living with them for lengthy periods. The couple had adapted the whole place to make it safe for people with limited mobility: everything on one level, no steps, no narrow doorways, everything at reachable height from a sitting position, one of the bedrooms with accessible ensuite bathroom. A long flat driveway led around to the rear where there was a huge concrete area and a carport. Bill could climb out of his car and wheel across to the back door, all on the one level. Beyond the concrete area was lawn, dotted with trees. The house suited Bill perfectly and as soon as the mortgage was organised he bought it.

Bill was 28, but he'd never lived alone and his parents were worried about the move. He'd never even prepared food for himself beyond the odd snack. To assuage their anxiety, Bill asked Grant, now 18, if he'd like to come and live with him for a while. It suited Grant perfectly as he'd recently started work as a DJ, but wasn't yet earning enough to live independently.

After the removals van had left, Bill and Grant ordered pizzas for dinner. Grant was due to start work at 9pm in a nearby pub. It began to weigh on Bill's mind that he'd be completely alone in the house for five or six hours without immediate assistance a few metres away, something he'd been used to all his life. He knew his anxiety was silly, but even so … What if he fell as he was climbing into bed? Or suddenly became ill and couldn't reach the telephone? He'd had a telephone installed on the wall beside his bed and there was another in the lounge, but if he fell or had a mishap anywhere else in the house he'd likely not be able to reach the phone. Mobile phones were still the size of a brick and weighed a ton, but Bill decided he'd get one as soon as they became affordable. A phone you could slip in your pocket was about fifteen years in the future.

As Grant got ready to go to work, Bill followed him around, talking nervously, hoping to delay him. Finally, Grant had to go, and Bill had to face the new reality. He couldn't call his parents; it would only convey to them his anxiety. He phoned a few friends, ostensibly to give them his new address and telephone number, then watched television, had a few beers, and fell asleep in his wheelchair. He awoke when Grant came home at 2am and sheepishly went off to bed. He never felt anxious again, even when

Grant moved out a year later. June and Adrian came over every Sunday to help with anything that needed doing, and June would cook a roast dinner, a tradition that continued till he moved in with me and the boys ten years later.

With his job and house in place, Bill now began researching the various Graduate Diplomas of Education on offer in Victoria, asking Bryn and the senior teachers for advice. He wanted to study in off-campus mode, maybe with some modules undertaken during weekends or in the school holidays. He found such a course offered by Gippsland Institute of Education (now part of Monash University), in Churchill in eastern Victoria, and enrolled. He was ideally placed to do the practical classroom components of the course, and did his teaching practice in Year 11 Legal Studies and HSC Politics. Teaching the latter subject remained his greatest passion. He completed his Diploma of Education part-time over two years and graduated at the end of 1986. He was now able to work as both an administrator and a secondary teacher.

The administrative load increased enormously when in 1988 Box Hill TAFE incorporated another campus into the Adult Evening School, one based at Box Hill High School, also adding it to the daytime HSC classes taught across two campuses. The whole ensemble now formed a division of Box Hill TAFE, entitled the School of VCE (Victorian Certificate of Education, the new program replacing the HSC), with Bryn in charge as Head of School. Increasingly occupied at higher levels of administration, rather than with the day to day running of the classes, Bryn delegated the supervision and administration of the Evening School to Bill, who became Coordinator of the combined Adult Evening Schools. Bill now had his own office at the Box Hill High School campus, where he worked from early afternoon to 10pm every day, returning to the Croydon Evening School when needed, and teaching his own classes of VCE Legal Studies and Politics.

In 1989 Bryn was promoted to an Associate Director position in the TAFE, and in turn he appointed Bill as Acting Head of the combined VCE

Evening Schools. This was the position Bill occupied when I met him in my first year at the Institute.

The following year it was decided to combine the daytime and evening programs, and to advertise for a Head of Department. The department would include Adult VCE, year 11 education, as well as some vocational courses, and would eventually be named the Department of Vocational Access and Education. Bill applied for the position of Head and was successful. He moved to an office in the Whitehorse Road campus of the TAFE, and persuaded the long-time secretary of the Evening School, Larraine, to go with him. Efficient and loyal, Larraine made Bill's years in this demanding position more pleasant and manageable than they otherwise would have been, until her retirement in the late 1990s. Meanwhile, my course was transferred to a different department, although we returned to Bill's department seven years later in the next restructure.

The combined Adult VCE program was now delivering 30 different subjects to about 1400 adult students in 135 classes at five locations. In Bill's first year in the role, the pass rate increased from 80% to 93%. Proving Dr Burke's words prescient, Bill was a first-class employee, if anyone was. But he didn't take his position for granted, and remained extremely grateful to Bryn, never forgetting the generous, first-class mentor without whom the glass ceiling of his career would have remained very low indeed.

2001: Taking Control

The moment when Bill told me of his decision is seared in my memory, replaying like an old newsreel whenever I summon it, and often when I don't. I will never forget that Saturday. It was in early December.

Arriving home about midnight, we'd just pulled into the driveway. In my mind I can still hear the motor running, can sense the rhythmic susurration of the windscreen wipers, the soft rainfall on the car roof. It was unseasonably cold, even for a capricious Melbourne summer. Before he'd even switched off the car engine, Bill turned to look at me.

'I've decided it's time for me to go,' he said. Just like that. He'd stop having dialysis, he went on, and let nature take its course. I knew that without dialysis the toxins would gradually build up in his bloodstream. Within seven to ten days he would be dead.

I also knew his doctor had phoned that afternoon to discuss the results of Bill's scans, wanting to admit him to hospital on Monday, although Bill hadn't given me any details. Now he did.

'The rod in my back is fractured,' Bill told me, 'and the broken ends are abrading the vertebrae and surrounding tissue. That's what's causing the pain.'

We'd just attended an end-of-year work dinner at the Institute. Even on this day, when he must have decided to take control of when he would die, it was unthinkable to Bill that we would miss a work event. He'd reminded me to bring the Panadeine in my handbag, although I hadn't needed reminding. Lately he'd been going through a packet every few days. During the evening he hadn't mentioned the scan results once, not even in the few quiet moments between speeches and presentations. But he must have been thinking of them. All evening I'd had the sensation of waiting. Too fearful of what he might say, I didn't dare ask him how he was feeling.

Now, as we sat in the car in front of our house, I knew I had been right to be scared. In his usual calm tone of voice he began to tell me of his decision. I felt suddenly hollow, as if all the blood were draining from my body through some unseen leak. I remember I began shivering. Now he was outlining the steps he would take in the same sort of matter-of-fact way he would discuss a new program at work. My sense of being caught in a nightmare deepened. I had to do something. Anything.

'No,' I said, turning to him swiftly, 'surely this isn't your only option. What about …' But he cut me off, something he rarely did, saying, 'Don't try and talk me out of it. They want to operate on my spine. It'll be similar to what they did when I was fifteen, only this time I don't believe it's repairable. I've been through it once, and I said I'd never do it again. Anyway, my whole body's starting to deteriorate because of dialysis. It's time for me to take control. But I'll need your help. Please, just say you'll support me.' His voice was controlled and firm.

'Okay,' I said slowly, although nothing felt okay about this. 'But I can't give you anything,' I said, meaning there was no way I could give him any medication that would hasten his death.

I don't necessarily believe euthanasia is wrong, and intellectually I feel people should have the right to die when they want to. It was just that I couldn't physically give another human being, not even my very ill husband, any drug that would hasten his death. Subconsciously I may also have been thinking of my two boys, still only 16 and 19. They were too young to lose their beloved stepfather and then have their mother arrested.

Bill's next words showed me he'd understood my thoughts: 'No, you won't need to give me any medication. Stopping the dialysis will be sufficient.'

A mental foothold appeared in my mind: he wasn't really going to kill himself, so it wasn't really full-on euthanasia, but a more passive type.

He might not even succeed, so it might not happen. But even as these thoughts circled in my head, I knew they were false. What he was going to do might be technically passive euthanasia, if the technicality really made any difference, but he was still going to die. It was a death he was choosing; something he would not be choosing if he were physically well. So technically it was an act of euthanasia that in 2001 was illegal in all states of Australia.

Bill followed his announcement by saying, 'I want it to be at home. If you can manage it.' I didn't need to deliberate about whether I could 'manage'. It was unthinkable that he would go off to hospital to die. In any case, he very likely wouldn't have been permitted to refuse dialysis in hospital due to the laws covering euthanasia at that time in the state of Victoria. He simply wouldn't have been allowed to choose to die.

At the time I had no more than a vague idea of the laws, but not long after Bill's death I discovered that each state in Australia had its own laws dealing with end-of-life issues, none of which clearly allow a terminally ill person to ask for and receive assistance to die. Historically there was briefly one exception to this, in the Northern Territory in May 1995, when the Territory became the first place in the world to pass legislation, The Rights of the Terminally Ill Act, giving the terminally ill the right to die and to receive assistance, once this law came into effect in 1996.

Nine months later the new law was overturned by the Federal Government, under Prime Minister John Howard. During the period when the law was in force, Dr Phillip Nitschke, a long-time euthanasia campaigner, was the first doctor to administer legally a voluntary lethal injection to a terminally ill patient who wanted to die. I remember how Bill and I followed these events in the media at the time. We were in our third year of marriage then; Bill was still relatively well and totally independent, and we never imagined euthanasia would be anything we'd have to face. At least, that's what I thought. In retrospect it struck me as odd that Bill had followed the story in the media so closely and yet had always been strangely silent on the topic.

In South Australia there was a law that allowed a patient to refuse treatment as well as to make positive directions about his or her own treatment that could, for example, include palliative care instead of dialysis. In Victoria, there was a similar law, the Medical Treatment Act 1988, under which a person wishing to refuse medical treatment can complete a form, in tandem with a medical practitioner, who certifies the person is "competent" to make this decision. Bill and I knew nothing about this form at the time, and none of the medical practitioners we told of his decision informed us about it.

In the years following Bill's death, as I looked more deeply into the patchwork of processes and precedents concerning end-of-life laws in the early 2000s in Australia, I could see that within the law more generally there exists the principle of autonomy or self-determination that applies to all human beings. Against this principle of self-determination, there apparently needs to be balanced a second legal principle: the principle of what is in a person's 'best interests', and whether that person is capable of judging what their best interests are; their judgement should not be clouded by depression, for example, in which case someone else should make the judgement.

Logically, the principle of autonomy can justify a person allowing himself to die by omitting treatment, such as refusing dialysis, although only if he is of 'sound mind' or 'competent'. This refusal does, however, need to be accepted by those who would otherwise give the treatment, an acceptance shown in Victoria by the doctor's signature on the Medical Treatment Act form, in those cases where the patient is made aware of the form. Characteristically, Bill's mind was not only sound but shrewd enough to devise ways to work around the various obstacles. But the enormity of what we were about to do made this the hardest thing I've had to deal with in my life, before or since.

I remember vividly the day I started writing Bill's story, in September 2010: by a very strange coincidence, my eyes fell on a news item in the Melbourne newspaper *The Age*. 'Euthanasia ad banned,' declared the headline. The euthanasia 'advertisement' had been made by the organisation Exit International, a lobby group for legislative change on euthanasia. I read that the advertisement was to have been aired that night but was banned at the last minute. The article described how the ad featured an actor as a terminally ill man, sitting on a bed in his pyjamas. He discusses the choices he has made in his life, but says he did not choose to be terminally ill, finishing with, 'I didn't choose to starve to death because eating is like swallowing razor blades … I've made my final choice. I just need the government to listen.' The newspaper article concluded: 'Euthanasia is not legal in Australia. State laws prohibit anyone from assisting or giving advice to another person to commit suicide'.

I went to the website of Exit International and watched the advertisement. It was very straightforward, not at all sensationalist. Apart from the exaggerated dark circles around the actor's eyes, he did not look particularly ill. But then I didn't think Bill looked ill either, not even in his last hours. I read on the website that the advertisement had been banned by a lawyer acting for the Commercials Advice Division (CAD) of the industry body, Free TV, which represents all of Australia's commercial free-to-air television stations. Although the CAD approved the advertisement for television at pre-production and post-production stages, two days before it was due to be aired, the CAD lawyer informed Exit International that the ban would be applied because the advertisement 'breaches s2.17.5 of the Commercial Television Industry Code of Practice Suicide: Realistic depiction of methods of suicide, or promotion or encouragement of suicide'. The lawyer continued: 'We have considered that an advertisement for voluntary euthanasia is a promotion or encouragement of suicide as voluntary euthanasia would be considered to be a subset of suicide'.

This final sentence, with its last eleven words emphasised by the lawyer, seems to me to be such a wilful disregard for the way the two terms, euthanasia and suicide, are commonly used and understood. According to my *Oxford English Dictionary*, euthanasia is about ending life peacefully, especially as a release from an incurable disease. The very term euthanasia comes from Greek words meaning 'good' and 'death'. To suggest that euthanasia is a subset of suicide is to ignore the very clear and commonly understood connotation of euthanasia as being something a person would consciously and rationally choose to do *only* in order to end great physical suffering.

The whole issue was very fraught, as evidenced by the multiple attempts over decades in many Australian states to legalise voluntary euthanasia. Four states have since passed euthanasia, or Voluntary Assisted Dying (VAD), legislation between 2017 and 2021, Victoria being the first. In each case, the passing of the bill is followed by an implementation period of around 18 months, permitting extensive consultation, following which the legislation comes into force. As I was finishing this book in early 2021, Victoria was still the only Australian state in which VAD was lawful, with Western Australia's VAD bill coming into effect on 1 July 2021. Tasmania passed its VAD legislation in April 2021, to commence in 2022, and Queensland's bill is about to be debated. The most recent state to pass VAD legislation is South Australia in June 2021, after 17 attempts to do so over 28 years. In 2016, the attempt was defeated by a single vote, a defeat for which the 'Right to Life' lobby group claimed credit. In New South Wales, the last attempt at a VAD bill, in 2017, was defeated by just one vote, but an independent MP intends to introduce it to the NSW parliament in September 2021. There are euthanasia campaigns in both the Northern Territory and the Australian Capital Territory, but since 1997 these territories have not had the right to legalise assisted dying, due to a restrictive legislation enacted after the federal government's overturning of The Rights of the Terminally Ill Act in the Northern Territory.

In Victoria in late 2017 the state Labor Government initiated debate about voluntary euthanasia with a model that involved two years of extensive consultation, and contained 68 safeguards, including a restriction to those expected to live for 12 months or less (so would not have applied in Bill's case if operational in 2001) with penalties for those who encourage a patient to die. Throughout this debate, the 'Right to Life' association was posting flyers to 260,000 homes in marginal seats, urging people to contact their local members of parliament to protest against the proposed legislation. This had little if any effect, and in November 2017 the Andrews Government's Voluntary Assisted Dying bill passed with amendments on a conscience vote, 22 to 18 votes in the Upper House. Patients wanting to access the scheme must be over 18 years of age, must have two independent medical assessments, and must in most cases administer the drug themselves, clearly preserving their autonomy.

Autonomy is the key concept here. In trying to understand more fully why Bill chose to do what he did, I came to realise the importance to us all of rational choice. After reading the work of researchers such as Sheena Iyengar, examining the human activity of choice, I realised that autonomous choice is an innate and very strong human trait. It must be about having control. Faced with an ill and damaged physical body that would no longer permit what he saw as a satisfying existence, Bill's choice to die was a form of self-determination, control, even power. Although it was a peaceful, loving death, surrounded by those closest to him, it was something he would not have chosen had he been able to look forward to a life he would find fulfilling.

As I got out of the car that December night and watched Bill's wheelchair descend slowly from the car roof on its electric pulley, before I unfolded it for him as always and lined it up with the open car door for his manoeuvre into the chair, I had no idea how we were all going to cope. I prayed that the boys would be absorbed in watching television, or still out with their friends, as I knew I could not look at them without my face betraying everything. Bill and I had yet to discuss all the practical points of how we were going to proceed, how we were going to break this to everyone, how I could support him as he died, voluntarily but slowly, in our midst, in the place and at the time he chose, in the company and care of those he loved.

December 2001: A Real Farewell

Sunday, the day after Bill's decision. He was in so much pain he stayed in bed all day, asking me to say nothing to anyone just yet. He didn't want to talk, he said, and just drifted in and out of sleep; perhaps he also needed some hours alone to think again about the course he'd chosen. For me this was the hardest day of all, in retrospect, harder even than the week to come. I felt so totally alone with my knowledge of his decision. It was almost too terrible to comprehend; my mind reacted by not comprehending it. Each time I went into the bedroom to check on Bill to see if there was anything he needed—painkillers, a drink or food, help with rolling over—it felt exactly like all the other times he'd been ill in the past eight years: something we didn't much like but would get through with medical procedures and patience.

A few times during that day I did approach a sense of reality—small windows through which I glimpsed the loss and absence and ultimate dislocation into which my sons and I were moving. At those times it felt as if steel encased my head and internal organs, while the rest of my body moved as if on automatic pilot. I had to concentrate very hard to avoid crying. Everything seemed meaningless and I wondered how I could possibly survive what Bill was going to do, how I could somehow salvage a carapace of family life for my sons, how I could proceed with a life in which I'd write 'widow' on official documents. Then almost imperceptibly this feeling would lift and the unreality returned, but with it a fake sense of 'normality'—resembling how I must have felt in life 'before', before Bill told me of his decision.

On Monday morning when Bill was still in bed, one of the doctors at the hospital rang to talk to him, probably to convince him to have the operation to try to repair his spine. Bill had said he didn't want to speak to anyone, so I took it upon myself to tell him of Bill's decision. Perhaps I hoped he would try and change Bill's mind, or at least convince Bill that the prognosis was not as grim as he thought. There was silence for a second before he said, 'I don't believe you,' adding that Bill had always been one of the most positive of his patients, so this decision didn't fit at all with his view of Bill. He demanded to speak to him. I took the phone into the bedroom and handed it to Bill.

After he'd rung off, Bill told me that the doctor wanted us to go and see the psychiatric doctor, and had made an appointment for us the following day. 'We'll go to keep him happy,' said Bill, 'but it won't make a blind bit of difference'. Bill then asked me to go out and buy him Coke, orange juice, chocolate, potato chips—all the things that are high in potassium and that the doctors had forbidden for the two years he'd been having dialysis.

On Tuesday I helped Bill to get out of bed and dress and drove him to the hospital for the 11am appointment. The psychiatrist grilled Bill for an hour and a half about his decision, his motivations, about his family and professional life. Then the dialysis doctor talked to Bill. They both said they wanted him to reconsider, to delay, but Bill was quietly firm. I said nothing. No one asked me anything anyway, which was fortunate, as I felt that if I were to try to talk, no sound would come.

It's likely that in their grilling of Bill, the doctors were only trying to establish whether he was capable of judging what was in his own 'best interests', as required by the legal principle against which the principle of autonomy needs to be balanced, a judgement that has to be accepted by doctors who would otherwise be giving him treatment to save his life. In other words, they were legally and ethically bound to respond as they did to Bill's choice to discontinue dialysis and die.

Finally, the psychiatrist said to Bill, 'I think you are of sound mind, and not depressed'. But the other doctor seemed unconvinced, saying he would like a second opinion, and told Bill he wanted him to see the head psychiatric doctor. They set up a meeting for five o'clock that afternoon, saying they could organise a bed in the renal ward where Bill could stay until the appointment. Tuesday afternoon was normally one of Bill's dialysis sessions, and I wondered if they wanted to keep him in so they could try to talk him out of missing it. I could see Bill was starting to get agitated just at the idea of being admitted to the ward, so I suggested we go home for a few hours and I'd drive him back to the hospital later. As we left the building Bill said, half smiling, 'Good thinking back there, 99. But we won't be returning.' He wanted to do a detour to the dialysis unit so he could say goodbye to the dialysis nurses. When we arrived, I could see from their faces that they knew why he was there, as he hugged those to whom he'd become close over the past two years. They had tears in their eyes, but said nothing to dissuade him.

At home, we sat around our dining table with Alex and Patrick, and Bill quietly told them what he'd decided. I'd already told them part of the story, that the steel rod in his spine had broken; now Bill explained that in his view it was not a simple matter of having an operation to repair it, that he believed surgery would probably cause him to lose the use of his one good arm, that dialysis was wearing out his body, and other problems were appearing; he would have to spend the foreseeable future in hospital, lying motionless, and even after that he might not survive long. He simply could not endure it. So he would stop his dialysis. The boys were too shocked to say anything. One bent over and rested his forehead on his folded arms, the other reached for Bill's hand.

Bill telephoned his parents and siblings to tell them. In the early hours of Wednesday, Bill's two brothers arrived. Wayne had driven non-stop from South Australia. Grant was alternately laughing and crying, a little high or drunk, or both. Bill had gone to bed, but he was expecting them. They sat on either side of the bed, the three of them sharing a joint. Their talk and laughter drifted through the house along with the subtle spicy smell.

At about 4am I started to unfold the guest bed in the study where Bill had suggested I sleep since his back pain had become even worse a week earlier, making him restless at night. But Grant put his hand on my arm, saying, 'I think you should go back to your bed'. I could see he was right, but at the same time I wanted to run away. This was too hard. I couldn't do it. But somewhere inside me a small but insistent voice said, 'You must'.

I put on my pyjamas, I cleaned my teeth, and I climbed into bed beside my husband, whose body was gradually closing down. I cuddled up to him, as if it were just a normal night, as if Bill were not choosing to die, as if he were not already embarked on his journey away from us. He couldn't hold me, he was too weak, in too much pain, but he was glad I was there. He told me the past ten years had been the best of his life.

The next two days were like living underwater. Every movement I made required terrible effort. Hours and hours passed and I could think of nothing that I had accomplished. I would try to go out to buy food but would find myself weeping in the supermarket aisle and would have to return home empty-handed. Friends brought around casserole dishes full of food they'd cooked for us.

One of our local doctors came at lunchtime on Wednesday. 'How are you feeling?' he asked Bill.

'Not bad,' Bill replied, 'as well as can be expected, under the circumstances,' giving a slight smile.

'Well, don't hold back on asking for medication if you feel uncomfortable,' the doctor said. 'I'll give you an injection of painkiller now, and one that's anti-nausea. And I'll come every day at this time.' This calm, compassionate man, saying just enough and no more, effectively supporting Bill in his decision, brought us great relief.

He told us he'd organised a palliative care nurse to visit Bill each day, and wrote prescriptions for morphine and a sedative. I walked to the nearby pharmacy, each step feeling like I was wading through deep mud. The pharmacist looked at the prescription and then back at me, her face full of concern, although she said nothing. In the afternoon, the palliative care nurse rang. She would begin her visits the following day.

It seemed as if people were continually coming and going. I moved like an automaton, answering the door, ushering people in, seeing them out, shutting the door behind them, receiving flowers, casserole dishes full of food. Bill's parents arrived, and his sister and her husband and their four children. Bill's brothers were, mercifully, almost always there with us. And not one of us, not his brothers, parents, sister, nephews or niece, tried to talk him out of his decision. At the required intervals I'd pour the prescribed dose of morphine into a small medicine cup and hand it to Bill.

On Thursday the palliative care nurse came around midday. She stayed for two hours, talking to Bill, assessing his needs, helping him in the bathroom. I changed the sheets, choosing our best ones. The doctor arrived a little later and discussed medication with the nurse, in case Bill became very uncomfortable towards the end, although they said I must call them if that happened. After they left I helped Bill shower and get back into bed.

Later that day the children's father arrived. He'd telephoned me the day before to ask if he could come and say goodbye to Bill. We'd always maintained amicable relations, and he and Bill would often meet at the boys' various sporting activities. They got along well.

'Thank you for being such a great stepfather to the boys,' he said to Bill now, unable to stop his tears.

In the evening Bill wanted to get up for a few hours. With his brothers he drank some champagne and shared a joint, but then became very tired so they helped him back into bed. I poured the prescribed amount of morphine into a small plastic medicine cup and handed it to Bill. He was having this three-hourly, and Valium too, when he asked for it. As he seemed happy and comfortable, Patrick went in to talk to him, coming back to the lounge and demonstrating how Bill had been lying back with his eyes closed, a contented half smile on his face.

Grant's wife arrived and, although this might seem strange if one has never been in this situation, a sort of party atmosphere developed. Bill's brothers were playing his favourite music on the small CD player in the bedroom, and when Bill went off to sleep they played the same music on the stereo in the lounge. We ordered in Chinese food and sat outside on the back verandah to eat it. Possums appeared on the branches of the trees. One ran along the gutter of the garage next to us before leaping into a tree. They were a mixture of small and large, ringtail and brushtail, all with dark brown fur. As they leapt from branch to branch, we could see their creamy-coloured underbellies.

Grant had to go and organise some sound equipment for a band at the pub where he worked. He asked Patrick if he'd like to accompany him and watch the band setting up. For a distraught sixteen-year-old it was the perfect distraction from the momentous event taking place in our house, as well as a sign that life continues.

Later, after Grant, Fran and Patrick had returned, we all sat around talking, and sometimes laughing, as if death were a normal part of life, which of course it is, but mostly we are all in denial about this. How rare and precious it is, to die when you choose, at home, surrounded by family.

On Friday morning, 14 December, I awoke at about seven. Bill was breathing very heavily and slowly. I had a sense that the end was near. I cuddled up to him, and he awoke, and I asked if he needed anything. He said he'd like some Valium when I got up.

A little later I said, 'I'm sorry if I've been a grump a lot of the time'.

'Don't be silly,' he said. 'I have no regrets. None at all.'

I asked him if we'd done the wrong thing when we persuaded him to start dialysis. He said, no we hadn't, he'd had a good two years.

I gave him the Valium he asked for, but he said he didn't want morphine as he had no pain. He gave me various instructions: 'Lilydale Crematorium, and a cardboard coffin like George Harrison's,' he said. 'No church, but prayers for the believers as that will comfort them. And for music, "Imagine". Maybe the boys can play it, if they can learn it in time.' He seemed to enjoy issuing these edicts. Unfortunately, as I discovered a few days later, Australian law does not permit cardboard coffins. But the boys went out and bought the musical score for John Lennon's 'Imagine'. Patrick, the pianist, started practising it straight away. A few minutes later,

Alex picked up his violin and joined in by playing the vocal line. The sweetly melancholic sounds harmonized, swirling into the empty spaces of our house, and into our heads too, where remembered snatches of the song would lodge, their gentle optimism sustaining us.

At lunchtime the doctor made his usual visit. Bill asked him if he could give him something to speed it up. The doctor said he couldn't do that, but the morphine would ensure he felt no pain.

Later that afternoon Bill's mother June and I went to the local shopping centre because she wanted to buy Christmas presents for the grandchildren. While we were gone, the boys and one of their friends looked after Bill. The friend had dropped out of school a year or two before and, at Bill's suggestion, she was going to start some VCE subjects in Bill's department in the new year in two months' time. By then he would be gone, I realised, and it would no longer be his department. Bill discussed with her which subjects it would be best to start with, and which teachers to avoid. Amid the jokes and laughter there was some serious advice, which the teenager indeed followed, completing her VCE over the next few years and eventually going on to further study.

By 7pm when we returned home, Bill was asleep. I curled up on the bed next to him. His breathing seemed different from how it had been earlier, but he was not noticeably in pain. The doctor had told me how to recognise the signs—a furrowed brow, agitated or jerky movement—but I could see none of that. I was nevertheless worried he might have an uncomfortable night, so I rang the number I'd been given for the palliative nurse, and an hour later she arrived. She spoke to Bill, but he didn't respond and seemed deeply asleep. After adding up the morphine doses he'd had that day, all of which I'd recorded on my sheet, she calculated how much he could have and gave him an injection, the only dose he'd not taken by himself while fully awake. We turned him on to his side and his breathing sounded softer. He was not to awaken again.

Patrick lay next to Bill while I prepared dinner. He later told me he'd talked to Bill, telling him how much he'd loved him, thanking him for the past ten years. He then went to his piano and played 'Imagine', leaving all the doors open so that Bill might be able to hear it, if indeed he was still hearing anything. Then, around ten o'clock we all ate dinner in the kitchen; me, the boys, and June.

Barely twenty minutes later our elder boy went to check on Bill but returned almost immediately. Bill didn't appear to be breathing, he said. We all went into the bedroom. Bill was lying on his side, his face relaxed, his forehead cooling, but his body still warm. I felt an ineffable sadness—one shouldn't have to die at 45. But I also felt a huge sense of relief that he'd died comfortably, at home, at the time of his choosing, with us nearby. I know for sure that he wouldn't have chosen to die if the quality of life he wanted and needed had been able to continue. But it hadn't.

Some time later, trying to write about this, I found a passage by Nietzsche that describes Bill's death so perfectly: 'One should die proudly when it is no longer possible to live proudly. Death should be chosen freely—death at the right time, faced clearly and joyfully and embraced while one is surrounded by one's children and other witnesses. It should be affected in such a way that a proper farewell is still possible, that he who is about to take leave of us is still *himself*, and really capable not only of valuing what he has achieved and willed in life, but also of *summing-up* the value of life itself.'[27]

Notes

1 Tulloch, Gail. 2005. *Euthanasia – Choice and Death*. Edinburgh: Edinburgh University Press, p.3.

2 Aidan Fennessy, discussing his play, *The Architect*, in the programme for the MTC performance, 27 September – 31 October 2018.

3 Couldry, Nick. 2006. *Listening Beyond the Echoes: Media, Ethics, and Agency in an Uncertain World*. Boulder & London: Paradigm Publishers, 2006, pp. 110, 125.

4 Aidan Fennessy, discussing his play, *The Architect*, in the programme for the MTC performance, 27 September – 31 October 2018.

5 Bryant, Nick (14 September 2015). 'Australia: Coup capital of the democratic world', BBC News. https://www.bbc.com/news/world-australia-34249214 Retrieved 4 December 2016.

6 Rich, Adrienne. 1984. 'From a Survivor'. *The Fact of a Doorframe. Poems Selected and New 1950-1984*. New York & London: W. W. Norton, p.176-7.

7 Frost, Robert. 1946. (29th printing, 1971). 'Two Look at Two.' *New Enlarged Pocket Anthology of Robert Frost's Poems*. With an Introduction and Commentary by Louis Untermeyer. New York: Washington Square Books, pp.215-217.

8 Rance, Carolyn (28 March 1992). 'Bill is an Inspiring Motivator', *The Age*, p.164.

9 Young, Jenny M. and Alister Browne, 'Choosing Death in Rehabilitation'. *Topics in Spinal Cord Injury Rehabilitation*, 2008: 13 (3), pp.18-29.

10 Brown, Brené. 2012. *Daring Greatly*. London: Penguin Life.

11 Marshall, Norman. 1978. *The Yooralla Story: A History of the Yooralla Hospital School for Crippled Children*. Yooralla Society of Victoria, *p.116*.

12 Devereux, Eoin. 1996. 'Good causes, God's Poor and Telethon Television'. *Media, Culture and Society*, Vol. 18, 1996, pp.47-68.

13 'Yooralla's 100 year anniversary celebrated on Channel 9's Today Show' https://www.yooralla.com.au/news-and-media/news-items/yoorallas-100-year-anniversary-featured-on-the-today-show Accessed 10/2/18.

14 Marshall, Norman. 1978. *The Yooralla Story: A History of the Yooralla Hospital School for Crippled Children*. Yooralla Society of Victoria, p.120.

15 Children entering the Yooralla school at Balwyn were given IQ tests to determine whether or not they had an intellectual disability. Personal communication with a former Yooralla supervisory staff member, February 2018.

16 *Goggin, Gerard and Christopher Newell, 2005. Disability in Australia: Exposing a Social Apartheid.* Sydney: University of New South Wales Press.

17 The Higher School Certificate or HSC was the then name of the final two years of secondary school in the state of Victoria. Students were required to pass a certain number of subjects in their final year in order to be admitted to university. In 1992, its name was changed to the Victorian Certificate of Education, or VCE.

18 Galbally, Rhonda. 2004. *Just Passions: The Personal is Political.* North Melbourne, Victoria: Pluto Press, p.3.

19 Hall, Lesley. 2010. In *Claiming our future.* Compiled by Rosemary Francis and Nikki Henningham, in partnership with the staff and membership of Women with Disabilities Victoria. 2010. https://www.wdv.org.au/documents/WDV_RTF_final_book.pdf. pp.18-21. Accessed 15/2/18.

20 Hawking, Jane. 2000. *Music to Move the Stars: A Life with Stephen.* London: Pan Books.

21 *Yooralla Annual Report 1972/73*, Medical Advisory Committee, p. 8.

22 *Yooralla Annual Report 1972/73*, Medical Report by P.L. Colville, Chief Medical Officer, p. 11.

23 *Yooralla Annual Report 1971/72*, p. 17.

24 Becker, Ernest. 1997. *The Denial of Death.* New York: Simon and Schuster (Free Press Paperback edition).

25 In the 1990s, Pembroke High School was amalgamated with two other schools to form Yarra Hills Secondary College.

26 Aidan Fennessy, discussing his play, *The Architect*, in the programme for the MTC performance, 27 September – 31 October 2018.

27 Nietzsche, Friedrich. 1911. *The Twilight of the Idols.* Translated by Anthony Ludovici. Vol. 16 of *The Complete Works of Friedrich Nietzsche.* The First Complete and Authorised English Translation. Edited by Dr Oscar Levy. Edinburgh and London: T. N. Foulis, p.89. Project Gutenberg: http://eremita.di.uminho.pt/gutenberg/5/2/2/6/52263/52263-h/52263-h.htm Accessed 23 July 2021.

www.ingramcontent.com/pod-product-compliance
Ingram Content Group Australia Pty Ltd
76 Discovery Rd, Dandenong South VIC 3175, AU
AUHW020835181125
419656AU00003B/141

9 781922 669025